PLAYING A PART IN HISTORY:
THE YORK MYSTERIES, 1951–2006

STUDIES IN EARLY ENGLISH DRAMA 10
General Editor: J.A.B. Somerset

MARGARET ROGERSON

Playing a Part in History:

The York Mysteries, 1951–2006

UNIVERSITY OF TORONTO PRESS
Toronto Buffalo London

© University of Toronto Press Incorporated 2009
Toronto Buffalo London
www.utppublishing.com
Printed in Canada

ISBN 978-0-8020–9924-2

∞

Printed on acid-free paper

Library and Archives Canada Cataloguing in Publication

Rogerson, Margaret, 1946–
    Playing a part in history : the York mysteries, 1951–2006 / Margaret
Rogerson.

(Studies in Early English Drama ; 10)
Includes bibliographical references and index.
ISBN 978-0-8020-9924-2

1. York plays.   2. Theater – England – York – History – 20th century.
3. Theater – England – York – History – 21st century.   4. Mysteries and miracle-
plays, English – England – York – History and criticism.   5. English drama –
England – York – History and criticism.   6. York (England) – History.   I. Title.

PN2596.Y6R63 2009   792.1'60942843   C2008-906304-X

University of Toronto Press acknowledges the financial assistance to its
publishing program of the Canada Council for the Arts and the Ontario
Arts Council.

University of Toronto Press acknowledges the financial support for its
publishing activities of the Government of Canada through the Book
Publishing Industry Development Program (BPIDP).

Contents

Illustrations

Preface

Terminology

The York mystery plays, or 'mysteries' for short, do not constitute a seamless whole but are a series of self-contained episodes based on the biblical history of God's relationship with humanity, beginning with the Creation and ending with the Last Judgment. In the surviving records of medieval York, where their first performance history extended from the late fourteenth to the late sixteenth century, they are referred to either as 'Corpus Christi' plays, a reflection of their customary performance on the religious festival of that name, or simply as the 'Play'; the episodes themselves are sometimes called 'pageants,' a word that can also refer to the wagon stages on which they were performed.[1]

The coinage 'cycle of mystery plays' appeared in the title of the York text published by Rev. J.S. Purvis for the 1951 Festival of Britain production, the beginning of their second performance history, which is the subject of the present study. Local community performances of such dramas were commonly referred to at that time as 'mystery plays,' and the name has been retained in this context ever since. But there are other designations that require some explanation since they are adopted in the academic criticism that I refer to in the course of this book.[2] Carl Stratman's scholarly *Bibliography of Medieval Drama*, which appeared in 1954, just three years after the first revival production of the mysteries in York, contains citations in which the nomenclature includes 'Corpus Christi play,' 'cycle' or 'craft cycle,' 'pageants,' 'mystery play,' 'miracle play,' and 'scriptural drama.'

'Corpus Christi' and 'pageant' are, as I have mentioned, original appellations. 'Cycle' is a fitting appropriation of the nineteenth-century literary sense of the word as it was applied to collections of interrelated medieval romances. 'Craft cycle' acknowledges the fact that the local 'craft' or trading guilds were responsible for the medieval productions, while 'mystery' has been explained by scholars as a reference to the subject matter, the 'mysteries' of the Christian faith, or to the original presenters of the plays, the guilds, which were sometimes referred to in the Middle Ages as 'mysteries.' 'Scriptural drama' is another attempt to foreground the subject matter being performed, while 'miracle' is validated in the title of A.C. Cawley's widely-read anthology, *Everyman and Medieval Miracle Plays*, where it is used in the sense of 'a vernacular religious play acted outside the church.'[3] Cawley specifically rejected 'mystery,' which dates from the eighteenth century, when it was attached to this form of drama by Robert Dodsley, who borrowed it from medieval French theatre, where the word *mystère* encompassed both biblical and hagiographic drama.[4]

Many scholars now favour 'York Plays' or 'York Play,' following Richard Beadle in his old-spelling edition of the fifteenth-century manuscript preserved in the British Library (BL MS Add. 35290), *The York Plays* (1982). Some of the other terms listed above, however, remain in favour, with Beadle and Pamela King, his coeditor of the modern-spelling edition of the text (1984), taking up the term 'mystery plays' in their title, and King, in her recent monograph (2006) referring to them as the 'York Mystery Cycle.' In the context of the history presented in these pages I prefer 'mystery plays/ mysteries,' with occasional lapses into the use of the word 'cycle.'

For convenience I adopt the title 'director' to designate the person in overall artistic charge of the York productions. Various descriptors have been used between 1951 and 2006, including 'producer,' a term commonly used in association with amateur theatre, 'artistic director,' and, in 2006, 'pageant master,' honouring the title given to the medieval guild officers appointed to oversee their group's contribution to the mysteries.

Plays and 'Players'

Appendix 1 gives a brief coverage of the music played in outdoor productions in York to supplement discussion of musicians and music in the main text. The names of major 'players' in the modern history of the mysteries in York recur frequently in the following chapters. These players include not only musicians and actors, but also directors, scriptwriters, choreographers, designers, academic and newspaper critics, local officials and local groups, volunteer workers, and others too numerous to list. While it is impossible to give full biographies of these 'players' here, in cases where the detail is not presented in the main text, some material relevant to this study is included in appendix 2 and supplements the lists of directors, actors, performance groups, and their plays in appendix 3.

At the beginning of my academic life I embarked on an archival project to investigate evidence of dramatic activity in medieval York; as a PhD student generously supervised by Professor A.C. Cawley of the University of Leeds I attempted to reach an understanding of how the mysteries were performed in the two centuries of their first flowering. Over the past several years I have found the piecing together of a history of the modern productions in the various physical and virtual archives now available for such a task equally challenging. It has also brought me great pleasure in the many new friends I have made in the process and in my reconnection with old friends. On a professional level, as I point out in the epilogue to this study, it has taken me back to my youthful preoccupation with one of the great conundrums still puzzling theatre historians, the logistics of processional performance on wagons in the narrow streets of the ancient city of York.

This study does not pretend to offer theatre reviews, which would be impossible since I have experienced many of the York productions discussed here only vicariously through the reports and reminiscences of others; nor does it prefer fixed-place productions over wagon plays or vice versa. It sets out to provide a history of the modern performance run to date, admitting freely that just as the medieval history of the York mysteries can never be told fully, nor can the modern one. This book, hopefully, can contribute to the continuing investigation of both periods, encouraging medievalists to look further into the modern phenomenon to inform and provoke their thinking about the past, offering the current stewards of 'medieval' theatre in the city a fuller sense of what has gone before, and providing the general reader with a broad view of the first fifty-five years of the revival of the mysteries in York.

Acknowledgments

Many people in York have spoken to me about their experiences with the mysteries, too many to be listed here, but my thanks are with them all. The University of Sydney assisted with study leave and two Research and Development Grants, and without the efficiency of the Interlibrary Loan section of Fisher Library my work would have been much more difficult. The Society for Theatre Research, London, has given generous financial assistance towards publication. I am particularly grateful to wagon play directors Jane Oakshott, Meg Twycross, and Mike Tyler for their advice and encouragement. The staff of the E. Martin Browne Archive at the University of Lancaster, the York City Reference Library, and York Minster Library have been unfailingly helpful. Delma Tomlin and her colleagues at the National Centre for Early Music, York, have also been most hospitable; their physical archive is ever-growing and their digital archive, available at http://www.yorkmysteryplays.org, is invaluable. I am deeply indebted to Rita Freedman and her assistants at the York City Archives, where archivists, scholars, and local volunteers work in cramped but productive harmony. Helen Bennett, Patrice Christie, Denise Ryan, Kirsten Tranter, and Liz Trevithic have given sterling research assistance at various times during this project. My long time friend and colleague Sandy Johnston has been a tower of strength.

Finally, and most of all, I wish to acknowledge my family – Mark, Anne, and Jim – whose patient support is beyond words.

PLAYING A PART IN HISTORY:
THE YORK MYSTERIES, 1951–2006

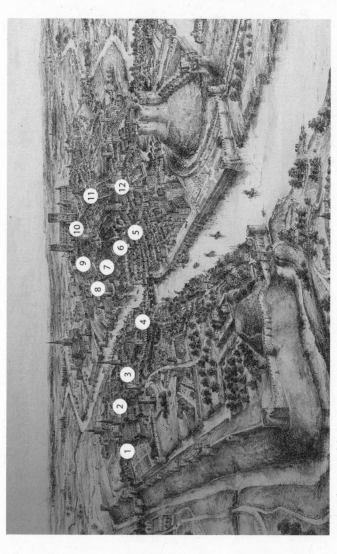

Map The route of the York mysteries in the Middle Ages showing the approximate positions of twelve playing stations:

1. Holy Trinity Priory church gates, Micklegate
2. Robert Harpham's house, Micklegate
3. John de Gysburn's house, Micklegate
4. Corner of Skeldergate and North Street
5. End of Coney Street, opposite Castlegate
6. Corner of Jubbergate and Coney Street
7. Henry Wyman's house, Coney Street
8. The gates of the Common Hall (i.e., the Guildhall), Coney Street
9. Adam del Brigg's house, Stonegate
10. Minster gates
11. Corner of Girdlergate and Petergate
12. Pavement

Prologue

Festival of Britain, 1951

During the 1951 Festival of Britain the citizens of York made history by staging the first major production of their mystery plays in nearly four hundred years. There had been previous twentieth-century 'revivals' of medieval plays in various places, but while these were important in the process of bringing early theatre to the notice of modern audiences, they were on a much smaller and much less public scale than what was being ventured in York in 1951.[1]

York was certainly not alone in reviving its mysteries for the nationwide festival. Chester and Coventry, communities with a similar medieval performance tradition, also seized the opportunity to put their venerable religious dramas on show, carefully dusting them off as historical artefacts that reflected uniquely on their place of origin and its current inhabitants. Audiences for all three productions were delighted, but the York mysteries had by far the greatest impact; Glynne Wickham, who saw the performance against the ruins of St Mary's Abbey in the Museum Gardens in 1951, noted the absolute astonishment of 'those who had come to gaze, even to mock' but in the event 'in an almost literal sense ... stayed to pray.'[2]

York had a number of advantages over its mystery play rivals, not the least of these being a guarantee from the Arts Council of Great Britain.[3] As an approved provincial centre for the Festival of Britain year, the city had the benefit of the additional finance, publicity, and encouragement that this status entailed, all of which Chester and Coventry lacked. The revival in Coventry was, of necessity, less impressive because the greater part of the original medieval text is lost and the Coventrians could offer only a Nativity play; and although the Chester mysteries were similar in scope to those of York – covering the panorama of biblical history from Creation to Last Judgment – their revival paled in comparison.

David Mills ascribes the lesser success of Chester's plays in 1951 partly to a later start on the project, a factor that deprived them of the services of E. Martin Browne.[4] The authorities in Chester approached Browne only after he was already committed to York as their mystery play director, and so they had to cast about for someone else. Browne was undoubtedly an asset. As Simon Shepherd and Peter Womack have commented, he was widely respected as 'a national ... scholar,' who 'as director of the British Drama League ... had been campaigning since the late 1940s for a theatre research centre, negotiating with the Society for Theatre Research and the Arts Council.'[5] An experienced director, Browne was adept at working with the press and was able to secure good media coverage for his York production, something that Mills points out was neglected in Chester.[6] The publication of the J.S. Purvis text that formed the base for the 1951 script, *The York Mystery Plays: A Shorter Version of the Ancient Cycle*, was an additional boost. Neither Coventry nor Chester could offer readers a modernized version of their ancient playbook at that time, and the York mysteries went out unrivalled to a reading public.

Playing a Part in History

Many people were involved in the 1951 exhibition of the mysteries in York; most were associated with the local amateur theatre groups, but a strong team of outside professionals was brought in to help meet the challenges of a production that was both ambitious in its scope and daring in its nature. All participants were essential to the success of the event, from Browne, the high-profile director, to the members of the Old Priory Youth Club, who acted as volunteer ushers and program sellers for the festival fortnight (3–17 June). In a report on the 1951 mysteries in the Youth Club magazine, these young men and women were reminded of how fortunate they had been to enjoy a 'first-class seat in watching history being enacted' and heartily congratulated on the fact that they, too, had 'played a part in history.'[7]

More than one academic critic has attached the word 'nostalgia' to modern productions of mystery plays in York and elsewhere, using it as a mildly derogatory term, or at best an equivocal one;[8] this study, however, stresses ways in which mystery players in York have looked back productively to the original performance conditions of the Middle Ages and to productions in the city from 1951 onwards. But these players have done more than look back; they have looked around them to the trends in the contemporary theatre scene, both amateur and professional; to other mystery play productions; to the current debates about medieval theatre in the academy; and to younger people in the community whose enthusiasm and effort are needed to take the plays forward.

The performance history that began for the York mysteries with the Festival of Britain is an ongoing one; its major landmarks and potential for continuation are considered in the pages that follow, revealing how the local players and the outsiders who have been associated with them have adapted to various constraints and opportunities presented over time. Chester and Coventry, like York, have maintained their mystery plays into the twenty-first century;[9] academic directors have brought together 'original-staging' productions; professional theatre practitioners in the United Kingdom and abroad have offered their own interpretations of the medieval originals; and local communities that are without an 'authentic' base on which to build have appropriated the surviving medieval texts and passed them off as their own with some success. The mystery play has indeed become a popular form, but York retains the prominence it achieved in 1951.

Dramatic Benchmarks

The success of the York mysteries in 1951 was not achieved without careful planning. Much advance publicity was required to entice an audience, particularly as mystery plays were virtually unknown as a dramatic genre in the mid-twentieth century. The York Festival organizers assiduously built up a frame of reference for their plays, inviting comparisons between the mysteries and two other antique dramas that were already well known and well regarded in Britain: Scottish court poet David Lindsay's sixteenth-century morality play, the Satire of the Three Estates,[10] abridged and adapted for the recent festivals in Edinburgh, and the seventeenth-century German Passion Play, proud possession of the village of Oberammergau.[11]

The Three Estates is a socio-political play, written, as Greg Walker puts it, when Scotland was 'struggling through the early stages of a religious reformation,' and 'informed' by 'a fierce condemnation of the Catholic clergy.'[12] In this it is unlike the York mysteries, which were written well before the English Reformation and, as I discuss further in chapter 1, remained thoroughly Catholic, despite cosmetic efforts to cover up their religious pedigree in the changing circumstances of Tudor England.

Tyrone Guthrie's production of the Three Estates was the undisputed triumph of the second Edinburgh Festival in 1948.[13] However, although it had been performed there in 1554 for the queen regent, Mary of Guise, Edinburgh could not claim this play as its own in the way that York could claim its mysteries, which had enjoyed a medieval performance run of around two hundred years within the city walls.[14] As York strove to establish itself as a festival city, even aspiring to eclipse the Scottish capital in this regard, the authenticity of its dramatic offering provided a competitive advantage.

Keith Thomson, the artistic director of the York Festival in 1951, was politely scornful of Edinburgh and the *Three Estates* as he extolled his own festival's innate superiority:

> What a superb opportunity awaits the City now, not to play 'the pale faint cygnet' to Edinburgh's swan – not, that is, to be content just to superimpose a collection of unrelated musical and dramatic events (however good) on to the town – but to design a Festival which is the artistic expression of York itself, which springs from its history and its traditions and is fashioned out of the beauty of the place, not fastened on to it. [15]

The *Three Estates* may have had its virtues, but, according to enthusiasts in York it could not compete with the mystery plays which were 'supremely York, belonging to the city in the same sheer sense as its architecture old and new.'[16]

The version of the Oberammergau Passion that would have been familiar to British audiences in 1951 was closer to the mysteries than the *Three Estates* in its subject matter and Catholic connections. It was compiled 'during the high tide of the Counter-Reformation,'[17] and its oldest extant manuscript (1662) is 'a composite of medieval and later sources,' principally 'a fifteenth-century playbook from a Benedictine monastery in Augsburg,' with a 'significant chunk' that can be traced ultimately to English Protestant Nicholas Grimald's Latin play *Christus Redivivus* (1543).[18] This ecumenical blend of sources and subsequent revisions by a series of Benedictine monks and, finally, by parish priest, Joseph Daisenberger, resulted in a text that was palatable to visiting Protestants from England prior to 1951. Those concerned with promoting the York mysteries were counting on this positive cultural memory of religious tourism to help them gather an audience.

The Oberammergau play, said to have originated in 1634 as thanksgiving for the delivery of the villagers from the Black Death, had been admired in England since Victorian times;[19] like the York mysteries, this play belonged to the place and its people in a special way. In 1950 its traditional owners, rescued by a loan of $300,000 from the American government, brought together their first post-war production, hoping both to restore the local economy and to liberate the play from the stigma of Hitler's endorsement of it in 1934. Oberammergau was in the limelight again in 1950 but when the show opened in May, a reviewer for *The Times* belittled it alongside the 'many genuine mystery plays ... played in England in churches at Christmas and at Easter and at various dramatic festivals'; the Passion Play had some 'historical interest,' this reviewer conceded, but the history of the English mysteries was much more interesting.[20]

In York, the festival organizers were keen to point out the added attractions of their local plays. Although they had the 'same inherent religious background' as the German play, they were more than just a Passion Play in that they presented the whole panorama of Christian history from Creation to Last Judgment; furthermore, according to the *Yorkshire Gazette*, the plays were not to be admired as thanksgiving for deliverance from the pestilence but as something much more impressive, 'the dawning of secular drama' that ushered in the brilliance of the English Renaissance.[21] Theatre scholars now decry this myth of origins as unflattering and untrue, but in 1951 the notion that the mysteries were the forerunner of the familiar and beloved theatre of Shakespeare's time was very good press.

Browne had long had his sights on the German enterprise as a benchmark. As early as 1932 he urged the formation of religious drama groups in his own country to bring theatre into 'God's service,' citing Oberammergau as an example of what could be achieved; indeed, he suggested, 'any English parish or Rural Deanery' could 'become an Oberammergau.'[22] If this was possible for the humble parish or deanery, surely much more could be achieved by York, a city that David Palliser presents as second only to London in the sixteenth century, the 'chief administrative centre' of the North 'until the seventeenth century,' and 'its social and intellectual capital until the early nineteenth century.'[23] In the mid-twentieth century York was determined to reassert itself in the climate of optimism fostered by the Festival of Britain; the revival of the mystery plays was a suitable means of affirming past glory and signalling a glorious future; as such it was in perfect harmony with the national celebrations.

Oberammergau has remained a benchmark throughout the history of the York revivals, although some have, strategically, continued to rate it well beneath the artistic and spiritual aspirations of the York enterprise. Purvis, who prepared the text for 1951, dismissed the German play as 'rather sentimental,' pointing out that the York mysteries were a 'much bigger conception' that included a Passion Play but much more besides.[24] Hans Hess, curator of the York City Art Gallery and artistic director of the York Festivals from 1954 to 1966, regarded the 'commercialising [of] the Mystery Plays and turning York into something like Oberammergau' as an outright danger to be avoided most strenuously.[25]

Recorded History

There is a recorded history of medieval mysteries in York covering a period of almost two hundred years, a history that came to an abrupt end in 1569. There is now a recorded history of modern mysteries presented there over a period of fifty-five years, a history for which there is currently no end in sight. John Elliott presented a brief account of the first thirty years (1951 to 1980) in his landmark work on the revival of medieval drama, *Playing God*;[26] and Katie Normington, in *Modern Mysteries*, offers a brief commentary on productions in the city to 2002.[27] Neither of these academic critics thinks well of York, a situation that the present study seeks to redress, not by arguing point by point with either of them, but rather by presenting the York story in greater detail than they could, given the scope of their work.

Between 1951 and 2006 there have been numerous small-scale mystery play productions by local church and community groups; this study, however, is concerned primarily with twenty-one larger productions (see appendix 3). Fifteen have been fixed-place performances of heavily abridged versions of the medieval plays, many of them offering a 'wagon play' as an ancillary event. The fixed-place productions were adaptations rather than re-enactments of the originals: twelve of them outdoors against the backdrop of the ruins of St Mary's Abbey in the Museum Gardens (1951–88), two in the Theatre Royal (1992–6), and one in the Minster (2000). The remaining six productions have been wagon presentations of selected episodes from the larger play directed by Meg Twycross (1988 and 1992), Jane Oakshott (1994 and 1998), and Mike Tyler (2002 and 2006). These wagon productions, the two most recent ones arranged by the guilds of York, who can claim descent from the original mystery players in the city, offered performances at a number of outdoor playing stations in imitation of the medieval processional performance method.

From 1951 to 1976 a York Festival of the Arts was held at three-year intervals, with the mysteries as its main event. The city council decided against the Edinburgh pattern of annual festivals, and although there were early hopes of a second festival in 1953, it was considered inappropriate to compete with the coronation of Her Majesty Queen Elizabeth II scheduled for that year. By the time a production for 1954 came under consideration, Browne could assure the board of the York Festival Society that 'the

Mystery Plays [i.e., the Purvis version] had been made a standard textbook in American Universities,' thus projecting an international audience similar to that attracted by the Festival of Britain events three years earlier.[28] With this second production, a modern mystery play tradition was on its way to becoming established in York.

After the success of the initial festival, the two-week program was extended to three weeks in 1954, while some later festivals ran for a month. There was a four-year break between the festivals of 1969 and 1973, a consequence of the effort and resources expended on the commemoration of York's 1900th year in 1971. The three-year interval was reinstated between 1973 and the next festival of 1976, but the city council ruled for a four-year gap between the 1976 and 1980 festivals, an interval that became customary from then on. Although the mysteries remained financially viable throughout the 1970s, there were growing concerns for their future at that time. Ominously the Arts Council, whose support for the local festival was seen as vital, expressed the opinion in 1976 that the mysteries had become 'over-exposed.'[29]

There have been several times in the history of the York revivals when it appeared that they were about to be discontinued. R.B. Dobson expressed fears in the late 1990s that the cycle was 'about to slide once more into oblivion' as the city council, claiming that the plays were of 'no interest to the ordinary citizen and ratepayer,' appeared to have withdrawn financial assistance.[30] In the early years of the twenty-first century, however, it is clear that there is a strong support base among local residents, whose affection for the plays is sufficiently 'extra'-ordinary for their history to remain open-ended for some time yet.

The city council has continued to back the mysteries, providing some administrative assistance and financial aid to the guilds in recent years, and allocating funding to a feasibility study for the York Mystery Plays Association to investigate the possibility of reinstating the mysteries in the Museum Gardens. At the time of writing the York guilds are aiming for 2010 as the date for their third wagon production, while it appears that the next fixed-place production could be in the Minster, also in 2010 or perhaps 2012, with the council pledging £100,000 to that venture over the next five years.

Infrastructure

Since 1951 there have been changes in the organizational structures behind the York mysteries. Initially, a York Festival Society was set up to administer the Festival of the Arts during which the plays were presented.

This was a matter of financial expediency because the local authority was not eligible to receive Arts Council grants; nevertheless elected members of the city council and its appointees dominated the Society's board. The sixth festival in 1966 was distinguished by a fiery conflict over the program between the artistic director, Hans Hess, a stickler for high culture, and Councillor Jack Wood, chairman of the York Festival Society, who advocated events aimed at a popular audience. Hess resigned and was only persuaded to return to his post when Wood stepped down, but the 1966 festival was a financial disaster and the Society was wound up and replaced by the York Festival Committee, a formal committee of the council.

In 1974 the council, worried about money, disbanded the Festival Committee, but mindful of local affection for the plays, they tapped into the enthusiasm and generosity of their constituents and encouraged the formation of a support group, the Friends of the York Mystery Plays and Festival.

This group was anxious to see a festival in 1979 and, at their instigation, two independent bodies were set up: the York Festival and Mystery Plays Ltd, with HRH the Duchess of Kent as its president, to organize future festivals; and the York Festival Trust, with the Earl of Harewood as president, to raise money for investment to assist in financing them. Dire predictions that there might not be a 1979 festival or that it would be a scaled-down affair were greeted by public expressions of dismay. The papers carried news of a possible cut-back in the council subsidy, but even as the city fathers hesitated, the Friends insisted that the plays were essential in 1979 'as an antidote to the gloom spreading through the social life of the country.'[31] Unfortunately, the time was too short for funds to be raised for 1979, but commercial sponsorship was secured for the first time in the history of the York Festivals for 1980, when the Midland Bank came to the aid of the mysteries with a donation of £20,000.

There were a number of potentially disastrous developments in 1984. Early that year the Arts Council announced that they would not fund any future York Festivals. The loss of the Council's customary £70,000 was serious, adding to the burden of fund-raising not only because of the shortfall itself but also because the prestige of the Council's support had been an incentive to other donors. In 1988 Jude Kelly, artistic director of the festival, commented that the 'coming to power of the Labour Administration in May 1984' suggested that 'the Festival's future was uncertain' because in previous years 'the Labour Group had declined to serve on the Festival's Board.'[32] This new administration had created the Leisure Services Department and with that, Kelly declared, came a challenge to see 'how the combination of a local authority leisure department and an independent Festival' could work. But a much more worrying challenge came when the festival of 1988 made a loss of over £80,000.

Another financial catastrophe in the unlucky thirteenth festival of 1992 ushered in significant changes and the council wound up the board of the York Festival and Mystery Plays. At this time the public airing of the behind-the-scenes dramas outshone even the histrionic resignations and counter-resignations of 1966. Eventually Margaret Sheehy, the artistic director of the 1992 festival and codirector of the mysteries, was sacked, her controversial proposal for a promenade production in the Museum Gardens was abandoned, and the plays went indoors for the first time, rescued by the Theatre Royal. The theatre, with financial support from the city council, staged the mysteries again in 1996, but despite protests, the old-style York Festivals of the Arts had come to an end and the mysteries were a standalone event. In another development, the Friends of the York Mystery Plays, with the aid of the Centre for Medieval Studies at the University of York, brought director Jane Oakshott from Leeds to orchestrate a multiple-wagon production in 1994 as part of the York Early Music Festival. With Oakshott's encouragement the guilds of York have since banded together to assume responsibility for the modern wagon tradition, with people who might previously have joined the Friends, who were disbanded in 2007 as a result of reduced membership, moving to support this enterprise.

In the medieval period, responsibility for the mysteries was shared somewhat unequally between the city council as general overseers and the guilds, whose members bore the economic and practical burdens of the productions. With the modern guilds taking over the financial, administrative, and practical arrangements for wagon play productions since 2002, history has, to some extent, repeated itself and the mysteries of the modern wagon play tradition have a strong infrastructure.[33] In the 1990s, Meg Twycross commended the administrative structure behind the original mysteries, an integral part of the 'existing organisational infrastructure of the working community,' as a major strength of the medieval tradition and in sharp contrast with what was then the York Festival's 'parallel *ad hoc* organisation.'[34] With the Early Music Festival maintaining an involvement and the guilds committed to the wagon plays, a relatively stable administrative base is in place once again.

Mysteries for the Modern World

Following the success of their wagon plays of July 2002, the York guilds began planning for their 2006 production. Around the same time, the then dean, the Very Rev. Raymond Furnell, looked back on the sell-out success of the mysteries in the Minster in 2000 and expressed a personal preference for another production in the great cathedral church in 2008 or 2010 in the hope that York would become 'an Oberammergau' in the north of England.[35] In 2003 the York Mystery Plays Association was established by the *York Evening Press* under the chairmanship of a former Lord Mayor, Keith Wood. The Association's agenda was to secure a return to the Museum Gardens, still widely regarded in York as the ancestral home of the plays. The feasibility study completed for this Association by event manager Ben Pugh in early 2004 concluded that a 2006 Gardens production was possible, but no action was taken.[36] Pugh's report also urged that, given the local enthusiasm for the plays at the time, the Association should consider a 'smaller scale ... promenade production in the late summer of 2004,'[37] an ironic suggestion given that the plays had been ousted from the Gardens in 1992 when a promenade was proposed.

While the feasibility study was underway the *York Evening Press* began a campaign through which it encouraged the idea of the plays as a site of tension between the devotees of specific performance venues and different performance modes. There are, indeed, rivalries in York over the mysteries, as inevitably there must be in any community-based enterprise, but many participants are happy to work in any performance space available and in both formats, fixed-place and wagon productions. The real issue for most of those concerned was not to resolve tensions or declare one faction the victor, but to draw attention to the plays as a York icon and thus ensure their continuation. Division need not be seen as weakness; rather it helps keep the mysteries in the public eye through the occasional skirmish in the newspapers. Mystery play veteran Dave Parkinson summed up the situation in a letter to the *Press* in which he stated that it did not matter if the mysteries were performed on wagons 'or in spaceships,' the challenge was to make 'medieval drama ... relevant for a modern audience.'[38] Perhaps it is true for York and the mysteries, as T.S. Eliot claimed to be the case for the cultural health of the war-torn nations of Europe in 1944, that 'there must be a certain amount of internal *cultural* bickering and jealousy ... to achieve anything in the way of art, thought and spiritual activity.'[39]

The mystery play revivals have had a strong impact on audiences in York. Some responses have been memorably expressed through the creative arts, such as Richard Eurich's painting of the 1954 plays (*The York Festival Tryptich*, 1954–5),[40] crime fiction novels by Barbara Whitehead (*Playing God*, 1988) and Reginald Hill (*Bones and Silence*, 1990), and

Peter Gill's award-winning play *The York Realist* (2001).[41] In addition, they have provoked, rather than inspired, other important mystery play productions to be discussed briefly later in this volume, such as Martial Rose's production of the Towneley ('Wakefield') cycle at Bretton Hall (1958) and Tony Harrison's *Mysteries* for the National Theatre (1977–85).

The modern history of the York plays is interwoven with the history of British theatre since the Second World War. At times the mysteries have adopted current theatrical fashions, notably in the Brechtian interpretations of 1960 and 1963, when the German playwright's theories were at the cutting edge of British theatre practice. At other times their own impact on the theatre has been considerable; indeed, the mysteries of modern York, which were instrumental in lifting the prohibition of the appearance of the deity on stage, can claim to have been a key element in the 1968 abolition of Britain's four-hundred-year-old system of theatrical censorship.

The York mysteries also intersect with developments in the academic study of medieval theatre, an area that has received increased attention since the revivals began. In 1951, in an article written before the Browne production, Waldo McNeir lamented that the mysteries received 'casual depreciation and quick dismissal' at the hands of his fellow scholars,[42] but by the late 1990s, Kimberley Yates, in her doctoral dissertation on scholarship devoted to the York plays, could claim that this was no longer the case, partly because of 'the immensely successful performances of the cycle for the York Festival in 1951.'[43]

In April of the Festival of Britain year, before the opening of the first York mystery play revival season, a 'Symposium on the Responsibility of the Universities to the Theatre' was held at the University of Bristol, whose Drama Department, the first in the country, had been established in 1947. Founding professor Glynne Wickham was determined that his department should be 'as much concerned with psychology as it is with literature; as much with the architect and engineer as with the man of letters; as much with theology as with economics; as much with the philosopher as with the actor.'[44] The symposium was organized with the idea of expanding the discussion of drama beyond the study of the written text to encompass all aspects of performance, and the focus on this occasion was on the connection between the professional theatre and the academy. Browne, then director of the British Drama League, attended as the representative of the amateur theatre movement. He did not mention his forthcoming production in York in his formal paper for this meeting, and the link between the amateurs and the universities that he was proposing was an educational one;

the universities were to produce graduates who were 'properly trained' as tutors for the amateurs.[45] In September 1974 a colloquium was held at the University of Leeds, 'The Drama of Medieval Europe,' and a series of academic papers was delivered there. This gathering was attended by Browne and York wagon play director Stewart Lack, but although they contributed briefly to the discussion that followed the papers, the academic participants were dominant.[46] In recent years the continuing York revivals have established a somewhat different nexus between the academy and amateur performers. In 2007, more than half a century after the Bristol symposium, the York Festival Trust hosted its own conference on the mysteries on behalf of the York guilds. The guild custodians of the local wagon play tradition shared their knowledge and experience with scholars in a joint program of presentations: the 'amateurs' were, to some extent at least, tutors to the academic theatre historians.

Outsiders, both theatre practitioners and scholars, have been important to the York mysteries throughout their modern history. The contributions of non-local participants, however, should not be overemphasized, as many of the local people involved in the plays have brought with them the skills of their own formal theatrical and academic training. The professional theatre and the academy have, moreover, not been the only constructive forces at work; belief in the power of drama in the service of religion and commitment to the expression of a local identity through amateur community productions have also been essential and enduring influences.

Impetus behind the Revivals

In 1951 the York mysteries were part of an officially sanctioned drive towards spectacular display of the past and an emphasis on the home-grown product in the Festival of Britain. Added to these circumstances, a large number of individuals, including representatives of the church, playwrights, directors, and actors, had long been intent on returning religion to the stage and were determined to convince both the church and the office of the Censor that the combination was both wholesome as an expression of faith and conducive to great art. Prominent among the members of this religious drama movement were Bishop George Bell, E. Martin Browne, T.S. Eliot, and Dorothy L. Sayers, whose names feature in this study. The anxieties about national renewal underlying the Festival of Britain and those other anxieties that fuelled the religious drama movement combined to generate a set of circumstances favourable to the revival of medieval theatre. In York, however, there was the additional impetus of an influential group of men, many of them members of the recently founded York Civic Trust, and all of them determined to advance the city and deeply interested in its history. R.B. Dobson has singled out a 'remarkable triumvirate of cultural entrepreneurs ... Eric Milner-White, Dean of York Minster; Canon J.S. Purvis ... and Alderman J.B. Morrell.'[47] But to these must be added the names of other local officials and enthusiasts, in particular Hess, the Art Gallery curator, Alderman A.S. Rymer, and the long-serving town clerk, T.C. Benfield. No list can ever be complete in this context because without the members of the local amateur theatre groups and the other largely unsung volunteers who played their part in 1951, the modern history of the York mysteries could not have even begun.

The Need for Change

As will become evident in the first two chapters of this study, the changes made to the mysteries in 1951 were violent, but it is the nature of theatre ever to be remade with the next performance. Dramatic works survive by enticing new participants and allowing new approaches. Change, although it often entails a need to renegotiate ownership, itself a challenging experience for all concerned, is to be desired rather than deplored, for reshaping a dramatic tradition to the needs of the present is a means of securing its future.[48]

The mysteries did not stagnate over their two-hundred-year performance run in the Middle Ages; the texts were revised, sponsorship of the individual episodes changed, and wagons were renovated or replaced. There was continuity and there was innovation, the same elements that have kept the mysteries going in the first fifty-five years of their modern history. Civic documents from the medieval period enunciate the establishment view that the mysteries were performed in honour of God and for the benefit of the city and its people,[49] thus allowing for contributors both then and now to fashion their understanding of the plays as an act of worship, a civic duty, a community theatre project, a re-enactment, or an exercise in promoting York through its dramatic heritage. Participants have continued to use the mysteries in different ways and for different purposes. The ownership of the plays has been and remains an ownership by many and their meanings are as varied as those who have participated in them and will do so in the future.

Sacred Theatre and Heritage

The mysteries were admired in 1951 because they belonged to the past; they were also admired as sacred theatre, even though local social historian

Seebohm Rowntree 'drew a very gloomy picture of institutional religion in York' in that year,[50] and the American philosopher Russell Kirk was even gloomier, claiming that only a 'select' audience that was 'generally upper-middle-class' saw the plays and that 'nine-tenths of the population of modern York ... prefer[ed] the carnalities of the cinema and the cheap press.'[51] For all this, many of the messages received by Browne spoke of the devotional value of the production. Cyril Garbett, the archbishop of York was an instant fan; in fact, he was a convert, since he had been doubtful about the production up until the first night. But he was not the only person to feel the spiritual impact of the Museum Gardens mysteries. A number of private letters to Browne witnessed to this, the Religious Drama Society sent a congratulatory telegram to express their thanks, and J. Ormerod Greenwood of the BBC's Religious Broadcasting Department wrote to say that the production was easily the best of the religious plays he had seen during the Festival of Britain[52] – ample proof of Wickham's observation quoted earlier in this discussion that audiences came to these unfamiliar plays and then, almost literally, 'stayed to pray.'

The religious aspect of the modern mysteries in York has been underlined since their inception in 1951 by formal associations with Christian practice. Their openings have been marked by services in the Minster; official chaplains have been attached to them; and post-performance prayers have been available for both cast and audience members. The local guilds who have taken up the responsibility for the wagon productions of recent years are, moreover, 'all inspired by a Christian ethic';[53] and growing numbers of church drama groups and choirs have performed in the wagon play productions since 1994. Sarah Beckwith has issued a challenge to the revival tradition in York by declaring the impossibility of replicating the sacramental aspect of the medieval mysteries as plays for the Corpus Christi festival. Dismissing the 1951 production as 'ruined history,' she argues that this and later efforts are 'an unavoidable part of a commodified heritage industry' and cannot recover what she terms the 'perpetually estranged, chronically anachronistic' originals.[54] Strictly speaking any sacramental aspect of the medieval mysteries should have disappeared when the Corpus Christi festival was abolished in 1548; from that moment the plays were 'estranged' from their former devotional context and, despite the residual sacramentality of the conservative York population, were from then on a heritage event.[55] Heritage has been much maligned, but the debunking of this 'commodified' industry has itself been discredited. As David Lowenthal urges, there is much to be gained by accepting even the un-'true past' sometimes packaged as heritage:

At its best, heritage fabrication is both creative art and act of faith. By means of it we tell ourselves who we are, where we came from, and to what we belong. Ancestral loyalties rest on fraud as well as truth ... We cannot escape dependency on this motley and peccable heritage. But we can learn to face its fictions and forgive its flaws as integral to its strengths.[56]

The performance of 'historical make-believe' is, as Raphael Samuel has described it, 'a trope which shows no sign of exhausting its imaginative appeal.'[57] 'Christian practice' may have declined in Britain over the past fifty years, but Edmund Cusick notes the rise of a 'passive religion' and the establishment of 'a "cultural Christianity" in which no orthodox spiritual faith in a divine Being is necessary.'[58] Cusick is, like Lowenthal, concerned with heritage. The 'growth in the heritage industry,' he claims, 'has in some ways filled a gap left in people's lives by the loss of a religious dimension,' with 'reverence for the past ... replacing the religious reverence of previous generations.'[59]

The mysteries were transformed from a medieval civic ceremony associated with the religious festival of Corpus Christi to a 'modern' theatrical event in 1951. Although the precise nature of the experience may have been difficult to pin down in the national celebratory mood of the Festival of Britain, it was an experience that did not replicate the Middle Ages but belonged to the present. In her recent wide-ranging study, *Uses of Heritage* (2006), Laurajane Smith stresses heritage as a performative cultural process. Although she does not discuss theatre as such, except briefly in relation to Aboriginal Australian dance theatre in northern Queensland, her comments on heritage as 'something vital and alive ... not something frozen in material form' are nonetheless relevant to the present study of the York plays:

Cultural meanings are fluid and ultimately created through doing, and through the aspirations and desires of the present, but are validated and legitimized through the creation and recreation of a sense of linkage to the past.[60]

The York mysteries fit this paradigm: Janus-like, they look back to the Middle Ages and at the same time forward into the twenty-first century, welcoming new participants as the show goes on.

1 From Medieval Religious Festival to the Festival of Britain

York's Festival of Britain 'Centrepiece'

The enthusiasm that greeted the 1951 revival of the mysteries in York established them overnight as the centrepiece of the local contribution to the Festival of Britain. Nearly 26,500 people from eighteen different countries came to see them and ticket sales reached £9,000, far in excess of the £5,000 expended on the production. For 1954 the 'York Festival of the Arts' was renamed the 'York Mystery Plays and Festival of the Arts' to give the mysteries their well-deserved top billing; and while other post-war festivals such as those at Malvern and Bath 'flickered and faded,' the York Festival, playing the mysteries as its 'trump card,' lost none of its initial brilliance.[1]

In subsequent festivals in the city other entertainments were devised to complement the main event: the wagon play of the 'Flood' and an exhibition of medieval alabasters at the York City Art Gallery in 1954, for example;[2] a production of three medieval Latin music dramas in the Church of St Michael-le-Belfrey in 1966;[3] a re-enactment of Richard III's 1483 visit staged in the Minster in 1980;[4] and Benjamin Britten's *Noyes Fludde* in Bootham School Hall in 1988.[5]

The 1951 Festival Program

In keeping with the objectives of the Arts Council of Great Britain, the emphasis in York in 1951 was on what Maynard Keynes, the first chairman of the Council, had called the 'civilizing arts.'[6] Among the musical attractions were concerts conducted by Sir John Barbirolli (Hallé Orchestra) and Sir Adrian Bolt (London Philharmonic Orchestra), and recitals of chamber music, folk song, and organ music. The visual arts were represented by masterpieces from the great houses of Yorkshire, medieval manuscripts, and antiquities from the Castle, Railway, and Yorkshire Museums. Architectural delights were provided by the city's ancient buildings and two new blocks of flats commissioned for the occasion. There were boating events on the River Ouse, a Georgian ball, folk dancing displays, and a brass band contest. *Standing Brass*, a new play about York's beloved 'railway king,' George Hudson, by local schoolteacher Leslie Burgess, and the musical comedy version of *1066 and All That* were presented at the Theatre Royal, while the York Amateur Operatic and Dramatic Society performed William Bullock's *Highwayman Love*, a romantic light opera set at Lovel Court, near York, in the early eighteenth century, at the Joseph Rowntree Theatre. Excellent as they may have been, however, these diverse offerings came a collective poor second to the mysteries.

Medieval Mysteries on Corpus Christi Day

In the Middle Ages the mysteries were the centrepiece of a very different kind of festival, the religious festival of Corpus Christi, a celebration of the Catholic doctrine of Transubstantiation, initiated by Pope Urban IV in 1264, established by Pope Clement V in 1311, and instituted in England not long afterwards.[7] The festival date was the Thursday after Trinity Sunday, the first Sunday after Whitsun (it varied from 21 May to 24 June). As R.N. Swanson has commented, in places like York, Chester, and Coventry the festival was 'hijacked by the urban elite,'[8] who transformed it into a civic ceremony. Clearly stamped as devotional by virtue of their focal position in the religious festival, the mystery plays were the official statement of the corporate faith of the lay people of York that, on the admission of the official documents of the period, conferred honour on the city and its rulers even as it paid homage to the Real Presence of Christ in the Eucharist.

The mysteries express a Christian view of the world and its history in which future time and the biblical past are interpreted through the lens of the medieval present. The biblical past, the English present of the original performers and their audience, and the common future for all humanity, when earthly time comes to an end on doomsday, form a logical continuum. The Holy Land of the Bible relocates to medieval England, its characters assume medieval anxieties, the actors anachronistically don contemporary medieval dress rather than 'historical' costume, and great moments of biblical history merge with contemporary life in the York streets. Richard Homan argues that the anachronisms of the plays were 'an effort to communicate actively with the scheme of redemption as it was believed to exist in the mind of

God.'[9] But as J.L. Styan has commented, it is difficult 'to estimate how much of devotional participation ... carried over into [their] secular presentation.'[10] The mysteries were not church-instigated or church-sponsored dramas; behind the outward show there could have been a range of secular motivations for some of the participants alongside a heart-felt desire of others to worship God on the festival day.

The first known reference to the Corpus Christi feast in York is in Archbishop William Melton's register of 1322;[11] but the earliest indication of civic-related dramatic activity associated with it is dated 1377.[12] In that year three Corpus Christi 'pageants' were housed in a building rented out at the rate of two shillings a year by the Masters of Ouse Bridge. This may not seem a particularly informative statement in itself, but subsequent medieval documentation has encouraged scholars to infer from it a spectacular panorama of dramatic presentations on wagons processing through the city streets. Tempting as it is to envisage such splendour, there may not have been fully fledged plays as early as 1377; this first known reference could be to an event that did not involve spoken drama at all but, rather, confined itself to visual display. Further, there may well have been a host of wagons at this time, but 'three' is the only number that is certain.

The mysteries as set down in the single surviving manuscript in the fifteenth century are a specialized form of history play. They dramatize the story of the Bible beginning with a series of Creation episodes and ending with the Last Judgment. Christ's birth, life, and death form the focus, with thirty-two of the forty-eight episodes devoted to events between the Annunciation and Christ's Ascension; eleven of the remaining episodes deal with Old Testament material and five with post-Ascension events. Almost one hundred years before the manuscript was compiled, in 1394, the York civic records describe the mysteries as an ancient custom.[13] Given the hyperbole of official language and the pride with which communities perceive their own traditions, it is by no means certain how long the plays might have been in place, whether it was decades or just a few years. What seems less debatable, however, is that the citizens and their leaders were intent on preserving them.

Originally the mysteries were one of two processional ceremonies orchestrated by the city council for the festival day; they shared the limelight with another civic event in which the Host was paraded from the church at the gates of Holy Trinity Priory near Micklegate Bar to the Minster gates, where the procession turned left to its final destination at St Leonard's Hospital.[14] By the late fifteenth century (c. 1463–77), when the council was in the process of recording the mystery play texts in their central playbook, usually known as the register, the performance had been elevated as the sole civic marker of the festival while the procession with the Host took place on the following day.[15]

As Pamela King comments, the register is a 'late-coming record' in the medieval archive;[16] it was compiled about half-way through the known history of the plays and so cannot be assumed to represent the mysteries throughout their medieval performance life. Although King and others have described the register as a 'script,' the word 'script' should not be taken to indicate a record of performance. The register is an official council record of the texts of the mystery play episodes owned by their guild sponsors at a particular time. It is dangerous to assume that the registered play was ever performed as a whole or that at any one performance the individual episodes were presented word for word as they are recorded. At best the register offers a view of the guild texts when they were called in to the office of the common clerk to be copied, and evidence of later efforts to correct its contents attest to its unreliability as a performance 'script' that would hold good through to the last known medieval performance in 1569.

This council register contains forty-eight separate episodes attributed to separate performance groups. Richard Beadle, in his definitive old-spelling edition, *The York Plays* (1982) has only forty-seven episodes, a reduction that results from his amalgamation of plays XVI 'Coming of the Three Kings to Herod' and XVII 'Coming of the Three Kings, the Adoration' as they are designated in the previous scholarly edition by Lucy Toulmin Smith (1885).[17] For the sake of clarity, especially in discussion of the Museum Gardens mysteries, which were based on Toulmin Smith's edition, this book refers to forty-eight episodes.

Medieval Infrastructure

Performances of the medieval mysteries were at the command of the York city council but there was conveniently little cost to the civic treasury. The financial burdens and most of the practical responsibilities fell to the trading guilds and, particularly, to their 'pageant masters.' The duties of these officers, although not known precisely, included collecting money to pay for the performance, seeing to the storage and maintenance of the wagon, costumes, and properties, and arranging for a 'reckoning' dinner held on the occasion of the presentation of their accounts. Undoubtedly scholars will continue to speculate as to whether the pageant masters operated as directors or acted in the productions as well as fulfilling their custodial and fiscal roles.

R.B. Dobson has suggested a causal relationship between the mystery plays and the formal establishment of the guilds, theorizing that in York, and in other places, it was 'the emergence of ambitious sequences of plays' that 'initiated craft organisation'; furthermore, Dobson argues that the plays provided the rulers of the city with 'an ideal mechanism for identifying ... crafts and their members.'[18] If the York mysteries were indeed associated with guild formation, there is a pleasing synchronicity in the late twentieth and early twenty-first centuries, with the continued existence of the modern guilds linked to a large extent to their steward-ship over the performance of the mysteries on wagons.

The Medieval Guilds

The dominance of the nineteenth-century social discourse on labour in the modern consciousness has resulted in the popular conception of the medi-eval guilds as forerunners of the trade union movement. This is in fact a mis-conception, but one that has had a fruitful effect on productions of mystery plays, as I consider later in chapter 5; however, in the context of understand-ing the past, it is important to recognize that medieval guilds cannot be aligned with any single modern equivalent and certainly not with trade unions. Indeed, they were much more complex than that, combining the varied features of 'clubs and societies (such as the Rotarians or Freemasons), unions, friendly societies, chambers of commerce and others.'[19]

Historians are divided on the precise functions of medieval guilds. Heather Swanson sparked debate in 1988 by challenging the long-held perception that the guilds were 'groups of men, pursuing a specific craft, joined with their fellows in exclusive associations ... designed to protect their interests against competition as well as to provide mutual support and friendship'; her contention was that while the guilds were undeniably interested in the occupational, social, and religious concerns of their members, they 'primarily served a political and administrative purpose' and had 'little, if any, relation to economic structure' and operated as 'agents of the civic authorities' to police the workforce.[20] Such an argu-ment runs counter to David Palliser's earlier assertion that the guilds were 'primarily economic organizations';[21] and, as Gervase Rosser has com-mented more recently, 'it has greatly underestimated the internal vitality of the craft organizations, which it is no less legitimate to see as potential resources, created and utilized at will by their members.'[22]

Guild membership could include everyone associated with a particular occupation, the apprentices, journeymen, and master craftsmen, men and (sometimes) women working in the same trade. There is no concrete evidence that women acted on the wagon stages in York, which are generally regarded as an all-male preserve, but the episode in the play with which their guild was associated was, nonetheless, a public face for the entire group.[23]

The guilds contributed to civic life in York in numerous high-profile ways: they served on the 'Forty-eight,' a group that came together from time to time 'to ratify an election or important decision' of the council or to protest against its actions;[24] they marched in civic processions; and they provided the money, the wagons, the playing gear, and the personnel required to present the mysteries. The council had to be obeyed, but individual motivation for continued association with the plays may also have been personal religious belief or any of the numerous social reasons now associated with participation in community projects. Yet another incentive may have been, as David Mills has suggested for medieval Chester, commercial, for to contribute creditably to such an event would have brought prestige to those involved, and prestige would, in turn, have been good for business.[25]

Sometimes the professional or religious practice of a guild was reflected in the episode from biblical history assigned to it. The local Shipwrights were perfect as presenters of the 'Building of Noah's Ark'; while the Fishmongers and Mariners ably steered the Ark on the waters of the 'Flood.' The Pinners, who manufactured nails, were a grisly and appropriate choice for the 'Crucifixion,' as were the Butchers for the 'Death of Christ.' And what could be more proper than that the York Carpenters, who worshipped together as the Guild of the Resurrection, should present the 'Resurrection' episode? Then for the spectacular 'Last Judgment' that brought the play to an end, who better placed than the richest of the local guilds, the Mercers and Merchant Adventurers? In this episode, Christ presides over humanity and shows how its ultimate fate is predetermined on the basis of the Acts of Corporal Mercy, community services in the days before state welfare: feeding the hungry; giving drink to the thirsty, shelter to the homeless and clothes to the naked; and visiting prisoners and the sick. Who better to present the 'Judgment' or to enact merciful deeds in real life than the wealthy merchants? Local people and visitors to modern York can see, just as their medieval counterparts could, a well-dressed fifteenth-century merchant performing the Acts of Mercy in the stained glass of All Saints' Church, North Street; in the Middle Ages those who came on Corpus Christi Day could see the fruits of mercy 'live' on the streets, courtesy of the players on the 'Judgment' wagon.[26]

The guilds used the plays to make various statements about themselves, but the mysteries had other benefits: they were also an occasion for having fun, sometimes, it appears, to the point of excess. While the civic establishment regarded the plays as morally uplifting, representatives of the church observed that some play-goers were intent on overindulging themselves: eating and drinking immoderately and otherwise engaging in behaviour that distracted them from attendance at divine services and hence deprived them of the benefit of the religious indulgences they could receive in return.[27] If the petition of the Masons for council permission to relinquish their responsibility for the pageant of 'Fergus' (the 'Funeral of the Virgin') can be believed, audience reception of the plays was not uniformly respectful. 'Fergus,' it seems, incited derision rather than devotion and violence rather than civil harmony, and scuffles broke out between members of the audience bent on insult and the affronted supporters of the pageant.[28] The plays may have been, officially, a statement of community faith, but we cannot assume that the audience response was uniformly sober.

Heather Swanson has suggested that the guild sponsors were resentful because of the economic burdens placed on them by the mysteries;[29] but other scholars, such as Clifford Davidson and Jeremy Goldberg, have disagreed with considerable vehemence.[30] Indeed, while room for debate on this issue will remain, it seems that the guilds coped with the burdens and, in many cases, turned them to their own advantage. Goldberg claims that they 'used their obligations ... to increase the muscle' of their organization, 'raising revenue that might in fact be used for a variety of purposes' and exerting their authority 'over those whose work impinged' on their own by insisting on financial contributions to the production costs.[31] Writing more generally of guilds rather than of the York situation specifically, Gary Richardson agrees that the 'bundling together of occupation and religious activities' helped guilds to 'enforce their rules' and hence made them 'better business operations.'[32] Clearly there is a basis for regarding the York mysteries as having something rather more worldly to offer the guilds as well as the spiritual benefits that would accrue from their performance as an exercise in piety. Complaints about costs, while they cannot be discounted too far, need not imply any serious resentment towards the plays; rather, they are best interpreted as sound economic strategy on the part of the guilds to maximize their gain while minimizing their output.

Medieval Processional Performance

In their heyday the mysteries were presented on a fairly regular basis, but as a once-a-year event only, for audiences at playing stations along a route similar to that followed by the civic procession with the Host, from Holy

Trinity gates across Ouse Bridge to the gates of the Common Hall and on to the Minster gates, where, departing from the route of the liturgical procession, the wagons turned right into the commercial heart of the city and on to the market place (see map).[33]

While the guilds were expected to give their all to the individual episodes that made up the play, the city fathers also had responsibilities. The council documentation from the period concentrates on two issues – keeping track of the content of the play and the guild sponsorship arrangements, and dealing with the logistics of presenting a large number of separate episodes 'in procession,' that is, with each episode performing along the route to different audiences at a number of playing stations. David Wiles has commended the practicality of this processional format that 'allowed a huge cast to perform before a huge audience in a city of confined spaces,' but he also notes that the 'logistical complications of halting the procession to play these dramas must have been enormous.'[34] That the system was both complex and difficult to control is indicated in council injunctions against playing at unauthorized places and threats of fines for those who did, and by counterthreats on the part of the guilds of withdrawing their services if the council did not regulate the event with sufficient rigour.[35]

The complexities of processional performance in York remain a frustration to theatre historians. The traditional view has been that each episode was performed at each of (usually) twelve playing stations along the prearranged route. In 1968 Alan Nelson shocked his fellow medieval specialists at the Modern Languages Association meeting in Chicago when he declared this system totally unworkable.[36] His solution was to abandon the notion of performing in the streets in favour of a single fixed-place production of the entire play 'in the chamber at Common Hall Gates.'[37] The academy was up in arms. Martin Stevens agreed in principle but would not accept the indoor venue, plumping rather for a single continuous performance on the 'Pavement,' the market place area, which was the last of the twelve traditionally appointed stations.[38] Stanley Kahrl suggested a combination of the spectacle of procession with occasional halts for performance; his scenario had each episode playing at only two stations in the streets rather than all twelve,[39] and some years later William Tydeman offered a variation on Kahrl's method, with '"shunted" starts and stops' whereby each episode played at three stations.[40]

Throughout the 1970s, other scholars strove in various ways to defend the notion of street performance on wagons. Some, like Alexandra Johnston (1977), Jane Oakshott (1975), and Meg Twycross (1977), turned to practical experimentation. In Toronto, Canada, Johnston was determined to prove that all the episodes in the surviving York text could be performed on wagons in a single day. In the United Kingdom, Oakshott in Leeds, and Twycross, in Lancaster, were more interested in proving the theatrical effectiveness of the street performance method, which had been indirectly but substantially slandered by Nelson. All three projects were certainly successful in demonstrating the power of this format for modern audiences and in explaining how some of its features worked, although not, as I discuss in the epilogue, in solving the riddle of how the practicalities were handled in the streets of medieval York. After reflection on the various productions of the mysteries in York that are considered in the intervening chapters, I conclude that medieval audiences at different 'playing stations' in the medieval city may have seen only a selection of the total number of episodes presented on the day of the performance, a selection that, arbitrary though it may have been, nonetheless had its own integrity and completeness for all participants.

Whatever the precise operational system may have been, it is clear that processional performance meant that virtually anyone could see the mysteries free of charge. There was no cost involved for those who stood on the street to witness the event or who watched the procession of wagons go past from houses along the route, although there was some revenue flow into the city's coffers from those who took out a lease on a playing station at their door. The station holders and their guests were an elite audience with a privileged view of the mysteries from the windows overlooking the street, and this was obviously a privilege worth paying for.[41]

In conjunction with the leased stations, there were four non-paying stations reserved for local dignitaries. The first was the station at the gates of the church at Holy Trinity Priory, where, from the early sixteenth century onwards the common clerk kept the register; and there were three other free stations: the Lord Mayor's station at the Common Hall gates, where he dined lavishly with the aldermen; the station at the Minster gates for the dean and chapter; and the Lady Mayoress's station on the Pavement, where she entertained the aldermen's wives. These three stations indicated the dignity of the medieval mysteries as a civic event and as a devotional act, approved – at least until the troubles of the late sixteenth century – by the local representatives of the established church.

Development and Demise

Some form of 'Corpus Christi' theatre was in place by 1377 and the register was largely completed to its present form about one hundred years later. During the religious struggles of the sixteenth century the mysteries came under attack, but, with some cosmetic changes to remove, reinstate, and then remove for a second time those episodes that dramatized the legends of the Virgin,[42] they survived the abolition of the Corpus Christi feast in 1548 and retained their customary title, 'Corpus Christi Plays.' Performances went ahead as usual on the date of the extinct festival, although the final medieval production in 1569 was on Whitsun Tuesday. In some years the plays were abandoned because of political upheaval or fear of the plague; in other years, community efforts went instead into one of the other local religious plays, the Creed Play or the Pater Noster Play; but, despite some grumbling, almost always about money matters, the citizens of York were happy to maintain the tradition.

The mysteries, whose origins were undeniably linked with Catholic ritual, were maintained in York long and faithfully, but as Palliser suggests in relation to the Northern Rebellion, it seems that the York council was eventually 'convinced, during thirty years of religious change, that loyalty to the Crown ... had priority,'[43] in this case over affection for local custom. Late in 1569, when the rebellion tested the Catholic tendencies of the city fathers, York did not side with the rebels and, perhaps not coincidentally, the mystery plays staged earlier that year were the last seen in the city until the twentieth century. The theatrical censorship that remained entrenched in Britain until the late 1960s was settling into place in York by the late 1560s; religion was no longer an acceptable topic of conversation on the public stage nor could the deity or other holy figures be represented there. Around this time York was deprived not just of the mysteries but of all three of its religious plays, and while the register of the mystery plays has survived, the texts of both the Creed and Pater Noster Plays have, sadly, disappeared.[44] The Protestant authority of Dean Hutton (appointed 1567) and Archbishop Grindal (appointed 1570) was accepted, and the shadow of the Minster darkened over the theatre of the York streets.

Another related factor contributing to the demise of the York mysteries and to that of religious theatre in other communities with similar traditions may have been the weakening of guild structure occasioned by the Reformation. Most of the guilds had a corresponding religious fraternity built into their organization; in York, the Carpenters were also the Guild of the Resurrection, for example, while the Mercers and Merchant Adventurers were the Guild of the Holy Trinity. Come the Reformation, these religious underpinnings were removed. As Vanessa Harding has stated, their 'character and preoccupations changed' even though the guilds 'still played an important role in social as well as economic' matters.[45] The guild infrastructure that had supported the mysteries in York was not as it had been in former years.

After 1569 and in some cases as late as the seventeenth century, the York guilds continued to elect 'pageant masters' and to collect 'pageant money'; it appears, however, that the wagons remained in storage except for a brief outing for those involved in the final production of the Pater Noster Play in 1572 and in the now-lost 'interlude' arranged by local schoolmaster Thomas Grafton for the Midsummer Shows of 1584 and 1585.[46] The council did agree tentatively to a performance of the mysteries in 1579, adding the cautious proviso that the archbishop and the dean be asked to peruse and approve the script.[47] There is no record of any contact between the civic authority and the Minster, nor was there a performance in that year. In 1580 a community delegation suggested to the council that the mysteries should be staged, but the response was silence; the show did not go on, and for the foreseeable future the mystery plays were no more.[48]

1951: Britain 'at home to the world'

Left behind in the suspicious gloom of pre-Reformation provincial practice, the York mysteries experienced a renaissance when England emerged from the gloom of the Second World War and its immediate aftermath. Even the pageantry of the royal wedding of 1947, coming as it did after the worst winter for many years, when 'there was rather less to feel good about ... than the euphoria of Victory in Europe Day in 1945 had suggested there would be,'[49] raised the spirits of the nation only momentarily. There were even more concerted efforts in this regard in 1951, however, when the country was declared 'at home to the world' for the Festival of Britain. The Labour government recognized the arts as a means of encouraging the population to have faith in themselves, their community, and their country. The York mysteries were highly appropriate as part of this secular festival, whose aspirations were similar to the commercial and communal goals that had combined with the devotional impetus to honour God on the Corpus Christi festival during the Middle Ages. Closed in the late sixteenth century because of their religious content, these home-grown plays were repackaged for the Festival of Britain and publicized as 'supremely York,' and, by extension, supremely British, neatly circumventing the Lord Chamberlain's concerns about sacred theatre by virtue of their antiquity.[50]

In 1951 antiquity was a means of encouraging belief in a splendid British future and a return to lost prosperity. Many communities chose to celebrate with a historic pageant, a genre invented in the early twentieth century by the great pageant master, Louis Napoleon Parker. To Parker pageant making was a 'Festival of Thanksgiving, in which a great city or a little hamlet celebrates its glorious past, its prosperous present, and its hopes and aspirations for the future';[51] he claimed that he had provided England with the 'National Drama' that it had been seeking, a drama that lifted 'our souls to God, and our hearts to the King.'[52] Historic pageants were a perfect fit with the aims of the 1951 Festival of Britain that was in essence, as Simon Trussler describes it, a 'nationwide civic pageant.'[53]

The Festival was seized upon as an opportunity to perform ancient British plays of various kinds. Shakespeare was a great favourite, Tyrone Guthrie's production of David Lindsay's *Satire of the Three Estates* was on show in Edinburgh again, and the amateur theatre program included several productions of the morality play, *Everyman*, well known since its revival by William Poel in 1901.[54] The Arts Council gave the British Drama League £2,000 for 'promoting the interests and activities of the amateur theatre' in 1951,[55] and accordingly both Derby and Coventry received financial assistance for mystery play productions. The Cathedral Players of Coventry performed their two surviving mystery play episodes, while the Diocesan Players in Derby, lacking a local medieval original, devised a fictional 'Revival of Trade Guild Plays' with a production of the 'Resurrection' from the Cornish *Ordinalia*,[56] the Chester mystery play episodes of the 'Flood' and 'Abraham and Isaac,' and *The Interlude of Youth* on 24 May, Corpus Christi Day. According to the published program for Derby, the plays were to be presented separately at a number of schools and factory canteens during the day with a combined performance in the market place in the evening.[57] This was an eclectic compilation unlike any of the surviving medieval mysteries in content or performance method, but E. Martin Browne, director of the British Drama League, praised the enterprise as an example of 'the mediaeval practice of playing for a whole day, on the Feast of Corpus Christi, at various "stations" all over the city.'[58] He also stressed the medieval connections of the efforts of the Holmfirth Amateur Dramatic Society that toured a one-act play of 'local interest' through their valley on a miniature proscenium arch stage set up on the back of a truck; the truck, declared Browne, was 'a successor to the mediaeval travelling stage.'[59] For Browne, of course, there was a very good reason for raising general awareness of early theatre in 1951 because he was heading the team that was, as he put it, about to 'bring to light' the York mysteries.[60]

Religious Concerns

It was not only medieval theatre that came out of the dark in 1951 but also Britain and its people. The Festival of Britain was a 'conscious celebration of a settled, successful society vindicated in the twentieth-century war with its eye (in imitation of the Great Exhibition of 1851) on the technologies and markets of the century to come.'[61] Some things had not changed in the hundred years since the Great Exhibition. The Medieval Court in the Crystal Palace of 1851 had been extremely popular and yet the official reaction to it had been apologetic, with the organizers keen to dissociate its glories from Catholicism, which underpinned the visual splendours of the period, but for which it was assumed most British visitors 'had an innate antipathy.'[62] Such squeamishness may not have applied strictly to the mysteries in 1951, but Browne did take the precaution in York of cutting the Marian episodes, thus replicating the removal of the same episodes in the sixteenth century. Originally these cuts did not save the medieval plays from their clerical opponents; as John Coldewey has remarked, their 'doctrinal core remained Roman Catholic' and the Reformers were not fooled by such transparent practices.[63] While cosmetic surgery failed to correct what was regarded as a severe blemish in the late Middle Ages, the same cuts in modern York raised the ire of some scholars, with John Elliott, one of the severest critics of the revival tradition there, deploring what he regarded as a downgrading of the original texts into a 'Protestantized version of the cycle.'[64] This 'Protestantization' was, however, merely a continuation of the medieval practice of adapting to circumstances to preserve the tradition, and with Anglicanism the dominant religion in twentieth century England, it was completely appropriate.

Browne had a deft touch with his material, so much so that the archbishop of York, Cyril Garbett, who had been apprehensive about the project, wrote after the first night to congratulate him on the 'religious teaching' and the 'dramatic skill' of the production, and to admire the 'silence and reverence of the audience.[65] Silence, particularly in the form of refraining from applause, a response to religious plays that was customary at the time, was enjoined on the audience in the 1951 program. Such reticence is something that both scholars and audiences might now regard as unmedieval and unnatural, but then, in a climate of general uneasiness about religious theatre, it was much to be desired.

Uneasiness about the 1951 Festival

The desire to celebrate in 1951 was not uniform and the Festival of Britain came in for considerable criticism. There were concerns over costs and about the appropriateness of rejoicing, especially given the outbreak of the Korean War in 1950 and fears that there could even be another World War. Rumours of disharmony spread abroad to the United States, whose citizens were being courted as potential visitors. Tania Long, a special correspondent for the *New York Times* informed trans-Atlantic readers that 'short of food, facing higher taxes and anxious about the state of the world, many Britons are wondering what indeed there is to be festive about.'[66] At home, the 'wags, as well as the Conservative press, had a field day,'[67] with Noel Coward, for example, satirizing the great event in the Lyric revue:

> Don't make fun of the festival.
> Don't make fun of the fair,
> We must all pull together in spite of the weather
> That dampens our spirits and straightens our hair.
> Let the people sing
> Even though they shiver
> Roses red and noses mauve
> Over the river.
> Though the area's fairly small,
> Climb Discovery's Dome,
> Take a snooze in the concert hall,
> At least it's warmer than home.[68]

Jokes about the English weather aside, the Festival was a success, lauded by Michael Frayn, again with meteorological reference, as 'a rainbow – a brilliant sign riding the tail of the storm and promising fair weather.'[69] After the opening in London by King George VI, Martin Ochs, another *New York Times* correspondent, enthused over the combination of 'the ancient pomp and an air of lightheartedness to match the times of the Tudors' and a 'warmth and a genuine uplifting of spirits among the thousands of spectators.'[70] The South Bank Exhibition, 'conceived in austerity and shaped by expediency, was a knockout.'[71]

The Dome of Discovery stood at the heart of the South Bank site, housing an exhibition honouring British geographical and scientific exploration past and still to come. Alongside the huge saucer-shaped Dome stood the Skylon, a vertical cigar-shaped structure that appeared to float above the ground without any apparent function at all. Paradoxically its function was this very lack of function: it was to stand as a statement of 'literal levity in the visual expression of weightlessness.'[72] Fun, the other kind of 'levity,' was an important emphasis of the Festival and the exhibits in the Dome were designed to be more than merely educational; they also assured their visitors of some real fun on their day out.

This 'state-organized fun' extended beyond London and, with or without central government funding, two thousand provincial cities, towns, and villages rose to the spirit of the occasion, organizing artistic events, making landmark 'civic improvements,' and 'restoring historic buildings.'[73] J.B. Priestley, who announced in the *New York Times Magazine* his own 'natural sympathy with the idea' of the Festival,[74] capitalized on the national euphoria with his novel *Festival at Farbridge* (1951), which came out in advance of the great event. The fictional council of Farbridge, a very ordinary market town in the South Midlands, rejected the idea of a local festival on the grounds of unnecessary expense; some strangers, however, put together an event and, eventually, those who had entertained doubts came round and were caught up in the excitement of the moment.

York, representing Yorkshire and the north of England, was chosen as one of twenty-two officially approved festival locations in the provinces and was granted financial assistance through the Arts Council. The sheriff, A.S. Rymer, and the mayor, J.B. Morrell, chairman and vice-chairman respectively of the board of the York Festival Society, demonstrated their personal allegiance to the local festival by undertaking a promotional trip to the United States and Canada at their own expense. But as in Britain at large and in Priestley's 'Farbridge,' there was some opposition in York. Questions were raised as to whether the city could afford to contribute to the Festival and if there was sufficient accommodation for the number of projected visitors. The proposed program also came under attack. Some objections were to become familiar in criticism of later York Festivals: it was elitist, weighted too heavily towards the 'cultural side,' and its ticketing was too expensive for 'ordinary people.'[75] But opposition was to no avail and the York Festival of the Arts went ahead with only three councillors voting against it.

Audience Responses in 1951

Somewhat to the surprise and much to the delight of those involved, the revival production of the local mystery plays was hailed as the York Festival's greatest ornament. The press was most complimentary. According to the *Yorkshire Evening Post*, the mysteries held their audience 'spellbound,' so much so that they forgot about the weather and noticed neither the 'failing light nor the increasing coolness of the evening.'[76] The reviewer for *The Times* pointed out an issue that so often troubles theatre historians: the gulf between audiences in the Middle Ages, who saw the plays 'with the eye of unconsidering faith,' and the less uniformly faithful audience that saw them in 1951.[77] This matter was raised only to be dismissed, and the reviewer implied that the lack of a religious mindset was no impediment to the experience of York's mysteries as a dramatic piece, a view that was shared by many others. Herbert Read for the *New Statesman* noted what he saw as infelicities: the severe cutting of the text, the poor sight lines, the 'rather baggy tights' worn by Adam and Eve, and the inappropriate predominance of BBC English, which, in a play belonging to the north of England, should, in his view, be heard properly only from the mouth of Satan; but Read, too, was ultimately full of praise and declared that the performance should be 'an annual event.'[78] Eric Keown for *Punch* was pleased to conclude that what 'might have been no more than an interesting pageant' was, in fact, 'utterly gripping, in places almost intolerably dramatic.'[79]

Strong statements were being made about British drama in the festival year, with Her Majesty, Queen Elizabeth, later the Queen Mother, laying the foundation stone of the National Theatre at its temporary site next to the Festival Hall. The York mysteries, along with those of Chester and Coventry, were viewed as part of the national estate. J.C. Trewin in the *Illustrated London News* went so far as to rank the York mysteries alongside the 'St. James "Antony and Cleopatra" as one of the master-works of the Festival' and to hope, like Read, that 'now that it has been rediscovered for the stage ... the Cycle will return year by year to adorn the "capital city" of the North.'[80] This was high praise indeed, especially as the Shakespearean production referred to starred the much-acclaimed husband and wife team of Laurence Olivier and Vivienne Leigh in the title roles. Trewin's ranking of Browne's largely amateur production in York with a fully professional production of one of the works of Shakespeare placed the mysteries firmly in the upper echelons of British drama, encouraging their recognition not just as a local artefact but also as a theatrical treasure that belonged to the nation. Like Shakespeare and Shaw, whose *Caesar and Cleopatra* was playing on alternate nights at the St James, again with Olivier and Leigh in the title roles, these anonymous fifteenth-century plays were, in Trewin's view, capable of capturing the imagination of the theatre-going public. Browne himself was later to write fervently of the dramatic power of his 1951 production:

It showed first that the drama of the age of faith, if accepted and acted for all it is worth by modern players, retains its power to move and exalt. And it restored the playwriting of the first great age of English drama to its rightful place in theatre and literature.[81]

Personal messages to Browne made favourable comparisons with the *Three Estates* and the Oberammergau Passion Play. Charles Landstone, associate drama director of the Arts Council, congratulated him on a wonderful production that was, to him, the most exciting presentation of a medieval play since Guthrie's *Three Estates*;[82] and the archbishop of York enthused that the mysteries had 'in some ways ... impressed [him] more than Oberammergau.'[83] Browne and York had achieved the kind of recognition they had aspired to: the mysteries were clearly ranked alongside the great theatre of the Renaissance, Edinburgh's acclaimed *Three Estates*, and the famous German Passion Play.

Whose Idea?

When the board announced their plans for York's mystery play revival late in 1949 they did not name any specific person as being responsible for the idea. Browne did not claim the distinction until 1971,[84] and it was not until 1989 that Elliott nominated the 1951 scriptwriter, Canon J.S. Purvis.[85] But others are equally eligible, particularly the members of the York Festival Society board, including J.B. Morrell and A.S. Rymer, the town clerk, T.C. Benfield, Keith Thomson, the artistic director of the festival, and Hans Hess, the assistant artistic director. These were all influential men with common interests in education, history, the arts, and most importantly, an overarching interest in York. Any of them could have known about the mysteries, which featured in the many histories of the city available and in the published collections of local records. Some of them could have seen mystery play performances in York, for although Browne was the first modern director to bring an abridged version of the entire cycle to the stage there, his mysteries were preceded by a number of other smaller-scale productions.

Early Twentieth-Century Mysteries in York

In 1909 Louis Napoleon Parker put together a memorable historic pageant for York, a four-hour-long extravaganza that included a pageant-within-the-pageant in the form of a wagon production of the Chandlers' episode of the 'Angels and the Shepherds.' The text was severely cut down from the original fifteenth-century version in the York register and emphasis was on visual pomp and elaborate ceremonial. While the individual wagons in the

Middle Ages had been accompanied by a small representation of about four of the guildsmen associated with them, this wagon was swept up in a colourful procession of guildsmen from a large variety of crafts, all bearing their heraldic banners, which were subsequently purchased by the Merchant Adventurers of York and still hang splendidly in the undercroft of their hall. This was not a replica of the past but a rendition of it that suited current purposes.

The *York Historic Pageant*, rather like the mystery plays in the way that it offered an episodic selection of highlights to its audience, covered the history of the city from BC 800, when it was founded by Ebrauc, to its surrender to the Parliamentarians in 1644. It was played in the Museum Gardens in an arena in front of the St Mary's Abbey ruins, lauded at the time by Charles Pascoe as a 'situation ... linking together the remote Past with the living Present.'[86] The pageant was an enormous success long to be remembered.

Parker's pageant involved around three thousand local people and drew on the services of all classes of citizen, including the dean of York, the Very Rev. Arthur Purey-Cust, who devised the heraldry and preached a sermon in the Minster to mark the end of the pageant season (26–31 July). His *Last Words on the York Pageant* commended the '*unity* required for a pageant' and the 'tact and unflagging good humour' needed to 'bring all divergences of opinion, which are nowhere more peremptory than in matters of taste and history, to a willing agreement.'[87]

The dean was only one of a number of prominent local clergymen involved in Parker's great undertaking; another was the vicar of St Olave's Church, Marygate, Rev. Charles Bell, who, in the lead-up to the event, gave public lectures on the subject of the history presented in the pageant, and later published a 'popular historical guide,' *Who's Who in the York Pageant* (1909). The revival of the 'Angels and the Shepherds' wagon play inspired Bell to arrange for the production of a play using six of the Nativity episodes from the York cycle at St Mary's Hall in the week after Christmas, 1909. The text, a modernized spelling version condensed for a two-hour production by Mr Wade-Gery, comprised extracts from the sequence beginning with the 'Annunciation' and ending with the 'Flight into Egypt,' and was published locally as *A Christmas Play* (1909). At this time and especially in the context of a church performance it would not have been decorous to debate the Virgin Birth, and consequently the bawdy domestic humour of the 'Joseph's Trouble about Mary' episode was excluded. Writing in the parish magazine, Bell confessed himself delighted with the result; in fact, he was able to record that those sceptics, who had come 'with disapproval effervescent within them went away touched, awed, a little mystified – and came again.'[88] He recognized that playing the roles of Mary and Joseph was 'difficult and dangerous' but was pleased to report that the unnamed actors had handled their responsibility in this regard with the 'refined reverence which can alone make possible such representations as these.' To all involved, Bell expressed his thanks, claiming that their play marked an important moment in history and making an enthusiastic prediction:

> In years to come, when thousands will fill the largest building in York [i.e., the Minster], to witness the Nativity Plays (give York five years and they will know all about it) then, dear performers and helpers, you will be proud men and women.

The projected five years stretched to almost a century, but the Minster did eventually open its doors to the mysteries as a gift to the city to celebrate the millennium.

Little has been recorded of subsequent mystery play productions in the city before 1951, but in 1919 the York Educational Settlement presented a program of unspecified mystery plays at Bootham School to open the spring term, offering two performances, one on Friday 24 January at 7:30 pm and the other on Saturday 25 January at 3 pm. In 1925 Edith Craig directed an *Old Nativity Play* at the Guildhall for the York Everyman Theatre.[89] In 1926 another Nativity based on the York plays, Paul Wright's *The Word of God* (1926), was presented at All Saints' Church, North Street, and the text was published in York for interested readers. Browne certainly underestimated local knowledge of the plays in asserting that they were a 'special treasure' in which York had 'shown no interest' prior to his involvement.[90]

Plans for the York Revival

At their second meeting on 16 December 1948, the board of the York Festival Society agreed that Thomson should prepare a plan 'under the following headings: – (a) Architecture; (b) Music; (c) Drama; (d) Pageantry; (e) Craftsmanship; (f) The River,' further instructing him to consult Hess and 'other officials necessary.'[91] The mysteries are not mentioned in Thomson's 'First Thoughts' presented to the board, although this document does consider various dramatic productions and possible venues. Early plays with religious connections, *Everyman* and Marlowe's *Dr Faustus*, were being considered for the Minster; an outdoor production of Shakespeare's *A Mid-summer Night's Dream* was a possibility; and an amateur production 'with professional assistance' of a historic pageant of York, possibly a repeat of 'earlier efforts [i.e., Parker's 1909 pageant], and performed, say, before the King's Manor.'[92] Parker's pageant remained under consideration as some-thing that 'might be worth doing' with Knavesmire and the Museum Gar-dens as alternative sites, but Thomson pointed out that historic pageants had 'the twin disadvantages of attracting bad weather and – on occasions – of being the dullest things known to man,' although they were 'very good fun for the schools and the thousands of voluntary performers and helpers who like dressing up and are doggedly prepared to risk catching their deaths of cold and/or getting drenched.'[93] York also considered enquiring about the possibility of a new play for the Theatre Royal by Priestley,[94] a very popular figure locally because of his Yorkshire connections, but as planning for the festival developed, so did the realization that the city needed neither a historic pageant nor a well-known local dramatist. York already had a play that, while it did not take the history of the place as its subject matter, was a reflection of the city's history and an authentic monu-ment to its medieval past.

Thomson first mentions the mysteries in his 'Second Thoughts,' where he indicates that there might be room 'for an adaptation of a York Morality Play,' with 'Morality' corrected to 'Corpus Christi.'[95] Then in his 'Outline Plan,' he lists *A Midsummer Night's Dream* and the *York Historic Pageant* as possibilities for the Museum Gardens, while the Minster and 'one or two of the Churches [could] be the setting for short performances of certain of the York Cycle of Morality [*sic*] Plays.'[96] This idea becomes clearer later in the plan in the more detailed suggestion of mounting guild processions 'mod-elled somewhat on the original "Corpus Christi" festival processions' that could be 'colourful and festive as well as being a backward glance at an old tradition'; these processions were to be accompanied by players who would perform in the Minster before continuing on to 'one or two of the other churches.'[97] The board made the decision on 29 September 1949 that 'instead of a York Pageant efforts should be made to see if it is possible to produce certain selected York Mystery Plays.'[98] Shortly afterwards the plan was announced in the press: York was to rival Edinburgh and the *Three Estates* by presenting a great drama that was truly native to the city. Both Browne, as director of T.S. Eliot's *Cocktail Party,* and Hess, on behalf of the York Festi-val Society, had been to Edinburgh in 1949; either of them – or Thomson or any member of the board – may have seen the *Three Estates* and made the necessary connection and suggested a large-scale revival of the mysteries.

Ongoing Mysteries

Not long after the Festival of Britain, novelist Evelyn Waugh, an implacable enemy of the post-war welfare state, predicted a bleak future. His satirical novella *Love Among the Ruins* (1953) includes a Nativity play. In Waugh's narrative, the Nativity is an 'obscure folk play ... revived and revised as a matter of historical interest' and shown on television on the eve of 'Santa Claus Day' (37). The Festival of Britain's splendid Dome of Discovery is renamed the 'Dome of Security' and stands cheerlessly at the heart of the dystopian new world. Waugh's characters interpret the Nativity play as a documentary on 'maternity services before the days of Welfare' (37), and when 'Food Production Workers' appear and 'declare a sudden strike,' leaving their sheep 'at the bidding of some kind of shop-steward in fantastic dress' (40), it takes on the added dimension of a political commentary on workplace relations. Just as his prophecy of the demise of the country house in *Brideshead Revisited* (1945) has been shown to be inaccurate,[99] Waugh's pessimistic view of the future of biblical theatre has been proven wrong. He was right though, and ironically so, in suggesting that 'historical interest' is a driving force behind the perpetuation of drama of this sort. As David Lowenthal claims, 'the cult of heritage' is a 'newly popular faith' in which the world can find solace.[100] In York this 'cult' has joined forces with more conventional devotional impulses to perpetuate the mystery play tradition, but we should remember that these were two of the forces that drove the original mysteries in the Middle Ages: the delight and the pride in preserving an ancient custom and the commitment to honour the Real Presence of Christ on Corpus Christi Day.

2 Dramatic Transformations:
Performance Spaces and Scripts

Although the splendour of the individual wagon stages would have varied according to the needs of the episode to be presented and the wealth and inclinations of its presenters, the performance space for the York mysteries was fairly constant over the two hundred years of their medieval history. The wagons, transported by manpower provided by the guilds, kept to their customary route, although there were variations in the number of playing stations: usually twelve, but sometimes as few as ten or as many as sixteen. Each station had its own unique configuration, but the cityscape remained as the permanent backdrop to the Corpus Christi theatre of the streets. This was community theatre in communal space. The city as stage, a natural characteristic of the processional mode, is a major distinguishing feature of the medieval mysteries, a far cry from performance spaces that were commonplace in the mid-twentieth century when the mystery play revivals began in earnest. The performance spaces that were familiar to audiences in 1951 were often enclosed and set apart from daily life rather than being an integral part of it.

The medieval scripts were subject to change: excisions, revisions, and amalgamations of episodes. In the early fifteenth century, the mysteries, assuming that they were indeed scripted plays by then, may have included more than the forty-eight episodes registered in the playbook in the second half of that century. This central register of play texts was nearing completion in about 1477, but even then change continued, and in the sixteenth century unrecorded texts were provided by the guilds for registration and the playbook was annotated to signal discrepancies between the official record and performance practice.[1]

Medieval Audiences

Since the 1950s, theatre practitioners have engaged with a variety of experimental formats and, consequently, street production has been restored to the range of possibilities enjoyed and expected by audiences in the twenty-first century. But the Corpus Christi theatre of the York streets was not 'theatre' in the sense that it was generally understood in 1951, when the proscenium arch was the norm. The open-air productions of the Middle Ages, with the natural light of the long summer's day playing on both actors and audience, had more in common with British playhouses before the introduction of advanced lighting techniques in the eighteenth century than they did with the enclosed and darkened auditoriums of the 1950s. As Edward Langhans has explained, those who went to the theatre in the seventeenth century were in a relationship with the stage that was unlike that of the mid-twentieth-century theatre where, 'except in Brechtian productions, directors usually [tried] to make an audience forget itself and succumb to the performance'; these audiences were 'less likely to remain quiet,' more likely to 'interfere with the workings of stage machinery,' and many of them 'went to playhouses for lack of anything better to do or to impress others or to search for sexual game.'[2]

In medieval York, the audience similarly had their own dramas to enact as they met their neighbours and encountered strangers visiting the city on the festive occasion. Among the onlookers in close contact with the wagons on the streets there was room for drunkenness and irreverence as well as the officially required sobriety and devotion. The civic leaders and their ladies also attended the mysteries in a markedly premodern manner. Comfortably indoors, at separate venues for men and women, and provided with generous quantities of food and drink, they watched the performance from their own enclosed spaces, or perhaps did not watch it as their fancy took them. With their attention divided between personal interactions indoors and the more distant performance outside, these elite audiences experienced 'theatre' as a civic-devotional-social ceremony. They thus had a relationship with the mysteries that modern audiences cannot fully share.

Scholars have long assumed that at least some members of the medieval audience were very early risers, eager to see the first wagon performance begin at 4:30 in the morning, but Meg Twycross has recently exploded this particular myth and urged us to 'forget the 4.30 a.m. start' until towards the end of the fifteenth century at the earliest.[3] The starting time, and indeed the running time, of the medieval event remains a mystery, one that will be encountered again in the epilogue to this study.

The 1951 Revival

Variations to the scripts and performance space that can be imagined for the Middle Ages pale into insignificance alongside the dramatic transformations made for the 1951 revival. The director, E. Martin Browne, and his team deliberately tailored the experience of 'medieval' civic drama to resemble modern professional theatre. In so doing they set the pattern that, in many ways, still holds good in the fixed-place productions in York, even though the venue for performances has been changed in recent years.

According to the 1951 program notes the mysteries were 'much compressed' for 'presentation in a single evening' on 'a single large stage.' Twenty-nine episodes were selected from the original forty-eight as edited by Lucy Toulmin Smith in 1885, and then these were further cut and 'dovetailed into each other so as to make a smooth running production in two parts' split by an interval after the 'Entry into Jerusalem' (see table 1).

Uncut and played at a single site, the York mysteries would run for at least thirteen and a half hours; Browne reshaped them for a three-and-a-half hour timeslot. The medieval script presents a leisurely unfolding of the biblical history of God's benevolent interventions in human affairs; Browne reduced it to a conflict between good and evil, with Christ and Satan as the central protagonists. In the Middle Ages there were multiple casts with 'characters' represented by different actors in succeeding episodes; numerous 'Gods' to perform wonders on the Creation wagons, for example; two 'Noahs,' one to build the ark and another to take his obstreperous wife aboard a second ark; and various 'Christs' for the Ministry and Passion sequences. Most scholars assume that the anonymous authors were 'parish priests, guild chaplains … chantry priests, or perhaps members of the monastic or mendicant orders.'[4] The combined script was overlapping, repetitive, and uneven in style and accomplishment.[5] The abridgement for 1951 stripped away many of these natural characteristics, transforming the mysteries into a seamless whole, smoothing out the wrinkles and refashioning the cycle for performance by a single cast.

Inventing an Author

In the preproduction publicity for 1951, the scriptwriter, the Rev. J.S. Purvis, represented the medieval playbook as the work of a single author, imaginatively costuming him as 'J. de Taystek,' a monk from the Benedictine Abbey of St Mary, and speculating that Archbishop Ralph Thoresby had instructed him to undertake the work.[6] To give this author further credibility, Purvis

Table 1
Episodes represented in the 1951 Museum Gardens mysteries

The forty-eight episodes in the original register of the play texts	1951
The Fall of the Angels	x
The Creation	
The Creation of Adam and Eve	x
Adam and Eve in Eden	x
The Fall of Man	x
The Expulsion	
Cain and Abel	
The Building of the Ark	
The Flood	
Abraham and Isaac	
Moses and Pharaoh	
The Annunciation and the Visitation	x
Joseph's Trouble about Mary	x
The Nativity	x
The Shepherds	x
Coming of the Three Kings to Herod	
Coming of the Three Kings, the Adoration	x
The Purification	
The Flight into Egypt	x
The Slaughter of the Innocents	
Christ and the Doctors	
The Baptism	x
The Temptation	x
The Transfiguration	
The Woman Taken in Adultery/ The Raising of Lazarus	x
The Entry into Jerusalem	x
INTERVAL	
The Conspiracy	x
The Last Supper	
The Agony in the Garden and the Betrayal	x
Christ before Annas and Caiaphas	x
Christ before Pilate 1: The Dream of Pilate's Wife	x
Christ before Herod	
The Remorse of Judas	x
Christ before Pilate 2: The Judgement	x

Table 1
Episodes represented in the 1951 Museum Gardens mysteries (*continued*)

The forty-eight episodes in the original register of the play texts	1951
The Road to Calvary	x
The Crucifixion	x
The Death of Christ	x
The Harrowing of Hell	x
The Resurrection	x
Christ's Appearance to Mary Magdalene	x
The Supper at Emmaus	
The Incredulity of Thomas	x
The Ascension	x
Pentecost	
The Death of the Virgin	
The Assumption of the Virgin	
The Coronation of the Virgin	
The Last Judgment	x

Note: The titles for the mystery play episodes used are, with the exception of 16 and 17, from the most recent scholarly edition of the original texts by Beadle. The titles of episodes 16 and 17, which Beadle combines as one ('Herod/The Magi'), are from the Lucy Toulmin Smith edition (1885) used as a basis for the script in 1951.

suggested that he may have been the compiler of Thoresby's *Lay Folks' Catechism*, someone close to the archbishop and 'much engaged with literary work and the writing of sermons.'[7] The invention of a single dramatist for York was tempting because Chester, a potential rival as a mystery play centre in the 1950s, could claim Ranulf Higden of St Werberg's Abbey as their equally spurious local author.[8] But the fictional monk of St Mary's had another powerful attraction: he lent authority to the choice of the performance space for the first revival production.

The Museum Gardens

In 1951 the mysteries were not made readily available on the streets of York but entertained an elite paying audience. Eager theatregoers sat in a custom-built outdoor stand to see the plays restored to their fictitious author as they were performed against the stately remains of St Mary's Abbey in the Museum Gardens, then a private space under the custodianship of the Yorkshire Philosophical Society and not freely accessible to the masses. Not only is there no proof of monkish authorship, but there is also considerable irony in that the mysteries were uprooted from the domain of the secular community and transplanted to the precincts of a religious community with whom the fathers of the medieval city had maintained a hostile relationship.[9]

Fear of the Censor

These mysteries were far from being a perfect facsimile of the original, but the program was encased in a reproduction of two folios of the 'Harrowing of Hell' episode from the fifteenth-century register of the plays (BL MS Add. 35290, ff. 208v–9).[10] This cover design was used for the next five Museum Gardens productions (from 1954 to 1966), thus foregrounding the notion of the plays as a 're-enactment.' A mantle of antiquity was assumed, shielding the production against the censor's scrutiny. Classical plays and modern works translated from foreign languages were subject to the 1843 Theatres Act and their scripts were examined accordingly. To avoid the possibility of such examination in York, efforts were made to downplay modernity and to suggest that the script had not been so much translated as simply transliterated to make it intelligible to the audience. In this context the use of the manuscript as a program wrapper was a visual guarantee of authenticity.

Censorship was an issue for the mysteries because Christ was in the starring role opposite Satan, and while the devilish hordes were quite free to inhabit the public stage, the deity and his close associates had been refused admission since the end of the sixteenth century. Although the Lord Chamberlain found no reason to intervene in York in 1951 or in the years to come, the local organizers feared his wrath until after the abolition of theatrical censorship in 1968: only then did the mystery play program change its format and in 1969 John Westbrook (Christ in the 1966 York production) carried the cross triumphantly across the cover.

There was another sign of relaxation in 1969. For the first time the program notes omitted the customary admonition that 'the audience will not wish to applaud' because of the 'nature of the subject.' In 1951 the audience was warned that this was 'not merely … a theatrical event,' and urged to see it 'as something with a deeper [i.e., religious] significance'; they were asked to suppress their natural instinct as theatregoers and receive the performance with the more circumscribed behaviour associated with church attendance.

Although York maintained a discreet silence about changes to the script that could have been challenged on the grounds of textual accountability,

the censor was not deceived. In 1956 the Lord Chamberlain's office bris-
tled with annoyance at the inconsistency whereby modern plays offering
a 'perfectly reverent, dignified and accurate life of Our Lord' were disal-
lowed while the York mysteries went on unchecked, approved by 'two
Archbishops' (i.e., the archbishops of York and Canterbury), and pro-
tected by their medieval pedigree, 'even though the version now played
has been edited and translated in the last few years.'[11] This inconsistency
was finally resolved early in 1966 when the 'absolute ban on the deity
appearing on stage in post-1843 plays' was removed, largely on consideration of the anomalies that had been apparent a decade earlier; the decisive
memo to the Lord Chamberlain stressed that traditionally no action was
taken on medieval plays 'provided they are produced in their original dialogue and setting.'[12] Browne claimed, and rightly so, that the revival of
the mysteries was instrumental in breaking the censor's ban on religious
plays and the stage presentation of the deity,[13] but in 1951 he was on dangerous ground because, as he knew and as the Lord Chamberlain most
likely also knew, the revived mysteries in York were 'original' in neither
their 'dialogue' nor their 'setting.'

Modern Audiences

Browne tested the endurance of his audience in 1951, exposing them to a
performance of an antique play that kept them outdoors at the mercies of
the weather for three and a half hours. This was, admittedly, a festival audience and perhaps they were, as T.S. Eliot maintained, theatregoers with
superior staying power and a large capacity for boredom. Speaking of *Murder in the Cathedral*, which he wrote for the Canterbury Cathedral Festival
of 1935, Eliot suggested that his audience consisted of 'serious people,' who
expected 'to have to put up with poetry' and went 'deliberately to a religious play' expecting 'to be patiently bored and to satisfy themselves with
the feeling that they had done something meritorious.'[14] Mary Kelly made a
similar comment about historic pageants, a genre with clear affinities with
the mysteries, and particularly relevant in York, where audiences may have
come to Browne's plays with a cultural memory of the *York Historic Pageant* of 1909. The audience for such pageants, Kelly claimed, went away
bored, but offered 'no serious criticism ... because of the social nature of
the affair,' and because they expected 'so little'; she did, however, entertain
the hope that the genre could be lifted 'into a fine and potent form of artistic expression' through which the pageant-goers would 'experience something that is thoroughly disturbing.'[15] Such was the outcome that Browne

desired for his 1951 mystery plays; there was far too much at stake to risk boring the audience.

Transformations for 1951

Much of the credit for the dramatic transformations of the mysteries for 1951 should be ascribed to Browne. In collaboration with Purvis he devised the cut-down scenario of twenty-nine episodes for the 'script' published by SPCK, later trimming it further for the production itself. The choices of performance space were limited as the city did not have a large concert hall, making an outdoor venue virtually a foregone conclusion. Browne refused to give any serious consideration to wagons, declaring that they could not be countenanced because of the potential disruption to traffic.[16] But he was not just anxious about traffic; he wanted to reach a large audience and believed that he could not achieve this using the 'intimate and leisurely method' of street performance.[17]

The director did not decide on the Museum Gardens immediately. He considered three possibilities: a site on the banks of the Ouse, a 'flat stretch with a hill rising up behind it'; the north wall of the Minster facing onto Dean's Park; and, his eventual choice, the 'ruined nave' of St Mary's Abbey.[18] The unspecified site by the river, possibly St George's Field, had the advantage of audience seating on the 'natural slope,' but there were 'difficulties in a backing consisting mainly of the river.'[19] At the abbey site the solid stones of the ruined walls offered a ready-made sounding board for the players; they also brought 'a strong character of [their] own' to the setting, something much desired by Browne and other directors of open-air theatre.[20] The famous historic pageant master Louis Napoleon Parker shared Browne's feelings about the value of appropriating existing buildings, preferring authentic ruins to a constructed set that might inflict on him the pain of seeing 'a Norman castle flapping in the wind';[21] in York Parker had, like Browne, chosen the area in front of the abbey as his 1909 pageant arena.

There was a rumour in December 1949 that the mysteries were to be staged 'almost certainly outside the west front of York Minster';[22] writing long after the event, Browne's designer, Norah Lambourne, implied that the Minster itself would have been a possibility had it not been fully committed to other events.[23] Given the uncertainties about the production expressed by the archbishop of York, Cyril Garbett, however, it is unlikely that the plays could have been performed there in 1951. The environs of the Minster may have been attractive to Browne, but as the building itself was used for concerts during the festival, there would have been serious problems with congestion and noise when the events coincided. The abbey site, on the other hand, was both self-contained and spacious, and these features, along with its proximity to the Tempest Anderson Hall, which could be used as a dressing room, and St Olave's churchyard, where actors could wait for their cues, were much in its favour.

Having chosen the site, Browne provided Lambourne, who worked with him at the British Drama League and was to be responsible for the design of his first three mystery play productions in York, with a specific blueprint for a fixed-place/multiple-setting stage, the Hubert Cailleau drawing of the Valenciennes Passion Play of 1547. In place of the raised platform for the main action at Valenciennes, Browne substituted the natural expanse of grass below the abbey walls. Leila Davies claimed that only 'a brave producer ... would risk these mighty scenes on the cramped picture stage of the modern theatre'; but her description of the stage, with the 'audience on raised seats facing it' suggests what was then a conventional modern stage writ large:

> [The stage] was the high grey wall of the ruined Abbey of St. Mary's, with its clerestory windows arching high in the air, and a great sweep of greensward stretching away at its feet. Clearly the one represented Heaven and the other Earth ... A long curving staircase led from one to the other, and in an angle of two walls stood a little hill with a tree bearing apples; the Garden of Eden. In the wall below was a dark doorway; the Sepulchre; and all along the lawn stood the 'mansions', the Stable, the house of Pilate and Caiaphas, and at the farthest remove from the steps to Heaven a yawning gate, framed in dragons' jaws; the mouth of Hell.[24]

Inventing the Crowd Scenes

The Oberammergau Passion Play may have influenced Browne's general approaches to his script and the stage on which it was performed, although he claims to have been unimpressed by it in 1930, unmoved by its 'pious conformity' and unawed by the 'hangar-like auditorium' with its 'glass-roofed inner stage' and 'huge forestage open to the sky.'[25] He was resolved that the work he was about to undertake as Bishop George Bell's Director of Religious Drama for the diocese of Chichester would not replicate Oberammergau's 'pietism' but would 'grow into our own century, free to find its own life.'[26] Despite these sentiments, he is unlikely to have obliterated the experience completely, particularly when he brought crowd scenes, a much-admired feature of the German play, onto his mystery play stage in York.

Having committed himself to the Museum Gardens, Browne found that he needed a crowd to absorb the spaciousness of the site, although he admitted that the medieval 'authors could not have included one on their pageants.'[27] His Valenciennes-style stage had to be filled with the colour and turbulence of a medieval city, and the large numbers in his casts rendered the open-air set as cramped as the imagined wagon-stages of the original mysteries (see plate 1).

The newly invented crowds were a cue for the scriptwriter to do some original composition. The leaf containing Pilate's decision to execute Christ is missing from the medieval text and so Purvis set about repairing the loss, although this was not made public at the time.[28] Browne was only too conscious in the lead-up to 1951 that such additions could be seized on by 'any competent lawyer' to prove that the script was 'not wholly medieval' and hence encourage the undesirable attentions of the Censor.[29]

The anachronistic crowds shouted 'Crucify!' and repeated the blood curse of Matthew 27:25, 'His blood be on us and on all our children.' Perhaps the Oberammergau crowd was uppermost in Purvis's mind, but he may also have been partly inspired by the convention of the Chorus favoured by modern religious dramatists such as T.S. Eliot (*Murder in the Cathedral*, 1935) and Dorothy L. Sayers (*The Just Vengeance*, 1946). Sayers's play is particularly relevant since her dramatization of the last moments of the life of an airman contains an embedded mystery play in which the Chorus shouts 'Crucify him!' and utters the blood curse.[30] Browne's Museum Gardens crowd scenes were to remain popular in York, despite John Elliott's scholarly frustration with 'a stage-area so huge that it has to be filled with a crowd of extras who can only get in each other's way.'[31]

The Satire of the Three Estates

Tyrone Guthrie's 1948 production of the *Satire of the Three Estates* in Edinburgh offered instructive precedents for the compression of a late-medieval text into a script suitable for presentation to festival audiences and for a radical change of performance space. Prior to the Guthrie revival, David Lindsay's play had been last presented in Edinburgh in 1554 in an outdoor setting as an estimated seven-hour production. Guthrie took the play indoors and his scriptwriter, Scottish playwright and novelist, Robert Kemp, devised a script that would fit into something closer to the conventional two-hour time frame of modern plays. Kemp had to add 'occasional lines of his own to cover the gaps' that resulted from the cuts made to the

Plate 1. 'The Road to Calvary,' Museum Gardens, 1954. The crowd follows Christ (Joseph O'Connor) as Veronica displays her veil imprinted with his image. The set is essentially a revival of the 1951 setting, with two of the 'mansions,' the thatched stable and the house of Pilate and Caiaphas, visible against the abbey walls. The soldiers carry the banners used to conceal the agonizing moments of the nailing and raising of the cross.

text, but was delighted 'by the ease with which audiences, many of whose members knew little or nothing of the Broad Scots speech, were able to comprehend the story.'[32] As they made the changes, Guthrie and Kemp kept the Lord Chamberlain in mind, judiciously removing 'most of the theology' and the 'bawdery,' because it 'might have caused more embarrassment than fun' and the Censor 'would certainly have banned all the best "lines" and all the funniest "business"' in any case.[33] A much more daring decision not to remove all of the 'magnificently highly coloured attacks upon the Roman Church' paid off; the 'performances aroused very little religious controversy' and the 'Church authorities took a very broad and tolerant line.'[34]

Guthrie chose an unconventional space for his production, the Assembly Hall of the Church of Scotland, where he built an apron stage on three levels that projected 'into the centre of the auditorium' with the audience sitting on three sides, an ideal configuration for 'the processions, heraldry and pageantry' of the play, and one that was, as Eileen Miller states, 'to revolutionize theatre building in Britain and America.'[35] Browne's adaptation of the Valenciennes stage for the York mystery play revival cannot claim anything like the international impact of Guthrie's work on stagecraft; curiously though, his choice of the continental stage plan in 1951 may have influenced medieval theatre scholarship. Before this time there was no scholarly backing for a Valenciennes-style stage on English soil, but in 1955, the year after Browne's second Museum Gardens production, Hardin Craig, who actually disliked the York revivals, suggested that the Valenciennes model might have been in use in southern England in the Middle Ages.[36] Craig offered nothing to substantiate this claim, but it may be that the Browne productions had prompted his thinking in this regard. By publishing this theory he gave the York director the academic authority he may well have desired, and as he prepared for his third production in the Museum Gardens in 1957, Browne cited Craig's pronouncements as justification for his importation of the Valenciennes setting.[37]

The Scriptwriter

After Guthrie's success, Browne had much to live up to and, with a base script almost twice as long as the original *Three Estates*, his task was more difficult. When he was Director of Religious Drama for the diocese of Chichester, he had himself adapted and edited a number of medieval mysteries, including 'The York Nativity Play,' for performance in churches. But for the York project he sought the aid of a local scriptwriter. Keith

Thomson, the artistic director of the festival, recommended Purvis, archivist to the archbishop of York since 1939, as 'a scholar who also had some of the gifts of a dramatist.'[38] Purvis had published numerous historical papers and had written and directed two historic pageants, the Cranleigh School pageant (1924) and the Eccleshall pageant (1925). As a clergyman and as diocesan archivist, he was also potentially a valuable ally in gaining the blessing of the archbishop and hence protection against censorship.[39]

The Local Dialect

Unlike Kemp, however, Purvis was not a professional writer, and while the *Three Estates* was delivered by professional actors, who delighted audiences with their 'Broad Scots speech,' many of the actors in York were from the local amateur theatre groups. David Mills states that these actors, like those who performed in the Chester mysteries that year, were 'primarily representatives of the middle-class business and professional community,'[40] a demographic that has subsequently been expanded somewhat, although to some extent it still holds good. Unsurprisingly, the favoured accent in the Museum Gardens in 1951, adopted by amateur and professional actors alike, was that of the BBC, although Davies reports that a 'wave of pleasure passed over the whole audience' when the Shepherds of the Nativity spoke their lines in 'good broad Yorkshire.'[41] Writing in 1963, perhaps with the benefit of hindsight in the climate of growing interest in regional accents in the professional theatre, Browne lamented that when he had contemplated leaving passages of the York mysteries in 'broad dialect' he 'could not find people to speak them.'[42] He later elaborated on this issue, insisting that 'only a very few of the north-country vowels' were in use in the city and that actors from the outlying countryside, 'mostly employed on the land and rising very early, couldn't face our late hours of performance'; although the shepherds were the genuine article, he claimed that any dialect used by other actors, 'was consciously studied,' and because he 'did not want to cumber actors with the care of *learning* a dialect: it seemed better to let each speak in his natural way.'[43] This may well have been the case, but it is also possible that the local amateurs, modelling themselves on their contemporaries on the professional stage, made an effort to suppress any native brogue.[44]

This dilution of the local dialect could be seen as a continuation of a process already under way in the fifteenth century. M.L. Holford argues that the 'rhymes' in the original York register of the plays 'suggest a good deal of dialectal diversity in the guild originals, including a number of more southerly forms' and that there was a deliberate policy on the part of the civic administration of discouraging 'regional language.'[45] Jeremy Goldberg provides a convincing reason for this, declaring it to be a 'policy of "spin"' designed to encourage a perception of York as 'second only to London in importance.'[46] When they published their modern-spelling edition of twenty-two of the original mysteries, Richard Beadle and Pamela King cited these same scribal practices as the beginning of a process that their own work brought to a fitting conclusion.[47]

The Impact of the Purvis Scripts

The Purvis text for 1951 undeniably has its faults, and the scriptwriter was aware that he lacked the appropriate literary and linguistic training for the task, admitting that he was 'no expert in Middle English verse, or in XV C. Northumbrian grammar.'[48] Nevertheless, when his expanded version came out in 1957, Browne praised it as a 'complete cycle for the modern reader' that combined 'scholarship with a sound sense of theatrical values' and was 'likely to become the standard text for the modern producer.'[49]

Elliott challenged Purvis's 'scholarship' and his 'sense of theatrical values,' despairing of his scripts as stumbling blocks to any director, regardless of his or her talent, and declaring that they were 'written in a language no one ever spoke.'[50] Despite Elliott's judgment, the Purvis text proved effective in practice, and even academic mystery play directors, such as those involved in the major wagon productions in Leeds (1975) and Toronto (1977), used the Purvis version, although other wagon play directors have used the more recent modern-spelling edition by Beadle and King or their own adaptations of the texts.

In 1951 J.C. Trewin described himself as one 'playgoer' who was 'profoundly moved' by the narrative and astonished by 'the sustained quality of the medieval rhymed verse.'[51] In the same year Yorkshire poet Tony Harrison was outraged by the production and conceived the idea of creating his own version, but his argument was with the southern tones of the actors rather than with the Purvis script. Bernard O'Donoghue's introduction to the published text of Harrison's acclaimed *Mysteries* goes so far as to praise the Purvis version as 'an effective, mildly modernized acting text' that 'served pretty well on the stage' even though 'nobody could deny that Harrison's, although it is both more colloquial and often harder to understand, has much more vigour and integrity.'[52]

Hans Hess, artistic director of the York Festivals from 1954 to 1966, conceded that the 1957 Purvis edition of the whole cycle might be preferable on 'purely literary and scholarly considerations,' but he recommended the use of the shorter edition of 1951 on the grounds of the 'greater ease of speaking and understanding of the parts' and its 'undoubted clarity and modernity' that made it 'better ... for dramatic performance in the open air.'[53] Browne agreed with him and used the 1951 version again in 1966. But by this time even Browne had reservations about using either of the Purvis texts and raised the possibility of 'starting again, on the lines of [his] original approach,' collaborating with a 'scholar (preferably at the University) to get a speakable acting version which an audience [could] follow, while retaining the original verse-forms and character of diction.'[54] But Hess was concerned about costs and also about 'petty quarrels or worse' – legal action on Purvis's part – that might result if a new version were attempted.[55] So it was that the Purvis texts were used until 1973, when the council commissioned Howard Davies, who worked as an editor, and had, according to the program, 'translated the Wakefield and Coventry Cycles for performances in the City of London festivals in 1971 and 1972,' to provide a completely new script for Edward Taylor's second production.

When Harrison began on his 'full-scale Yorkshire acting version' of the mysteries for the National Theatre (1977–85) he dreaded neither the Censor's ban nor the scholar's scrutiny. Harrison's work was clearly an adaptation and, as such, could claim licence for any departures from the originals he desired. Such freedoms were not available in the 1950s when nervousness over the possibility of a public outcry dogged the York mysteries right up to the opening night.[56] The 1951 script had to be passed off as a faithful transliteration from medieval to modern English; it could not be mistaken for an adaptation or a free translation. Purvis explained his 'guiding principles' in his edition of the full cycle in 1957; his aim was 'to alter nothing that could possibly be retained ... so long as the result might be clear to a modern audience.'[57] He kept some archaisms and 'dialect words,' but admitted that he made free with the rhymes, using deliberate mistranslations in some cases, and omitting the rhyme completely or replacing rhyme-tags with a 'token phrase' in others.[58] Rhymes that depended on pronunciation in dialect were, of necessity, lost when uttered by non-Yorkshire-speaking actors. Little wonder, perhaps, that from the point of view of medieval specialists, the result was, as Elliott so scathingly puts it, 'a language no one ever spoke.'

For all their faults the Purvis editions brought lasting benefits to the academy as well as to general readers. Browne's productions were, like all theatrical productions, essentially ephemeral; the Purvis texts, on the other hand, were a tangible memorial to the York revivals and to the mysteries of the past. Until the publication of the modern-spelling edition by Beadle and King in 1984, the Purvis volumes were the only ready access to an extended reading of the York mysteries available for the non-specialist. For those who could read Middle English, there was the Toulmin Smith edition of 1885, long out of print by the 1950s, reissued in 1963, but only superseded in 1982 with the publication of Beadle's old-spelling edition. Purvis clearly filled a gap, and in doing so made the York mysteries prominent.

As founding director of York's Borthwick Institute of Historical Research, Purvis embarked on a number of lecture tours to the United States during the 1950s. He visited universities, libraries, and learned clubs, and became known internationally as an expert on York and its medieval mysteries. At that time no one inside or outside the academy – perhaps not even Browne – rivalled Purvis in putting medieval English theatre on the map.

The royalties from the 'shorter' and 'complete' versions were divided between the scriptwriter and the York Festival Society, and for many years the mysteries were fiercely guarded against infringements of copyright. Productions outside York were scrutinized carefully and any other production of the York scripts in Britain in the same year as the local festival was forbidden. In 1976, Purvis's beneficiary, his sister, Hilda Purvis, signed the royalties over to the English Department at the University of Leeds, which then established two 'Purvis Prizes' for academic achievement. The Purvis legacy thus remains associated with scholarship, while local admiration for his work is such that in a recent publication, the discovery of the fifteenth-century playbook (actually purchased by the British Museum from the earl of Ashburnham in 1899) is erroneously attributed to him while 'cataloguing the archiepiscopal archives.'[59]

The Script for 1951

In the text published for 1951, only twenty-nine of the forty-eight episodes in the medieval text are represented. In Browne's production, only two of these, the 'Fall of Man' and the 'Temptation,' were left reasonably intact, while the remaining twenty-seven suffered further heavy cuts. Purvis made several attempts to secure an agreement with SPCK to publish an acting edition that would reflect more accurately what was presented on the Museum Gardens stage,[60] but his publishers, after two successful editions of the 'shorter' version, and mindful that an acting text might not be stable in perpetuity, were unwilling to go ahead, opting instead for publishing the 'complete' version. Purvis thus 'curb[ed] his dramatic tendencies somewhat and completely translate[ed] the nineteen previously omitted plays.'[61] This undertaking opened up the entirety of the original text for directors in the Museum Gardens and provided ready-made scripts for the wagon plays that were attached to the fixed-place productions as ancillary events.

Browne and Purvis chose the twenty-nine episodes for the 1951 publication in November 1949. The Browne/Purvis scenario stripped away most of the opening speeches to change the 'tempo' for the modern audience 'for whom [Browne believed] the ponderous progress of the pageant carts, most of their plays starting with a declamatory speech of "pomping" by the chief character or "telling" by a narrator, would have a boring slowness.'[62] Even the deity had his lines cut. God the Father was allowed to keep his opening lines for the first episode, the 'Fall of the Angels,' for example, but had to give up the reminiscences of the Creation that ran throughout the original texts as well as the review of human history at the 'Last Judgment.'

Elliott notes that the 1951 Purvis script was 'essentially a Passion Play with a Prologue and Epilogue' that 'purged the cycle of some of its more controversial legendary and apocryphal accretions, especially the Mariolatrous matter.'[63] All the Old Testament episodes other than those chosen from the Creation sequence were lost and consequently the production was skewed towards the Life and Passion of Christ, thus accentuating what was already a strong characteristic of the original text.

The Purvis text for 1951 contained an almost complete version of the 'Crucifixion' episode but this was cut at the request of the archbishop, who 'did not want the Passion scenes, with their physical brutality, to be shown.'[64] Browne responded by concealing the nailing of Christ and the raising of the cross behind the banners held by the Roman soldiers. The horror was obscured both verbally and visually as Browne cut the lines that enunciated this action from the acting script. Christ's potentially disconcerting direct address to the audience inviting them to gaze on his wounds and consider his suffering was also removed as was the soldiers' callous drawing of lots for his coat at the end of the original episode. Browne expressed his own concerns over the Passion scenes in 1956, declaring them so terrible that 'we probably could not endure' to see them played.[65]

Christ versus Satan

While the cuts made in the Purvis edition of 1951 and the subsequent cuts that Browne made for the production itself are interesting, what was not cut is even more significant. Browne was committed to the idea of drama as 'an art of contrasts' in which 'absolute goodness' could only be shown against 'the worst evil of which men are capable';[66] with this in mind he strengthened the Christ versus Satan contrast. Satan was allowed to retain his 'pomping' in the 'Fall of Man' and the 'Temptation' episodes in order to focus the narrative as a battle between the cosmic representatives of good and evil and to emphasize Christ's resistance to Satan's enticements as the prelude to the Redemption. In the original York mysteries devils have speaking roles in only six of the forty-eight episodes; Browne's production brought Satan upstage. For the millennium production in the Minster, professional writer, Mike Poulton, also made alterations to the script that enhanced the good versus evil conflict, keeping his Satan on stage to fight to the very end in the 'Last Judgment' scene by combining the 'Harrowing of Hell,' which, strictly speaking, should have been played earlier, with the grand finale.

Browne continued to revise the script after the 1951 text had been sent to the publishers, not only with further cuts, but also with one significant addition to reinstate some of the lines previously excised.[67] These lines, which later appeared in slightly altered form in the 'complete' version (225–6), involved Satan, Percula, and her son on the night of Christ's first trial before Pilate.[68] In keeping with the Christ versus Satan pattern, the additional material had the effect of bringing Satan to the fore as he entered the bedroom of the sleeping Percula. Satan, as the arch-enemy of God and humanity, tries to prevent the Crucifixion and therefore prevent the possibility of Salvation, choosing as he did in the case of the 'Fall of Man' to exercise his influence through a woman.

Browne's decision to focalize Satan as the enemy may inadvertently have had the effect of shielding the mysteries from the charges of anti-Semitism so frequently levelled against the Oberammergau Passion Play.[69] The differences between the mysteries and the Passion Play in their presentation of the enemies of God could account for the differing perceptions of anti-Semitic bias. Oberammergau lost its devils in 1811, when monkish reviser, Otmar Weis, decided to excise everything that was without 'biblical authority'; according to James Shapiro, this left a 'structural problem' since the removal of the 'infernal powers' as the 'opposition to Jesus' left a gap, which Weis then filled with the crowd and particularly the 'Jewish priests and merchants, who now became Jesus' main persecutors and were given biblical names and stereotypic attributes.'[70] Browne and Purvis added the crowd and the blood curse in imitation of Oberammergau, but Lambourne dressed the Jews in the costume of medieval England, aligning them with the citizens of York rather than emphasizing their Jewishness. More significantly, however, far from removing devilry for 1951 as Weis had done for Oberammergau,

Browne made Satan the real foe for Christ by enhancing his role. John van Eyssen played Satan in 1951 and 1954, and his graceful athleticism and allure almost stole the show.

Alternative Performance Spaces and New Scripts

Although Browne remained popular with audiences and the local actors who worked with him in the Museum Gardens, the board of the York Festival Society was keen to introduce change. Urged by Hess, they sought other directors after the 1957 production. By March 1958 they had agreed to invite Tyrone Guthrie to undertake the work, and by December he had accepted 'provisionally.'[71] Guthrie inspected some alternative performance sites including Dean's Park and King's Manor, but the board insisted on the Museum Gardens and by January 1959 he had withdrawn, apparently not charmed by the romance of the ruins.[72]

In the 1970s the need for change was being discussed once again. In 1973 the issue was raised in the press and local freelance theatre director Richard Digby Day suggested a move to Dean's Park against the wall of the Minster, one of the sites Browne and Guthrie had considered, or even inside the Minster itself, or more outrageously, a wagon production, while Wilfrid Mellers, Professor of Music at York University, suggested a radical new translation that would be 'a bang-up-to-the-minute one by a modern poet like Ted Hughes.'[73] But it was not until 1992 that changes of this magnitude took place and then under extraordinary circumstances. The artistic director of the festival, Margaret Sheehy, engaged Scottish poet, Liz Lochhead to write a new script, a major departure from all previous versions. At the same time Sheehy put forward a plan for a promenade production in the Museum Gardens. The year 1992 marked radical changes to both script and performance space, but not quite as Sheehy had envisaged. In the midst of a considerable tumult, the artistic director was sacked, and although the Lochhead script was used, the mysteries did not promenade in the Museum Gardens but went indoors to the Theatre Royal. The next dramatic transformations were in response to another set of special circumstances, this time of a much less contentious kind, when the Minster opened its doors to the mysteries for the millennium and Poulton rescripted the text for the occasion.

Using the Ruins and the Purvis Script

From the end of the 1950s to the aborted Museum Gardens production of 1992, directors and designers responded in different ways to the abbey ruins; some, like William Gaskill and John Bury in 1963 all but ignored the ancient walls, while others, like Edward Taylor and Patrick Olsen in 1969, constructed sets that blended into the permanent backdrop. There were some variations to the script, too, as directors made their own choices from the Purvis texts and added touches of their own.

In 1973 local director Edward Taylor worked with a completely new script, which was put together by Howard Davies, who based his work, as Purvis had done, on the 1885 Toulmin Smith edition.[74] Davies cut the 'Baptism' and the 'Slaughter of the Innocents,' added the 'Stretching and Nailing of Christ' and a 'Last Supper' of his own invention to supply a gap in the original manuscript, and interpolated some material from the Towneley cycle, a practice that has medieval precedent although the borrowings in the Middle Ages seem to have been in Towneley's favour.[75] Elliott complained that Davies, like Purvis, had shaped the text into a 'kind of Protestantized Passion Play.'[76]

Other directors were not entirely happy with the Purvis scripts or the shape of the cycle refashioned in 1951. Jane Howell chose the 'Ascension' rather than the 'Last Judgment' as the finale to her production in 1976, and Toby Robertson restored the Marian episodes of the 'Assumption' and 'Coronation of the Virgin' in 1984. Finally, in the last change before the Lochhead version, Steven Pimlott's assistant director in 1988, Andrew Wickes, prepared a substantially new adaptation based on the Purvis text of 1957.

Suggestions for the Future

After his last Museum Gardens production in 1966, Browne made some suggestions about the future of the mysteries, stressing the need for change to keep the tradition healthy.[77] He commended the example of Oberammergau's ten-year cycle for their Passion Play and the practice at that time of performing Old Testament plays in the intervening years to maintain interest and continuity. His suggestion for York was to keep the triennial festival but to present the abridged production of the whole Creation to Last Judgment story only once every nine years; he envisaged that at the two intervening festivals the text could be split into two sections thus allowing for more episodes to be seen and for the individual texts to be presented with fewer cuts:

First triennial festival   'Creation' to 'Last Judgment' cycle
Second triennial festival   'Fall of the Angels' to 'Entry into Jerusalem'

Third triennial festival   'Conspiracy' to 'Pentecost'
Fourth triennial festival   'Creation' to 'Last Judgment' cycle.

This scheme allowed the two 'parts' to end on a note of triumph but also
reserved the 'Last Judgment' as the unique finale for the complete version.
He further suggested that the 'Death,' 'Assumption,' and 'Coronation of
the Virgin' be omitted from these productions as, showing his Anglican
bias, he did not believe they belonged to the central story. At the same
time he was not suggesting a complete ban on these episodes, proposing
that, because of the music associated with them, they be presented separately from time to time in a church setting, using as the analogy the success of his own production of medieval Latin music dramas in the church
of St Michael-le-Belfrey in the 1966 York Festival.

With the Festival Society on the brink of being wound up after the 1966
event, it is not surprising that Browne's suggestion was not taken up, nor
is it surprising that he was also ignored in 1973, when the future of the
festival was again under discussion. At that time, based on the assumption
of quadrennial festivals, he floated the idea of a three-part split along the
lines of his suggestion in 1966 with a 'condensed version only every
twelfth year.'[78] In the difficult economic times of the 1970s, those in
charge of the festivals in York were not taking any chances by varying a
successful formula.

Browne knew the mysteries and the local community through and
through, however, and his thoughts were to some extent prophetic. The
pattern that has since established itself in the city, with the guilds mounting their full-text selections of wagon plays every four years, and the
Minster potentially offering the next abridged cycle on the tenth or
twelfth anniversary of the millennium production, is similar to what the
inaugural director had in mind as the way forward in the late 1960s.

Modern Wagon Plays

Radical changes to medieval practice occurred when Browne inaugurated
the modern wagon tradition with the production of a single play of the
'Flood' as an adjunct to and advertisement for the Museum Gardens event
in 1954. As I discuss in chapter 8, the modern wagon tradition has under-
gone various other transformations since then. The scripts have usually
been normalized towards modern English but have remained virtually
intact, although only a fraction of the original cycle has been performed
in the processional format. Meg Twycross opened a precious window of

opportunity onto the physical dimensions of the past in 1988 and 1992, when her wagons played on a section of the original pageant route, and Jane Oakshott, although unable to use these narrow streets for her wagons in 1994 and 1998, restored the tradition to the descendants of the original guilds, who have maintained their stewardship through to 2006.

3 A Leap of Faith

The decision to stage the Museum Gardens mysteries in 1951 was a spectacular leap of faith. The York Festival Society risked the success of their enterprise by abandoning safe options such as Shakespeare or a local historic pageant, while the mystery play director, E. Martin Browne, staked his professional reputation on a virtually unknown dramatic text and a largely amateur cast.

E. Martin Browne

Browne trusted in the power of the mysteries and in the dedication of his team not just to put on an entertaining show but also to convince church authorities that Christianity 'might find a new dimension' through theatre.[1] His years of experience meant that he was well placed for success. He had made his debut as an actor in 1927 and had a scholar's interest in theatre history, having taught theatre studies at the Carnegie Institute of Technology in Pittsburgh in the late 1920s. He had worked with amateur players in the mining community of Doncaster, where he was warden of the Educational Settlement from 1924 to 1926; and in 1930 Bishop George Bell, a major force in the modern religious drama movement, who as dean of Canterbury had established the Canterbury Cathedral Festival, appointed him as Director of Religious Drama for the diocese of Chichester. This connection brought him into contact with T.S. Eliot, and he subsequently achieved prominence through his association with the poet's career as a dramatist.[2] From 1948 he was director of the British Drama League, a group particularly important for amateurs, founded in 1919 for 'the encouragement of the art of the theatre, both for its own sake and as a means of intelligent recreation among all classes of the community.'[3] His professional theatre work included touring with the Pilgrim Players during the war and productions of modern verse drama at the Mercury Theatre in Notting Hill from 1945 to 1948. He was accustomed to working in straitened financial circumstances and on makeshift stages, and he saw value in combining amateurs with professionals, frequently calling on members of his professional circle to strengthen and encourage amateur productions.

Browne was sensitive to the integrity of the medieval plays and believed that modern productions should avoid the 'temptation ... to broaden the rustic realism into farce, to burlesque the "baddies" and oversweeten the "goodies", to "go to town" with "business,"' any of which could, in his view, result in loss of 'the poetry and the faith of those in whose power the plays were created.'[4] He had adapted the Coventry 'Nativity' for Doncaster (Christmas, 1925) and his first production for Bishop Bell in Chichester was 'The York Nativity Play' in Eastbourne Parish Church for Christmas in 1930. He followed with 'The Play of Maid Mary,' an adaptation of the N-Town episodes of the legendary birth and early life of Mary, presented in the gardens of the Bishop's Palace in August 1931.[5] His Pilgrim Players had numerous mysteries in their repertoire, including 'The Merry Play of Christmas,' an amalgam of episodes from the York, Towneley, and Coventry cycles. By the time he came to the Museum Gardens Browne had been offering glimpses of the medieval cycles for almost thirty years, but his previous efforts had been much less ambitious than what he intended in York and had usually been staged in church settings, where they were beyond the reach of the Censor and assured of a polite reception.

Browne's 1951 venture was fraught with danger. Even in academic circles, where the mysteries were known to a small number of specialists, the prospect of large-scale productions for twentieth-century audiences was not uniformly welcomed. In 1929, for example, George Coffman looked forward to the day when 'an English town or city ... may give us a revival of one of the preserved cycles,'[6] but in the following year Robert Withington put a dampener on such ardour, advising that it would be unwise to attempt it because he was 'not sure that even the professors could stand the whole of a cycle' and quite convinced that a performance 'based entirely on an historical interest [was] not likely to be effective.'[7] Browne was, of course, not attempting a 'whole cycle' as envisaged by Coffman or Withington, since his script was an abridgement of the medieval version; nor was it a 'historical' reconstruction, as the performance was on a fixed-place stage rather than on wagons. But even with these compromises to modern sensibilities, Browne's faith in the mysteries, in the local performers, and in his professional support group had to be strong for the attempt to be made at all.

The inaugural director brought to York more than his faith as a theatre practitioner in 1951. His personal religious commitment and his belief in the cohesive bonds of community were also important factors that were expressed pointedly in his practice of beginning 'rehearsals and perfor-mances with a public prayer.'[8] As an undergraduate he had 'read for honours in Theology at Oxford,'[9] and had it not been for his deep interest in drama and his consequent meeting with professional actor, Henzie Raeburn, who became his wife and partner in his theatrical enterprises, he may have entered the church. As he led the Pilgrim Players around the country per-forming religious plays he was particularly aware of the power of coopera-tive effort. He had founded the Pilgrims with a specific agenda:

> We would do religious plays. Let the Oxford Dictionary define religion: 'Human recognition of a superhuman controlling power, and especially of a personal God entitled to obedience.' We would do plays showing the effect of such recognition on conduct and mental attitude.[10]

Actors joined him with a sense of mission, 'giving up certainty, stability, comfort and the bright lights and applause of the "real" theatre; and giv-ing them up, not because [they] had to, but because [they] wanted to.'[11] But they joined for diverse reasons:

> There were definite Christians, who wanted to offer Christian ideas through their art. There were agnostics, who disapproved of the outspokenly Chris-tian plays, but felt that the theatre had a duty to the people ... There were pacifists, who saw in this self-denying ordinance for the actor a way of ser-vice compatible with their conscience.[12]

Despite this diversity Browne regarded the Pilgrims 'as a community,' with a single purpose of making an 'artistic' rather than a charitable 'offering to the Church' to convince audiences that a religious play was essential 'food for the spirit ... that, like any other food ... must be paid for.'[13] The literal rationing of food in Britain did not end with the war but continued until the summer of 1954, and by this time Browne had directed two mystery play seasons in York. This too was a 'community' effort and was, indeed, rich 'food for the spirit' that was eagerly received by those with the money and the inclination to pay for it.

The community that presented the mysteries in York was as diverse as that of the Pilgrim Players, yet it held together under Browne's direction for the three consecutive festivals (1951, 1954, and 1957) and welcomed him back in 1966. The initial leap of faith paid off for all concerned, acknowledged in the awarding of New Year's Honours to a number of the key players in the undertaking. Browne himself and the artistic director of the festival, Keith Thomson, received CBEs in 1952, while the scriptwriter, J.S. Purvis, and the assistant artistic director (and artistic director from 1954 to 1966), Hans Hess, received OBEs in 1958.[14] More importantly for York, however, in the euphoria that followed the success in 1951, the plays, albeit unrecognizable to a time-traveller from the Middle Ages, were reinstated as an 'ancient custom' towards which a section of the local community felt a deep fondness and, consequently, an obligation to preserve.

Local Contacts

Browne certainly won the affection and gratitude of the city and of individuals who worked with him on the mystery play project, but long before he was feted as the revival director, he had friends locally. In 1923 and 1924 he had worked as a subwarden with the York Educational Settlement, and in 1934 and 1935 he was, briefly, a director for the York Citizens' Theatre Company that had been formed in 1934 under the chairmanship of the influential Quaker and social historian, Seebohm Rowntree, to save the Theatre Royal from the dubious choice of being 'converted into a cinema or closed down.'[15] This background gave him a solid introduction to the city and a network of acquaintances who had the experience, expertise, and enthusiasm to assist him in his dramatic enterprise in 1951.

The Educational Settlement had been established in York by the Quakers in 1909 as a centre for men and women who 'wish[ed] to combine education and fellowship'; it was available to all regardless of 'social class, political party or religious faith' and offered a variety of activities, including lectures and recreational and craft classes.[16] Drama featured at the Settlement from its inception, and as noted in chapter 1, the opening of its spring term in 1919 was marked by a performance of mystery plays at Bootham School. In 1922 the Rev. John Hughes formally set up the York Settlement Community Players. During his lengthy service as warden (1921 to 1930) and through to his last production for the Settlement in 1935, Hughes worked with a number of people who were later to become mainstays of the York mysteries, including Browne himself and Edward Taylor, who was Museum Gardens director in 1969 and 1973. In his memoirs, Browne recalls important local contacts made through Hughes and the Settlement: Leonard and Lilian Pickering, John Kay, Alec and Kathleen de Little, and Reginald and Olave Dench, parents of acclaimed actor Judi Dench.[17] These were friends he acknowledged in fulsome terms in his tribute on the death of Alec de Little in 1976: 'Without them the great adventure – foolhardy as it seemed to many people – of reviving the Mystery Plays in 1951, could not have come to success.'[18] His old friends took key speaking roles and performed vital ancillary functions in 1951 and for many years to come, but Browne, and indeed other directors in York, also relied heavily on those who came season after season as members of the onstage crowd or to labour behind the scenes in less visible ways.

Browne's work with the Settlement in the early 1920s included lectures and discussion groups and in December 1923 he directed three plays for the Settlement Players: John Synge's *Riders to the Sea*, George Bernard Shaw's *The Dark Lady of the Sonnets*, and the 'Drunk Scene' (act 2, scene 3) from William Shakespeare's *Twelfth Night*, with Hughes as Malvolio and Browne himself as Sir Andrew Aguecheek. A decade later, when he joined the York Citizens' Theatre in 1934, he was grateful to Hughes for his pivotal role in fostering 'the considerable band of amateurs who had kept on doing good plays which the professional theatre had failed to provide.'[19] By this time, Browne asserts, the Settlement Players had 'become one of the leading companies of the north, recruiting also dress-makers and property-makers and building up a good wardrobe.'[20] Their success had encouraged the formation of other local dramatic groups, whose combined strength was such that Browne was asked to direct an amateur production of Clifford Bax's historical romance *The Rose Without a Thorn* for the Citizens' Theatre, with Leonard Pickering in the role of Henry VIII and Barbara Hughes, daughter of John Hughes, as Katharine Howard. Despite the apparent promise of the situation, Browne's tenure as codirector at the theatre and that of his wife, Henzie, as a member of the permanent company, were short-lived. He resigned because of his uneasiness over what was then his lack of experience in the professional theatre and a deepening antagonism between himself and his more-experienced fellow director, Roy Langford.[21] Brief though this second period of employment in the city was for Browne, it had the advantage of cementing local friendships and thus contributed to the ease of his return for the 1951 mysteries.

Other friendships formed during Browne's mystery play seasons themselves have had a significant effect on the ongoing history of the revivals in York. The Heppell family, for example, who owned a local construction firm, was involved in the building of the Museum Gardens sets for many years, and Ossie Heppell, who played a Roman soldier in 1951, continued to act in later productions and was codirector and set-designer for the wagon play of the 'Temptation of Christ' in 1998. Another significant new friendship for Browne was with Stewart Lack, a local secondary school teacher who, like Heppell, was a member of the Settlement Players. Lack's first mystery play role was that of Peter in 1954, and he was pivotal to the development of the modern wagon play tradition that will be discussed in chapter 8. Lack's support, along with that of many other local enthusiasts, was just as necessary to the director as the network of professional theatre colleagues that he also depended on.

Professional Contacts

Browne insisted that his mystery play productions needed professional input. He was adamant that 'the nonprofessional, who holds a strong conviction and is willing to work hard, can in certain circumstances do this job as well as a professional,' but he was equally convinced that it did 'not at all follow that the show can do without professional skill' and that 'the simplicity and directness which serve an actor best in this kind of work still need the disciplines of the theatre.'[22]

Professionals were used in all areas of the 1951 production. Lighting was provided by Percy Corry of the Strand Electric and Engineering Company; Alan Wicks, former assistant organist of York Minster and now at Canterbury Cathedral, was the musical director and the music itself was composed by James Brown, a lecturer in music at the University of Leeds; Geraldine Stephenson, a teacher at the Art of Movement Studio, Manchester, devised the movement; and the set and costume design was by Norah Lambourne, who had joined the British Drama League in 1949 as a staff tutor in Costume and Stage Decor. In 1951 Browne declared that 'the two chief parts [i.e., Christ and Satan] must be played by professionals,' reasoning that these roles would be too demanding on amateurs already tired from their normal 'day's work.'[23] Ultimately he employed sixteen students from Esmé Church's Northern Children's Theatre School at Bradford and a total of eight professional actors, including his wife, who also functioned, unpaid but acknowledged in the program, as associate director:

Joseph O'Connor   Christ
John van Eyssen   Satan
David Giles   Archangel Gabriel

Joyce Rankin	Eve
Tenniel Evans	Archangel Michael
Dudley Foster	Lazarus
Henzie Raeburn	Mary Magdalene
Esmé Church	Mary Cleophas

This casting of professionals, along with the enlistment of the Harrogate Dramatic Group, an amateur company with which Browne had worked in the previous year, caused a degree of discontent in 1951,[24] and tensions were to increase in the ensuing years as the local drama groups tried to influence the casting process in favour of the York amateurs. When he called for actors for what was to be his final production in 1966, Browne promised that 'recruitment of professionals would not start until after auditions in York,'[25] but the practice of employing professionals in key roles that he established in 1951, with the exception of Edward Taylor's all-amateur production in 1969, continued for the Museum Gardens mysteries, although as time went on the number of professionally paid actors dwindled to just one to take the role of Christ.

The Role of Christ

Browne theorized that because 'God took flesh ... and became a man,' the Christian faith was the 'closest of all religions to ... drama, wherein the actor offers his own self as the medium through which a new self is created before his fellow men.'[26] Little wonder, then, that he treated the casting of the role of Christ with particular care as he prepared for the 1951 mysteries. Although he was willing to be flexible regarding the other actors, he announced through *The Times* that the actor for this central role must be 'a Christian'; added to this, he must have 'considerable histrionic ability and some stamina,' looks that conformed 'roughly with the common idea of what Christ looked like,' and, by no means least important, he must also agree 'to remain anonymous.'[27] Anonymity was also required of Noel Shepherd, the local actor who played God the Father. Because of the religious sensibilities of the time and, perhaps more pertinently, because of anxieties about possible censorship, Browne and the York Festival Society were treading warily.[28] As Browne himself put it, anonymity, which was customary for religious plays at that time, was a precaution adopted 'to allay the fear that the appearance of the deity in visual form would be a blasphemy.'[29]

In 1951 Joseph O'Connor, the Dublin-born professional actor playing Christ, was not named in the program. O'Connor had only recently made his debut on the London stage and hence was relatively unknown. He was a devout Catholic and an experienced actor in religious plays, having appeared as Michael in Dorothy Sayers's *Zeal of Thy House* at the Canterbury Cathedral Festival in 1949 and as in Malcolm in Robert Kemp's *Saxon Saint* for the Edinburgh Festival in 1950. In his *New Statesman* review of the York production Herbert Read observed that 'only the Church of England (or Holman Hunt) could have groomed this curly-headed, beardless Nordic Jesus';[30] there were some complaints, however, about O'Connor's clean-shaven face, prompting Browne to consider a beard for 1951. Experiments at rehearsal convinced both him and O'Connor that facial hair 'blanketed expression and that appearing clean shaven was more aesthetically correct.'[31] Browne was perfectly happy with his star's looks and with his 'magnificent voice and gentle, tolerant expression [that] enable[d] him to invest a most difficult role with dignity and deep understanding.'[32]

O'Connor's anonymity did not last beyond the first night in 1951. He was recognized immediately by *Daily Express* theatre critic John Barber, who announced his identity to the world, praising his 'noble humility' and describing him as 'as effortlessly magnetic as the North Pole.'[33] Browne was later to rejoice in this disclosure, although, at the time, the York Festival board expressed outrage that Barber should not have observed the proprieties as other reviewers had done. Many must have recognized O'Connor but decided, like Eric Keown for *Punch*, to respect 'the convention that leaves *The Christ* anonymous.'[34]

With O'Connor unmasked and the 1951 mysteries declared a success, the anonymity requirement evaporated, and in later years there were concerted efforts to attract well-known actors to the role of Christ. For the 1960 production (dir. David Giles), for example, Hess, as artistic director of the festival, approached Paul Scofield to play Christ, George Rose to play Satan, and Paul Robeson to play God the Father.[35] He was not successful and similar disappointments followed in later years. In 1980 director Patrick Garland entered into negotiations with Michael York, whose surname as well as his fame made him most desirable, but filming commitments prevented him from accepting.[36] Eventually the role was taken in 1980 by Christopher Timothy, the TV 'vet,' whose long-running series *All Creatures Great and Small* had just come to an end. Timothy was not the first small-screen star to perform in the mysteries, nor was he to be the last, although not all of those who followed him, as will be seen in chapter 7, were as well received as 'James Herriot.'

The Crowds

The mysteries were not dependent merely on star actors to take the central roles, and when preparations were underway in 1951, Browne put out a call for three hundred performers.[37] Stephenson was presented with the task of devising the movement for the crowd of two hundred and fifty extras. Daunted by this prospect she sought advice from Hungarian choreographer Rudolph Laban, who suggested that she 'make three lots of thirty, eleven groups of ten, and split the remaining fifty into two groups, then put [her] students in charge of these groups' so as to be able to 'create separate bodies of movement.'[38] Her work with the crowds was still remembered by A.L. Laishley in 1980:

> As they rehearsed she watched carefully to see how her people were developing, and then selected her characters accordingly, so that, as nearly as possible, they could keep something of their own personality – shy or talkative, gentle, bold, unassuming. She would suddenly pounce on someone and demand, 'Who are you?' and woe betide that man, woman, child, who was still a nebulous nobody without even a name.[39]

David Henshaw, a lecturer in movement and drama at St John's College, York, who was Browne's choreographer in 1966, emulated this approach, dividing his crowd into groups representing families, neighbours, and friends. According to Browne, this treatment of the crowd was a means of showing to the audience how the Ministry and Passion of Christ were taking place 'in a city of people like ourselves.'[40] He saw the crowds as an opportunity to create a sense of a community of participants encompassing audience and actors, the same sense of community that can be read into the original mysteries.

The Guilds

In 1951 Browne sought to foreground the York guilds, thus making a statement about the place of the plays, past and present, in the formal structures of the local community. The ancient guilds featured in the publicity that accompanied his production, while the modern guilds were targeted to fill the roles of the burghers for the 'Entry into Jerusalem,' the triumphal finale of Browne's first act. Browne called for actors from the ranks of the 'four [sic] existing York guilds' to ensure 'a real link between past and present,'[41] and at least two guildsmen performed as burghers: Hubert Dryland, a member of the Merchant Taylors, and Charles Mein, of the Merchant Adventurers.[42] Dryland demonstrated his ongoing loyalty to the mysteries as a member of the Mystery Plays Advisory Board that was formed in 1954 and was cast as Noah in the wagon play of the 'Flood' presented as an adjunct to the Museum Gardens production in the same year. Mein did not perform again but showed his continuing interest when he wrote to Browne as a member of the 1957 audience, complaining, but with the utmost courtesy, about various changes that had been made, including the costumes, the acting, and the setting, which he considered did not fit well with the abbey ruins.[43]

Browne as Director

Browne's instruction to his casts was dispensed with unfailing courtesy and a conviction that 'specific acting choices should be made with full input from the actor in the role and not pre-planned by the director.'[44] Dale Savidge comments that he 'tended to direct actors in a more objective, traditional fashion (he rarely, if ever, referred to Stanislavski's theories)':[45]

> Sometimes [he] would read the play aloud to the cast, trying to give some semblance of the quality of delivery he would be seeking. He considered this the beginning and foundation to the production – learning to ride on the rhythms, not consciously but unconsciously, like breathing.[46]

Rhythmic delivery of lines, along with 'uncluttered stage space ... ritualised and processional movement, symbolic costuming and properties, [and] unobtrusive ... lighting' were the hallmarks of his work.[47] His actors were instructed in a rhythmic mode of walking in a 'free' and 'regular' manner, 'with the shoulders held straight and the head well poised,' something that was encouraged by trial runs in the medieval stage costumes.[48] The costumes had yet another virtue in that they gave the production additional armour against the Censor by dressing the play in a facsimile wardrobe as a period piece. Despite the fact that medieval actors wore contemporary costume Browne disapproved of the 'temptation' of using 'twentieth-century dress,' arguing that 'in performance it can import certain realistic questionings that may separate the audience from the experience rather than unify them with it.'[49] Although purists might say that he was missing the point, there would have been no point at all in risking emulation of the medieval practice in 1951.

A director with strong views, Browne was clearly a delightful personality, 'often characterized as gentle, soft-spoken and unhurried ... Henry Sherek ... jokingly called him "Saint Martin."'[50] Judi Dench performed in three of Browne's mystery play productions in her native city, graduating from attendant angel (1951) to angel at the tomb of the Resurrection (1954) and, finally, just before embarking on her brilliant professional career, to Virgin Mary in 1957 (see plate 2). Dame Judi now looks back on those days with great fondness: her 'first real taste of acting' and her 'first real experience of being part of a company,' very much a family time in which she and her parents, Olave and Reginald Dench, all 'had huge fun.'[51] She also recalls the impression Browne made on her: 'an adorable man, like a kind of crane, with huge hands, a very storky kind of person.'[52] All the same, he was a man of firm decision; Lambourne, his mystery play designer in the 1950s, recalls that his correction of his casts was 'totally final and absolutely crushing.'[53]

Browne and the Amateur Players

Although Browne believed that a medieval cycle 'belongs to, and reflects the characteristics of, its own location,' he remained convinced that if this particular 'dramatic heritage' was 'to be kept fully alive, the amateurs cannot be left to do it unaided.'[54] When the Festival board was preparing for the 1954 production he approached the matter of casting delicately, anxious not to offend the local players, but equally determined to maintain standards. He expressed the opinion that 'about three professionals' would be needed for the production 'unless, quite unexpectedly, a local genius should arise.'[55] He clearly thought that this was most unlikely, and although he 'would willingly give York Players the very first chance,' he asserted his prerogative as the director 'to fill each part with the right player.' Furthermore, he made the point that 'the Bradford Theatre Group [i.e., students from the Northern Children's Theatre School] would be needed, as the players [had] a special athletic training and were used with great effect in the crowd scenes, where they served as focal points for less well-trained amateurs.' But the local amateurs clearly wanted a greater level of input than they had been allowed in 1951, and in 1953 Alec de Little wrote to the board of the Festival Society suggesting a list of names of people to act as a Mystery Plays Advisory Board:

G.W. and J.L. Pickering, Reginald Dench, and Alec de Little (Settlement Players)

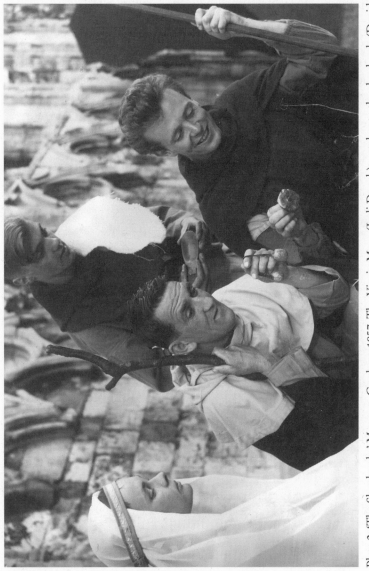

Plate 2. 'The Shepherds,' Museum Gardens, 1957. The Virgin Mary (Judi Dench) watches as the shepherds (David Smith, standing, and kneeling from left, Cyril Edghill and David Cobb) present their gifts to the Christ child.

John Watson (Rowntrees Players)
Edward Taylor (Co-op Players)
J.H. Blenkin (York Amateur Operatic and Dramatic Society)
H.H. Dryland (York Musical Society)
A.S. Rymer (Chairman, York Festival Society, 1951).[56]

Browne was delighted with the suggestion and approved the formation of this group on the proviso that it worked strictly under his authority.[57] Although he was not about to hazard the quality of his production by putting his faith solely in the talents of the local amateurs, he kept faith with them by listening to their advice, and they, likewise, kept faith with Browne as an old and respected friend.

Initial Reactions to the Browne Formula

Just over a week into the festival season in 1951, Purvis wrote to Browne in emotional, humble, and highly appreciative terms, according him, as director of the plays, the right to speak the words of God the Father as a means of stating his relationship to the mysteries:

Take ye now here the breath of life,
And have ye (here) your souls of me.[58]

The press was uniformly enthusiastic, praising the mysteries as expressions of faith, as drama, and sometimes as a combination of both. The *Church Times* approved of Browne as the 'appropriate producer,' declaring that the end result was 'not of art, but religion,' but also enthused that this was 'something startlingly different from the devout little religious dramas so often done in church.'[59] The same sentiment was reiterated in response to the 1954 production, when John Buckingham for the Christian journal *British Weekly* pointed to the York mysteries as a shining example of brilliant writing, a work of 'supreme genius,' whereas modern religious drama, he contended, was 'disgraceful stuff.'[60] J.C. Trewin wrote glowingly for the journal of the British Drama League, speaking for the audience when he said that the 'unknown author ... chilled us as no modern dramatist within recollection.'[61] Russell Kirk, despite his reservations about the 'generally upper-middle-class' audience already mentioned in the prologue to this study, was delighted that York had had 'intelligence and piety sufficient to conjure up the ghost of ... communal faith' in 1951, predicting that the city would continue the tradition and, over-optimistically perhaps, that the 'consequent influence upon belief and art in York' would be 'interesting to observe.'[62]

Some prominent members of the audience, however, were not quite so impressed. Dorothy L. Sayers, a close friend of the designer, attended opening night in 1951;[63] she reflected affectionately on Lambourne's work, declaring herself 'privileged to stitch silver braid all round Pilate's Centurion [sic] in the intervals of a slightly frantic dress-rehearsal.'[64] But although she wrote to her friend to congratulate her on 'a marvellous job of work,'[65] she was surprised and scandalized by what she saw as Browne's mishandling of the 'Harrowing of Hell' episode and singled it out as 'bad religious drama' both doctrinally and theatrically.[66] Ever a stickler for correctness, Sayers complained that by having the actor playing Christ leave the tomb for the 'Harrowing' and return to it via the front door before exiting again for the 'Resurrection,' Browne had failed to distinguish between the 'entry of the disembodied soul into Limbo, and the raising of the whole Humanity, body and soul, at the Resurrection.'[67] One reason for Sayers's ferocity on this matter may have been that she had herself taken meticulous care in this regard in her play for the Lichfield Festival of 1946, *The Just Vengeance*. Sayers's play presents the 'Persona Dei' as both God the Father and Christ in a truncated mystery cycle embedded within the larger play. She was conscious of the need to distinguish the two persons through their costume and to signal the distinction between Christ at the Crucifixion and his post-Resurrection appearance in heaven by means of 'a very difficult costume change which had to be exactly timed.'[68] Sayers may have been overly severe though, and few, if any, other members of the audience are likely to have agreed with her that the 'Resurrection' in York came as a 'complete anti-climax.' They are more likely to have been as impressed with it as Janet Leeper, the reviewer for the *Spectator*, who declared that the 'Harrowing' was 'a most impressive piece of medievalism.'[69]

The theatre scholars also had their say. Arnold Williams was of the view that the 1951 production was 'fascinating to both critics and the general public' and recommended the Purvis version of the text to the 'general reader,' who would not want to struggle with the original-language edition of Lucy Toulmin Smith.[70] Glynne Wickham not only approved, but also claimed that the 1951 revivals in York and Chester shook the 'basically Victorian attitudes' towards medieval theatre that saw it as 'at best some primitive, gothic prologue to Shakespearean drama.'[71] Audiences in 1951, he claimed, could well challenge scholars and ask why they 'should never have been told what they might expect of these mediaeval plays, or why it was that they had been so seriously misled by historians and critics.'[72] The 1951 experience, he said, had 'aroused suspicions of a possible misjudgment between literary and dramatic values,' and thus, very much in keeping with the mission of his Drama Department at the University of Bristol, which he had joined as founding professor in 1947, he threw down the gauntlet to those academics who still claimed that 'drama is literature or nothing.'[73]

American Hardin Craig, retired professor of English, however, was of the old school and was scornful of Browne's 1951 production, declaring that the application of 'modern histrionic and theatrical techniques simply did not seem appropriate':

> The performance was right enough, no doubt, but was not the York plays. As for mock holiness, in places almost as artificial as *Murder in the Cathedral*, it seemed a poor exchange for the simple piety of mediaeval people. There is no harm in going through what are thought to be mediaeval motions, but in fact mediaeval religious plays seem to be lost in the tide of time. Acting may present certain pleasant pictures through the senses, but the method of scholarship, which proceeds by way of reading, study, and reflection, is possibly the better hope.[74]

Could there have been an element of professional defensiveness or even jealousy in Craig's dismissive reaction to something that he saw as 'not the York plays'? Cultural historian David Lowenthal's remarks are instructive when we seek to reconcile the purist approach of some literary scholars with the audience applause for mystery plays. 'History' and 'heritage' are closely related activities, he claims, and their exponents might well see themselves as rivals, 'competing for the same terrain,' yet in this competition, 'heritage often comes out ahead.'[75] Similarly, the revival mysteries reached a public in 1951 that was far beyond anything that scholars of the time could dream of reaching – they were certainly coming out 'ahead.'

Some negative reactions to the Browne productions have proved extremely fruitful. The first of these was an academic enterprise organised by Martial Rose, then head of English and Drama at Bretton Hall Teacher Training College.[76] Rose was 'deeply impressed ... bewitched ... fascinated ... and moved' by Browne's 1954 revival of his first production in the Museum Gardens, but felt that it was 'far from the medieval spirit in which the original performances must have been imbued.'[77] Disturbed by the lack of authenticity in the fixed-place condensed cycle, he was prompted by the 1954 York wagon play of the 'Flood,' another Browne innovation, to begin preparations for his 1958 production of the Towneley cycle in the grounds of the college. These plays were then commonly known as the 'Wakefield'

plays, named after the town in which they were thought to have been performed on wagons after the manner of York, both of which assumptions
have subsequently been questioned.[78] The original text was not as heavily
cut as in the Browne/Purvis model for York, but this production was also
performed on a fixed set, although Rose also used two moveable wagons
to augment his main stage, thus acknowledging what was then believed to
be the original performance method.[79] There were further important
flow-on effects from the Bretton Hall production itself: in 1961 Bernard
Miles used the Rose text of the Towneley mysteries at the Mermaid Theatre in London for what was the first mystery play production on the
professional stage, slipping past the Lord Chamberlain's ban on 'imper-
sonation of Christ or the Deity' by claiming faithfulness to the 'basic simplicity' of the original text.[80]

Beyond the academy, Yorkshire poet Tony Harrison was annoyed by
Browne's 1951 production, largely on the grounds that the northern text
had been delivered in rounded southern tones. From his conviction that the
plays had been displaced from their original language and from what
he perceived, incorrectly, as the working-class identity of the guilds came
Harrison's acclaimed *Mysteries* for the National Theatre.[81] This professional
theatre project developed over a number of years, with the first part, *The
Passion*, performed in 1977 and the final Creation to Last Judgment text
directed by Bill Bryden in 1985. Harrison's Yorkshire-accented play is a
condensed cycle based on the York text with additions from the other three
surviving English cycles, Chester, Towneley, and N-Town. The impact of
Harrison's *Mysteries* has since been felt in York itself, where the hard hats
and the building-site set used in the Theatre Royal production of 1992
recalled the Bryden interpretation of Harrison's work. Harrison has also
inspired other adaptations such as the Katie Mitchell/Edward Kemp *Mysteries* for the Royal Shakespeare Company in 1997;[82] his influence also
extends beyond Britain with, for example, the Bernard Sahlins and Nicholas
Rudall production for the Court Theatre, Chicago, 1992, which acknowledges a debt to the 'English National Theatre's production of the mid-1980s
and its adaptation by Tony Harrison of these medieval texts.'[83]

Browne believed that the mysteries could be appreciated as religious,
theatrical, and historical artefacts. In 1956 he admitted that not all his
mystery play actors were religious, but although few of these 'modern
actors' shared the 'faith which inspired' the original writing and performance of the mysteries, the life of an ancient city' had 'deep roots' and
local people taking part in the plays were 'stirred by emotions which,
though old,' were 'very close to the heart.'[84]

Bryden reminded the audience for Harrison's National Theatre *Mysteries* of 1985 that the 'faith' presented in modern adaptations of the medieval cycles can have many interpretations:

> These plays are ... about the faith of the common people ... They make sense today, at a time when the church is virtually nowhere, because they help us to remember our faith and our struggle for that faith, whether it is in our family, our home town, our union.[85]

This diversity of interpretations of 'faith' that can encompass notions of religion, class, personal identity, and heritage remains important to the York mysteries in the twenty-first century. The very elasticity in the definition means that participants come together as a community to present and to receive the plays from a variety of viewpoints.

Arguments for Change

The successful 1951 formula was reapplied in 1954. Although audiences were delighted again, Hess was adamant after the experience of his first year as artistic director of the festival that there must be change, arguing that the 1951 production had been 'fresher, truer and more dramatic' than its revival and that there should be 'no firm pattern of production and no continuity of the same people.'[86] He believed that any directorial pattern would become 'outmoded' and advocated 'new thoughts to work out the style of the production' every few years. Although he was by no means ungrateful to Browne, Hess was convinced that the plays were greater 'than the men' and foresaw that 'each generation will have to solve its artistic problems anew.'[87] His admiration for Browne and his desire for change were in conflict as he outlined his plan for the 1957 festival:

> To appoint a new producer has much to commend itself but is fraught with many risks ... He might be very enterprising but unless the new man has the same and manifold high qualities of Martin Browne we may be faced with a great display of theatrical showmanship but lacking in the depth and love which Martin Browne has brought to the production.[88]

Change was slow in coming and the Festival board played it safe, seeking continuity along with change. For the 1957 production they tried to recruit O'Connor as associate director of the plays, hoping that he would also play the part of God the Father,[89] but although he expressed his willingness to work as Browne's assistant, O'Connor's preference as an actor was to take over the diabolic role in which van Eyssen had been so spectacular.[90]

The Role of Satan

O'Connor's aspirations to the diabolic role in 1957 are understandable. Even in the uncertainty leading up to the 1951 opening, the anonymity restriction that applied to him did not extend to his opposite number and, besides, van Eyssen's Satan had been a splendid success. Leeper, for the *Spectator*, commented that 'it was the devil-scenes which were enjoyed most in this spirited revival ... [the] Devil always seems to get the best of it, even in a mystery play.'[91]

Some part of the Satanic success must be ascribed to Stephenson's thoughtful choreography. She recalls van Eyssen as 'a man of great charm' and describes her work on the pattern of his fall in some detail:

> Sometimes with quick movements, sometimes slow as he held onto the railing. This allowed him to deliver his lines. The devils tore off his white and golden robes as he tumbled down ... and he landed at the bottom of the stairs in black and tattered array. I had also been asked to choreograph a small dance as the devils made their way from the bottom of the stairs to Hell's Mouth, and this went down very well, but Martin Browne said that it was too good and would steal God's thunder. So it was cut right down.[92]

Satan must be allowed to shine, albeit not too brightly, and his athleticism became traditional in Browne's mysteries. Robert Rietty in the role in 1957 was commended in the *New Statesman* review for his 'splendid agility of mind and body';[93] while Henshaw, who played Satan in 1966, as well as providing the choreography for the whole production, was also praised for these qualities.

Troubles for the Brownes

Browne did not always have matters go entirely his way in York and trouble was brewing in the lead-up to the 1957 festival when Hess presented his outline plan. The board of the York Festival Society agreed that Browne was to be invited to direct the mysteries, but also ruled that Hess 'should be authorised where necessary to exercise control over [Browne] on any particular desire of the Board with regard to the production of the plays' and that O'Connor was to be invited as associate director, a position previously filled by Browne's wife, Henzie.[94] Ultimately O'Connor did not come to York for the 1957 event and Henzie assisted her husband unofficially and no reference is made to her or any other 'associate director' in the program.[95] Judi Dench recalls Henzie's direction of the 'Resurrection' in the 1954 production in a way that suggests that she was every bit as firm as her husband:

> I played the young man guarding the door of the tomb ... I wasn't allowed a chair. Henzie said not, so I had to sit there with bent knees ... It was most uncomfortable.[96]

Martin Browne and Henzie Raeburn were accustomed to working as a husband-and-wife team.[97] Henzie regularly took starring roles in his productions and wrote a number of plays for him to direct, including *Disarm!* (1932), *Beginning of the Way: A Nativity Play* (1941), *The Green Wood: A Dramatic Liturgy* (1961), and *Who is There to Ask* (1963).[98] Browne was somewhat ruffled in Doncaster in 1925 when he presented the Coventry Nativity 'in a church so hidebound that the vicar would not allow Henzie to play in it because she was a professional actress, of the devil's brood,'[99] but he took some satisfaction in using her, dressed as a nun, as a prompter for this production. On another occasion, when he was working with theatre manager Henry Sherek on Eliot's plays in the early 1950s, Sherek 'like most other managers,' was opposed to the notion of a director's wife in the cast; Browne accepted this but described the situation as 'bitter for us both.'[100] The Brownes may have felt some bitterness again when Henzie was excluded from the York mysteries in 1957.

In 1951 and 1954 Henzie had been associate director and had also played Mary Magdalene. She was in charge of the Mary scenes and Sister Bernarda Jaques, whose invaluable doctoral research on the Museum Gardens mysteries (from 1951 to 1969) was supervised by Browne, credits her with the 'brilliant invention' in the 'Nativity' episode, where the 'Virgin prostrated herself with her circular cloak spread over her whole body ... parted her hands and arms and raised them as if they were enfolding wings in a gesture of love and humility to reveal the Babe hidden in the straw.'[101] A letter from Browne to Alderman G.S. Bellerby, chairman of the York Festival Society board, in 1954 clearly outlines Henzie's duties, all of which were covered by Browne's own fee as director.[102] As she had done in 1951, Henzie was to 'undertake the bulk of the work of training the amateur actors individually,' including the early weeks of rehearsals when Browne could not be present, and was to 'assume authority over the cast' and liaise with the artistic director on 'all matters pertaining to the production' during any of her husband's absences.[103] This arrangement was not, apparently, entirely harmonious, and when he wrote his report after the 1954 festival, Hess commented that the performance of the mysteries 'suffered from a good deal of sentimentality mainly in the roles of the Marys,'[104] a pointed criticism of Henzie's work.

In March 1957 Henzie wrote to Hess to voice her surprise and disappointment at the board's decision not to reengage her in that year. Her letter has not survived, but the reply from Hess implies that there had been official concern over the matter for some time:

> Already before the 1954 Festival the Board informed Mr. Martin Browne that no engagement of actors or Assistant Producers shall be made without the prior sanction of the Board ... It was at the Press Conference in 1954 that Mr. Martin Browne made the – to us unexpected announcement, of your re-engagement. We let it by. For the 1957 Festival, however, it was made very clear from the outset that it was not the Board's intention to engage you, for the Mystery Plays, neither [sic] as an actress nor as an Assistant Director.[105]

The Brownes may have felt bitter, but there is no specific indication of it in their memoirs. Browne describes Hess as a 'prickly little man who made, and rather enjoyed making, enemies,' and one with whom he had 'many quarrels,' but acknowledges him as 'a man of integrity and of artistic judgement which he would stand by to the utmost,' according him the honour of being largely responsible for the 'quality and vitality of the York Festival, and of successive productions which kept the Mystery Plays fully alive.'[106] Hess had a record of conflicts during the festivals with which he was involved and he often gave offence, having little time for members of the press, and ruffling feathers locally on more than one occasion. Even in his enthusiastic comments on the 'perfection' of the 1951 festival, he concluded waspishly that 'York had discovered its soul; it may not have known it had one.'[107]

Hess was intent on influencing the recruiting of performers for the mysteries and pressured Browne to recast the Maries for 1957.[108] The board also agreed that 'it would be advisable to engage professional Actors who [had] not taken part in previous productions for the main parts.'[109] Henzie was thus effectively excluded. After the 1957 festival Hess moved against Browne himself:

> Theatrically speaking, the Mystery Plays have reached a dead end, the third 'Martin Browne' production should be the last. It is impossible for a man, if he

has any stature, to change his views and in spite of many outward changes, some of which were improvements, the production was a repetition of former years ... there was too much third rate acting amongst the professionals and a complete absence of coherence in the style of acting ... The Abbey walls, the text, and a new mind must come together for a fresh start.[110]

In 1966, however, Browne was brought back after two experiments with other directors and he was quick to preempt Henzie's exclusion by announcing – to the surprise and annoyance of Hess and the board – that she had been cast as Mary the Mother of Christ. Although Hess appears to have made some form of protest, the casting was allowed to stand.[111] Henzie's subsequent performance as an 'agonizing Mary the Mother' was reportedly 'one of distinction.'[112]

A Leap of Faith

Browne's initial leap of faith had landed him on his feet. He had shown in 1951 that Christianity 'might find a new dimension' through the theatre and hence fulfilled the dream so long held by Bishop Bell and the members of the religious drama movement. The York mysteries, once the expression of a community's piety, had proven their worth as modern community plays, bringing people together time and time again as they explored their city's past and affirmed its present identity through theatre. The community bonded even as it overcame – or at least contained – the internal conflicts and the frustrations that accompany the organization of any major local event. Heritage awareness, a new 'faith,' as David Lowenthal claims it to be,[113] ran alongside the more conventionally defined faith that many individuals brought to the experience of playing in the mysteries.

Browne had made good use of the York heritage in his campaign to put religion back onto the stage and by the time his last production was underway in the Museum Gardens in 1966, his leap of faith had had a profound effect on British theatre. His mysteries, because they had been so enthusiastically embraced by the public, much more so than the mysteries of other revival centres, had, as discussed in the previous chapter, alerted the Lord Chamberlain's office to the hypocrisy of the banning of modern religious plays when the ancient religious plays of York were allowed to go on unchecked. The leap of faith had taken British theatre a giant step towards the abolition of stage censorship by bringing an end to the centuries-old ban on the stage representation of the deity.

4 Theatre of Cruelty

BARBARA: Our George was cruel in the crucifixion, though.
MOTHER: Too cruel.

Peter Gill, *The York Realist*

Writing between the wars, French surrealist Antonin Artaud insisted that the twentieth century needed a theatre to wake the 'nerves and heart' with 'immediate and violent action.'[1] Moving away from the passive voyeurism encouraged by the 'ordinary psychological theatre' he proposed a 'Theatre of Cruelty' that would 'resort to a mass spectacle ... [and] seek in the agitation of tremendous masses, convulsed and hurled against each other, a little of that poetry of festivals and crowds when ... people pour out into the streets.'[2] He rejected the conventional separation of audience and actor, and envisaged the spectator absorbed into the action itself, bombarded with elements of surprise, 'masks, effigies yards high, [and] sudden changes of light.'[3] According to Artaud only this would make theatre 'possible,' and because of the degenerate condition of society it was 'through the skin that metaphysics must be made to re-enter ... minds.'[4]

The professional stage in post-war Britain experienced the aftershocks of no less than three European theatrical movements. Artaud's 'Theatre of Cruelty' finally impacted in the mid-1960s, but the energy of the 'Theatre of the Absurd' from France had already been felt in the mid- to late-1950s;[5] so too had the 'Epic Theatre' of Artaud's contemporary, German playwright and director Bertolt Brecht.

The Berliner Ensemble in Britain

Brecht's work had been known in England since the 1930s, but the decisive moment for British theatre history came in 1956, shortly after his death, when the Berliner Ensemble came to London to present *The Caucasian Chalk Circle*, *Trumpets and Drums*, and *Mother Courage*. The plays were delivered in German, which few members of the audience could understand, and hence it was 'the visual effects of the productions and the physical aspects of the company's acting that had the greatest initial impact.'[6] William Gaskill, described by Maro Germanou as 'the warmest advocate of British Brecht,'[7] recalls that the experience of seeing the Ensemble at work changed his life.[8]

Immediately after the 1956 visit, Gaskill's mentor at the Royal Court Theatre in London, George Devine, directed a production of *The Good Woman of Setzuan*, and Gaskill himself went on to direct many of Brecht's works, including *The Caucasian Chalk Circle* for the Royal Shakespeare Company in 1962, which won the *Evening Standard* Best Play of the Year Award, and *Baal* for the National Theatre in 1963. His interest in Brecht showed through in his treatment of the Museum Gardens mysteries in 1963, and, as will be discussed further below, Gaskill, like David Giles before him in the 1960 festival, parted company dramatically with the Browne tradition.

Brecht's Plays at the York Festivals

The York Festivals were well acquainted with Brecht in the 1950s. German-born artistic director Hans Hess, who had fled the Nazis in the 1930s, introduced his former countryman to his new fellow citizens in England's North in 1957. He advocated the inclusion of Brecht in the festival program for that year and when preparations were underway late in 1955, he was planning a production of *The Threepenny Opera*.[9] He had undertaken to translate the work into English himself, but when he had almost completed this difficult task, he reported to the board of the Festival Society that there was a possibility of a production in London in 1956. Sam Wanamaker was indeed preparing a production for the English Stage Company in February of that year and Hess decided that it would not be 'advisable for it to be performed during the 1957 Festival.'[10]

Undeterred, Hess suggested *Galileo* for the Theatre Royal.[11] He then approached Brecht for permission to stage the play, invited Charles Laughton, who had taken the title role in the 1947 English-language premiere in New York, to join the production, and secured the promise of a 'producer from the Berliner Ensemble' to direct it jointly with the York Repertory Company.[12] As was so often the case when the famous were invited to York, however, Laughton was unavailable; nevertheless Hess went ahead with planning for two unspecified Brecht plays.[13] Eventually *The Caucasian Chalk Circle* had a one-week run at the theatre, performed by students from the Royal Academy of Dramatic Art, and directed by John Fernald, who had been appointed as principal of RADA in 1955. Hess contributed a note on the author to the program, extolling his virtues as a major influence on contemporary theatre in England and abroad.[14]

Local reaction to Brecht in 1957 did not match Hess's refined enthusiasm, especially as there was already concern that the festival program was too highbrow for the average York citizen. The board of the Festival Society insisted that it was their duty to provide quality events for visitors, but Bill Lang, writing for a special festival issue of *Yorkshire Life Illustrated*, concluded that 'certain York people who know what they like in the way of entertainment will not ... be at the Theatre Royal ... to watch *The Caucasian Chalk Circle* by Bertolt Brecht ... certain York people might have preferred Priestley.'[15] Well-known and well-loved, Bradford-born Priestley would inevitably win local favour, especially over a German playwright, whose work, as Hess admitted in the program notes, was 'not difficult to enjoy ... but ... less easy to understand.'

Robert Speaight for the *New Statesman* received the Brecht play favourably, noting that it had 'a most interesting affinity with the Mysteries,' and suggesting that it was 'a happy, and perhaps accidental, thought to have presented these plays in contrast.'[16] Whether or not it was 'accidental' in 1957, when Hess included *The Good Woman of Setzuan* in the 1960 program, again performed by RADA students under Fernald's direction, he made it quite clear that the choice was deliberate, explaining that the 'parable play by Bertolt Brecht has the same epic and eternal qualities and, as a counterpoint to the medieval plays, spans the centuries and shows not so much the gulf as the link between them.'[17]

Artaud, Brecht, and Medieval Theatre

Artaud's 'poetry' of festival crowds infiltrating the world of the performance recalls the dynamics of the medieval mysteries and their audiences in York on Corpus Christi Day; and his insistence on the link between metaphysics and cruelty is suggestive of the affective piety that characterized the religious practices of the laity in the fifteenth and sixteenth centuries. Intense concentration on the symbols of the Passion in personal devotions focused the medieval mind on the physical torments of Christ, while in the mystery plays the people of York and their visitors could see this cruelty represented against the backdrop of the workaday world of the walled city. Physical cruelty certainly made a lasting impression on at least one member of the original audience for a Corpus Christi play in the town of Kendal in Westmorland (now Cumbria). The Puritan divine, John Shaw, was appalled to discover this when he questioned a man, who was then about sixty years old, in 1644. He asked him what he knew of the 'way to Salvation … by Iesus Christ God-man, who … shed his blood … on the crosse'; to Shaw's disgust this man was ignorant in matters of religion, remembering only that he had heard of 'that man … in a play at *Kendall* … where there was a man on a tree, & blood ran downe.'[18] The last performance of the Kendal play was probably around 1604, forty years prior to this interview, but the memory had lingered, perhaps because the impression had entered, as Artaud puts it, 'through the skin.'

Brecht freely admitted his debts to earlier drama, turning 'frankly and self-consciously … to Shakespeare's and Moliere's theatre and … to the mystery and passion plays of the middle ages.'[19] Brecht strove for his now famous 'V-effects,' disrupting 'the viewer's normal or run of the mill perception by introducing elements that [would] suddenly cause the viewer to see familiar objects in a strange way and to see strange objects in a familiar way.'[20]

These features of the Brechtian aesthetic, and others, such as episodic structure and direct address to the audience, can be traced in the lineaments of the medieval mysteries, whose anachronistic treatment of the biblical story as if it were unfolding in present-day England, imperfectly seamed plots, expository figures, and opening speeches of self-display render them 'Brechtian' before their time. Cutting-edge theatre practice thus fortuitously replicated York's original mysteries, and in the late 1950s this was a means of promoting the revivals to the theatre-going public. As Speaight claimed, considered alongside Brecht, the mysteries emerged as timeless and immediate, 'concerned with the same primary themes of good and evil,' and resolving the 'antimonies of man's existence with the same fundamental optimism.'[21]

Brechtian Mysteries

Brecht made a profound impression on theatre scholars as well as theatre practitioners. Richard Southern, for example, dedicated his *Medieval*

Theatre in the Round (1957) to the memory of the German playwright and 'to the Berliner Ensemble in recognition of a theatrical experience among the greatest of our time.' But the analogies between Brecht and medieval theatre were not clearly articulated in the academy until 1970 when Martin Stevens suggested that by understanding Brecht, scholars could better understand the 'non-representational drama' of the Middle Ages.[22] In this instance theatre practice was well ahead of scholarly theorizing; long before the Brechtian aesthetic was applied to the professional study of medieval drama, professional directors were using it to bring the mysteries to festival audiences in York.

Browne's mysteries opened in 1951 to an audience that had no cultural memory of them, but by the end of the decade they were aligned with the new wave of British theatrical culture. In 1957, drama critics recognized that Brecht started 'from a position diametrically opposed to that of the mystery-play authors,' but he was 'not so far from them in method'; both Brecht and the mysteries were 'overtly didactic and brimful of humanity,' and both were 'equally far from the cliché-characters of our "realistic" drama.'[23] Browne himself noted the connection in 1958 when he was promoting the 'sturdy faith' of the original mysteries, emphasising their lack of sentimentality and their 'avoidance of emotion for emotion's sake' in the hope of attracting an audience that consisted of more than just the faithful.[24] He was certainly conscious of the excitement over Brecht in the 1950s, but it was younger directors, Giles in 1960 and Gaskill in 1963, who turned Brecht's appropriation of ancient theatre around and applied his theories to the Museum Gardens mysteries.

Change in the Museum Gardens

Neither Giles nor Gaskill had been the first choice of the York Festival Society as mystery play directors. For the 1960 festival Hess suggested inviting 'a great producer like Tyrone Guthrie ... or ... a scholar like Dr. Richard Southern ... [with] an assistant producer with practical stage experience ... like Anthony Yates ... the choice between showmanship and scholarship.'[25] Michael Croft, who had founded the National Youth Theatre in 1956, actually began work on the 1963 mysteries but was compelled to withdraw because of ill health, leaving an opening that was taken by Gaskill.

Hess was determined to find a new director for 1960, declaring that 'good showmanship' would 'pay us better' but that he 'should prefer scholarship if first-rate showmanship [was] not available rather than a mediocre production full of good intentions.'[26] Both Guthrie and

Southern were known for their inventive approaches to stagecraft and their broad understanding of early theatre. Guthrie's triumph with the *Three Estates* in Edinburgh, his subsequent success with the thrust stage in Canada and the United States, and his trademark production style, which consisted, as Gaskill puts it, 'of swirling banners and crowds in endless movement,'[27] would certainly have appealed to those who had acquired a taste for spectacle in the Museum Gardens. Southern, already the author of an impressive number of books on theatre, was an attractive alternative.[28] His recent scholarly work on the *Castle of Perseverance* made him formidable as an expert in medieval drama and also linked him to the contemporary interest in playing in the round, thus supplying him with additional credibility in the context of current theatre practice.[29]

After the 1957 mystery play season, American filmmaker Cecil B. DeMille, fresh from the success of his 1956 biblical epic *The Ten Commandments*, which was nominated for an Oscar for Best Picture in 1957, offered 'to organise a York International Festival of Mystery Plays.'[30] The board of the Festival Society ignored him. Amazing though the impact of *The Ten Commandments* had been in 1956, DeMille's cinema credentials may not have been perceived as sufficiently high-culture to allow him admission to the mystery play community.

DeMille's was not the only offer to be turned down; when Browne contacted the board in mid-1958 to indicate his willingness to direct in 1960 he was informed that they were already in negotiations with Guthrie.[31] There must have been high hopes of this new director, because he was to be paid a fee of £1000 (plus expenses), far in excess of the modest £400 (plus expenses) paid to Browne in the previous festival.[32] Guthrie, who had an aversion for the familiar setting against the backdrop of the abbey ruins, visited York with his designer, Tanya Moiseiwitsch, to inspect possible performance sites, but the board would not budge from the Museum Gardens and within a month of the site visit he had pulled out of the project.[33] Undaunted, the board considered Peter Ustinov and Peter Brook. Ustinov was ruled out as he was then in the United States while Brook simply did not reply to Hess's letter. The next move was to ask for suggestions from Eric White, secretary of the Arts Council of Great Britain, and Fernald from the Royal Academy of Dramatic Art.[34] Finally the position was accepted by Giles, who was among a number of 'young outstanding' directors approached by Hess after he had been authorized to 'vary at his own discretion' the previous decision of the board that the director must be a 'famous' one.[35]

The David Giles Production, 1960

Giles accepted the traditional performance site, but both he and his designer, Kenneth Mellor, agreed with Guthrie and Moiseiwitsch that the 'ruined abbey-wall was too romantic for the Plays' and, consequently, set up a 'construction of wood, stone and iron' to 'counteract' the romance of the ancient masonry.[36] Because of the evening damp rising from the ground and the possibility of further dampness falling from the heavens, a slightly raised stage area was constructed in front of the ruins, a partial answer to Judi Dench's complaints about discomfort as a kneeling angel in 1954. Rather than submitting to the ruins and accepting them as the natural backdrop for the mysteries, Giles and Mellor positioned their stage at a distance of ten feet from the walls, which were obscured by canvas-backed towers in which key scenes of the play were presented.

Giles in 1960 and Gaskill in 1963 were criticized for their departures from the Browne pattern, particularly for their treatment of the performance space. Ironically, Hess had insisted that Browne himself change his approach to the site in 1957, with the result that the stage stood 'out from the ruins rather than blending into them'; Browne disliked this new setting although he admitted that it 'did help the director.'[37] *The Times* drama critic approved in 1957, declaring that the 'roughly carved eminence serving for the Garden of Eden and for Calvary no longer pretends to be the ancient stone of the abbey but is frankly theatrical and all the more effective for that,'[38] clearly appreciative of this step towards Brecht.

Reactions to Giles's Brechtian production of the mysteries in 1960 were mixed and the local paper made the most of the controversy. Innovations were measured against the Browne blueprint, 'from which, as in Gilbert and Sullivan operas, no one must deviate a hair's breath.'[39] One letter to the editor would praise Browne's 'beautiful meditation on the miracle of the Bible' and condemn Giles for having 'given us the medieval Plays, ugly, vulgar, silly and utterly soul-less';[40] the next would decry those who wanted a 'romantic pretty-pretty production in the style of the pseudo-religious Technicolour film.'[41] Some locals took advantage of the mood of dissatisfaction to call for an all-amateur cast and a local amateur director;[42] while others insisted that this year the plays had been saved from 'being a total flop' only by the skills and talent of the professionals in the cast.[43] The reviewer for the *New Statesman* joined the litany of complaints, admonishing Giles for failing to follow the Browne formula:

> [He] should have filled the vast, 30-yard stage with movement ... He should have told his professionals that just because the York Cycle is poetry it need not

be rolled out like so much solemn elocution, delivered with meaningful glances and in statuesque poses. He should have cut down on the stage machines, as cumbersome and slow to work as something out of a medieval siege. He should have used instead the beautiful ruined windows of the setting.[44]

The mystery play scriptwriter J.S. Purvis wrote to the board about the production; he 'agreed with the Archbishop's opinion given to [him] unofficially, that it was a greater performance than the last Festival's, with a deeper spiritual impact,' but he had some serious quarrels with the designer.[45] He objected to the influence of Brueghel on the costume design, stating that German medieval costume was not the same as English, and that, for him, the angels were 'dingy' and the devils 'ineffective.' Worse than this, he considered that Mellor had let the director down with an excessive set design. Worst of all was the 'monstrous Cross and the towers which were a consequence of the height of the Cross'; these were, according to Purvis, 'cumbrous and ugly ... [and] held up the action.'

Giles may well have been pleased with these critical remarks, particularly the references to the cross, for in the 'Theatre of Cruelty' that he was working with in 1960, he was dwelling deliberately, visually and intellectually, on the cross and its monstrousness (see plate 3). It was in his staging of the central event of the Crucifixion that he was at his most outrageous, most cruel, and most Brechtian. Sister Bernada Jaques describes Giles as a 'modern realist,' who shared with medieval realists an aversion for 'falseness and sentimentality' and a view of 'the central issues of life as ethical.'[46] It was her opinion that his 'desire to make the story of the Cycle real ... strongly influenced the designing of the set, the choice of stage properties ... the making of costumes,' and his decision to be 'true to the medieval spirit' meant that he did not avoid the brutality of the Passion sequence.[47] Browne had cut the crude jesting of the soldiers in the torture scenes, but Giles chose to retain the original text in this instance. Browne had used the historic pageant approach of 'sweeping movements and statuesque tableaux' with the abbey ruins as the main scenic unit, but Giles and Mellor, in the manner of Brecht, envisaged a more complex and unashamedly theatrical set on which to 'present a contemporary interpretation of the plays and their message in good strong theatrical terms.'[48] According to Jaques, the 'realism' in the Giles approach could not be reconciled with the 'powerfully romantic ruined wall of St. Mary's Abbey'; she also stressed, however, that Giles was not seeking to subvert the ruins but rather to arrive at a set that would 'relate' to them.[49] Other observers, like Purvis, were less generous and interpreted the design as an insensitive and ill-advised move that deliberately obscured the traditional backdrop.

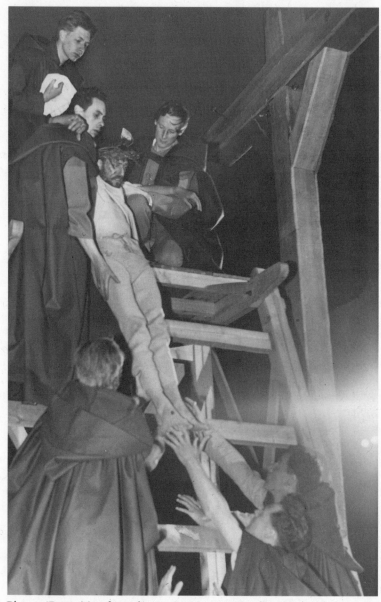

Plate 3. 'Deposition from the Cross,' Museum Gardens, 1960. Christ (Tom Criddle) is lowered down the tower behind the cross.

The 1960 set, however, took its inspiration from the original York text. As both Giles and Mellor were at some pains to point out, the towers that enraged Purvis were prompted by Pilate's reference to 'this tower-built town' in the 'Conspiracy' episode that opened the second half of the Museum Gardens production. Jaques describes the set as 'exceedingly original ... five enormous square towered gantries ... constructed of unpainted boards, posts, and beams arranged in a series of platforms with numerous stairways.'[50] The platforms and stairways that connected the towers functioned like streets enabling the characters to move between the acting areas concentrated in the towers. The set, with its approximation of the 'tower-built town,' acknowledged that the plays belonged to York, a city still bristling with church towers, themselves surrounded by the towers of the medieval walls. The original players and their audience were part of this city and, as the mysteries of 1960 implied, so too were the current performers on the 'tower-builded' set. Movement between the acting areas in the tower rooms suggested the movement of pageant wagons through the streets – a partial salute to the theatre of the streets that had been supplanted by the fixed-place stage.

There were other ways in which the Giles production encouraged the integration of the surrounding town and the audience with the dramatic action, breaking down, as Artaud and Brecht would approve, the familiar 'fourth wall' of the modern theatre. On cue for the 'Entry into Jerusalem,' the bells of the nearby St Olave's Church rang out in rejoicing, and at the very beginning of the play, God the Father made a surprise entrance through the audience rather than appearing, as he had in the Browne productions, framed distantly in the central arch of the abbey ruins.

This new perspective on the Creator was devised to unsettle not only preconceived notions of mystery play productions in modern York, but also preconceived notions of the actor/spectator relationship. God was an actor who clearly emerged from the domain of the spectators; in this production he moved impressively up the staircase leading to his tower, creating as he went, until finally he created Lucifer at the very top.[51] The ascent made the point of the great honour bestowed on Lucifer as 'bearer of light' at the top of heaven's tower, a point that was accentuated as he tumbled down the same flight of steps to the very bottom in his transformation into the fallen Satan.

Professional actors took the roles of God the Father (Robert Eddison), Lucifer/Satan (Harold Lang), Adam (Peter Brett), the Prophet of the 'Nativity' (Clifford Parrish), and Christ (Tom Criddle). The most significant of these roles from the point of view of Giles's Brechtian agenda is that of the Prophet. Although Browne had introduced Isaiah and another Prophet in 1957 to bridge the gap between the 'Expulsion' and the 'Nativity,' Giles included more of the original prophetic prologue to the 'Annunciation' episode and strengthened the role by giving it to a professional actor. He encouraged his audience to consider the Brechtian notion of the importance of narrative and asked them to engage actively with the meaning of the impending birth.

The influence of Brueghel, who was also a strong influence on Brecht, can be traced not only in the costuming that annoyed Purvis but also in the way that Giles used the rooms in the various levels of the towers.[52] Peter Woodham, the lighting designer, was able to 'isolate' a desired room so that 'it glowed like a small jewel.'[53] For Giles, this allowed for concentration of action, reminiscent of those paintings of Brueghel that isolate important sections of the narrative on the canvas by framing them in buildings that are open to the viewers' eye. Theatrically the lighting also allowed switching between rooms where action could be imagined as unfolding concurrently, or to areas outside the tower rooms where other types of action involving larger numbers of characters were underway.

Giles demonstrated concern for the life surrounding the central narrative events, particularly in the 'Baptism,' where the stage area in front of the towers became the river along which people sat 'as if it were the bank'; the fishermen 'cast their nets from the bank; boys with fishing poles sat on the edges, and girls dangled their bare feet in the water.'[54] The audience, seated metaphorically on the opposite bank of the 'river,' were cast as part of this crowd. For Giles this was a play about ordinary people and it belonged to their lives, but it was also a play about the sublime story of Christian Redemption and the high point was the 'Crucifixion.'

In this production God the Father had entered the action through the audience and up the stairs to the heaven tower, thus presenting a view of his back for a considerable time during the opening sequence; Mary also, in a new approach to the 'Nativity' that displaced the Henzie Raeburn method, turned her back on the audience to obscure their view of the stable before the infant Christ was revealed in the manger. Both of these back-views were innovative, but they might not have prepared the audience for the most startling back-view of all when the cross was raised. Not for Giles the iconic face of the crucified Christ; he chose to challenge his audience by forcing them to take a very different view of the event from behind the cross.

Just as the audience had occupied the opposite bank of the river, looking across to the townspeople as a mirror image of themselves observing the 'Baptism,' now at the 'Crucifixion' they took up their places on Calvary. Jaques describes a cross standing thirty-feet-tall and seated in a 'socket made for it on the very edge of the pavement nearest the audience.'[55] Christ dragged it to the centre of the stage before he was manhandled by the Roman soldiers 'up the stairs to the platform above the inner stage' in the central tower, and for the first time in the modern York mysteries, the audience now saw Christ 'struck and abused by the soldiers' while 'other soldiers pushed two medieval siege towers toward the center of the acting area ... clambering over the siege towers even as they were moving ... [and then] used guy ropes from the towers to raise the cross and place it in the socket ... eight feet from the platform upon which Christ was held by his enemies.'[56] During the abuse of Christ and the simultaneous movement of the cross into place, there was another simultaneous action on the part of the crowd, who were 'excited greatly' by the activity, and 'whose faces looked ugly and brutal in the half light.' A drawbridge was then lowered from one of the towers to connect to the platform where Christ was being tormented. Again for the first time in modern York, Christ was taken to the cross and fastened to it 'in full view of the audience,' but with his back to them.[57]

Viewing the cross from the back, the audience saw only Christ's hands and the 'outline of his body'; the faces that they saw were the 'strained white faces of the crowd looking upward.'[58] Jaques reports that Woodham's 'most challenging problem was lighting the mob' in this scene; he lit it from below, and so 'the open mouths and eye-sockets of the screaming, frenzied mob appeared as deep wells of blackness with the lights cutting across their faces as they alternately surged forward and fell back.'[59] The audience watched from the darkness and heard the final words of Christ rise from their midst. Giles's production had brought 'Theatre of Cruelty' to York and challenged the spectators to look at the mysteries from a different perspective, from within the scene rather than from outside the picture frame.

The William Gaskill Production, 1963

The advance publicity for the 1963 festival stressed that the mystery plays would be different that year. Anticipating disapproval or perhaps simply encouraging ticket sales, Hess, as he had done many times before, insisted that 'there is not one right way and one wrong way' of presenting the York mysteries and warned, yet again, that 'the repetition of a set pattern ... would bring interest in the Plays to an end sooner than would new conceptions, even controversy.'[60] Purvis advised audiences to come with an open mind, admitting that the Museum Gardens stage, the size of 'about three normal theatre stages set side by side' was a challenge to any director, and that the greatest difficulty was the 'almost too impressive' setting of the abbey ruins, their 'overwhelmingly ecclesiastical and medieval' character being something that was 'not always the character or the spirit which is required at all points in the Plays.'[61]

John Bury's 1963 design offered a solution to the problem of the ruins. His stage filled the 'whole expanse under the ruined Abbey windows' and there were two 'realistic two storey houses with thatched roofs,' one at either end of the stage, heaven on the right and hell on the left, and between them, three platforms where the action took place.[62] Jaques comments that there was no attempt to add 'naturalistic detail' but that the set suggested locales rather than representing them pictorially.[63] The design did not obscure the ruins as did Mellor's in 1960, 'it simply ignored them.'[64]

Prior to seeing the production, Purvis was supportive of Gaskill's rumoured directorial decisions, reprimanding those who expressed doubts about the proposed reduction in the crowd numbers. Such doubters, he said, 'should realise that this, too, is closer to the original performances'; after all, even for the grand finale of the 'Last Judgment,' 'the original book calls in the stage direction for 13 characters only.'[65] Open-minded before the event, Purvis suggested that people would 'benefit most' by attending the performance 'in expectation, not to carp but to understand and to enjoy, to hear the message of the Plays, [and] to let [the] imagination range free.'

The review of the 1963 opening night in the *Yorkshire Evening Press* was ambivalent: while the actors were praised, the production described as 'effective,' the set as 'simple and versatile,' and the 'alien conventions' of the masks as something that the 'mind ... soon attunes itself to,' the reviewer had obvious misgivings.[66] Yorkshire born Alan Dobie was commended for his double role as God the Father and Christ, but the reviewer regarded the Brechtian style of production as putting a 'severe' and perhaps unnecessary strain on even Dobie's considerable abilities; and the 'tone of the performance ... to underplay ... the moments of high drama' was regarded as 'too often carried to an insensitive extreme.' This reviewer was disappointed with the 'Raising of Lazarus,' complaining that the greetings of his sisters when he rose from the dead were no more effusive than they would have been if he had 'just come back from a week in Bournemouth.' Worse still, the 'Hails' of the 'Entry into Jerusalem' sounded like 'railway station announcements,' and the 'throw-away acting' reduced even the cosmic tensions of the 'Temptation of

Christ' to 'nonsense.' Worst of all, perhaps, the Royal Court trademark 'kitchen-sink whine' marred the emotional scene between Peter and Christ in the Garden of Gethsemane, but such whining, according to the reviewer, was only a 'temporary fashion.'

The critic's reference to the 'kitchen-sink whine' was inevitable given Gaskill's recent association with the Royal Court Theatre, the home of 'kitchen sink' drama. By 1963, however, 'kitchen sink' had made its presence felt in the professional theatre and in the academy, where Shakespearean scholar G. Wilson Knight wrote glowingly of the movement's capacity 'to bring new health to the insane paradoxes of a decaying culture.'[67] Brecht and the kitchen sink tradition were by no means destined to be 'temporary fashions.'

The *Spectator* reviewer, Bamber Gascoigne, was positive about Gaskill's 1963 mysteries.[68] He praised the 'superb realism' of the 'Crucifixion,' the authenticity of the thatching of the on-stage houses, and the release of pigeons during the 'Creation.' The lowering of Lucifer from heaven by means of a crane and Annena Stubbs's costuming of Adam and Eve, 'not the usual ridiculous pink tights but a strip of canvas above their peasant clothes with a plain drawing on it of a properly naked body,' were also noted favourably. Gascoigne praised the crowd scenes as 'brilliant,' and the 'Temptation' episode as magnificent with Satan 'bounding through the audience ... and dress[ing] as a friar before our eyes.' The Brueghelesque use of simultaneous stage settings with Christ 'being scourged in one place, Judas ... regretting his treachery in another and the high priests ... waiting to continue the trial yet elsewhere' was also approved. Here was one reviewer, at least, who appreciated the Brechtian aesthetic and saw that it worked for the mysteries.

Another of Gaskill's innovations was the doubling of the roles of God the Father and Christ by Alan Dobie. This was a doctrinally sensitive decision that emphasized the oneness of the Godhead and, along with the inclusion of the 'Slaughter of the Innocents,' was copied by Browne in 1966. In Gaskill's production the meaning of the dual role was emphasized in the Brechtian treatment of changeover between the two persons. A 'larger than life mask made from material which resembled blue steel' that identified God the Father was a deliberate signal to the audience that the actor was changing roles.[69] On cue for his first appearance as the adult Christ at the 'Baptism,' Dobie simply removed the mask and became his other self. Jaques describes the 'Ascension' as 'pure Brechtian': when Dobie reached the top of the stairs to heaven, he disappeared behind a blue cloth held by angels and immediately reappeared with the mask as

God the Father ready for the 'Judgment' scene, removing it again when he had to descend to earth as Christ.[70] Once the 'Judgment' was over and the other actors had departed, Dobie took up the mask again, 'surveyed the vast empty sky, and slowly walked off the stage, alone.'[71]

God the Father was not the only masked figure in the Gaskill production. The other supernatural characters, the angels and the devils (with the exception of Satan), were also masked. Reviewers were scornful of the angels, divested of the wings they had worn in previous productions and ridiculous in their golden headpieces that looked like 'hair-dryers.'[72] Despite negative reaction to the masked angels, it can certainly be said that, in his Brechtian treatment of the angels and devils, Gaskill was experimenting with ways of differentiating between good and evil and anticipating the arguments that Meg Twycross and Sarah Carpenter have since put forward for the masking practices of the medieval theatre.[73]

'Theatre of Cruelty' came even further upstage in this production than it had in 1960. The 'Slaughter of the Innocents' was included for the first time in the modern revivals and the 'Crucifixion' episode was emphasised, complete with the two thieves crucified alongside Christ. Gaskill expressed satisfaction that 'people used to faint at many performances.'[74] Almost forty years on, Peter Gill's prize-winning play *The York Realist* (2001) was to focus on the idea of cruelty using a mystery play production in the Museum Gardens as his context and one of the soldiers at the Crucifixion as his 'realist.'[75]

Gill worked on the Gaskill production as assistant director and noted the theatrical brilliance of the 'Crucifixion' episode, observing that the 'dialogue covering the nailing took just long enough for the soldiers to accomplish it technically' and commenting that the scene's 'special fascination and strength' arose from its 'strange combination of the sublimity of the sacrifice and the crudeness of the humour.'[76] In Gaskill's mysteries, the soldiers featured in this episode became 'a working-class chorus to the action' and remained on stage 'almost continually' in the 'second half of the performance as identifiable characters.'[77] While foregrounding the cruelty of the events they also fostered the mistaken but appealing notion of the original mysteries as a product of working-class initiative and the medieval guilds as the equivalent of modern trade unions already discussed in chapter 1.

The opposition between the oppressors and the oppressed was noticeably channelled through an emphasis on tyranny and physical cruelty. Professional actors were given pivotal 'cruel' roles: Annas (Henry Woolf), Caiaphas (Peter Bowles), Pilate (Shay Gorman), and the four soldiers of the Crucifixion (George Innes, Brian Osborne, Declan Mulholland, and Tim Preece). The *Yorkshire Evening Press* reviewer particularly commended the callous insensitivities of the Passion sequence commenting with admiration on the 'hideous brutality and ghastly competence' of the soldiers.[78] The audience was no longer looking at a pre-Raphaelite version of the torments of the Passion; cruelty was etched in black rather than blended into the idealized background as it had been in the Browne mysteries. There was no attempt to soften or distance man's inhumanity to man; in fact it was quite the opposite.

Gaskill claimed that the medieval theatre of the people had been 'performed by ordinary people, for ordinary people, and ... done in a straightforward way.'[79] One strategy used to recover this theatre was a determined effort to reinstate a recognizably Yorkshire sound to the local mysteries. He therefore chose 'professional actors with Yorkshire voices' for the major roles and, as far as he could, recruited amateurs who were able to 'use their native Yorkshire accent.'[80] Browne had been concerned that actors from the countryside who would have the appropriate accent would not be able to attend rehearsals or deal with the 'late hours of performance';[81] Gaskill was undeterred and simply accepted that his amateur actors had large demands on their time outside the play. He was to recall later that one member of the cast had to miss some rehearsals 'because the shearing of his sheep could not be postponed for another day.'[82] The perception that the local dialect was appropriate for the mysteries was, of course, entirely in keeping with the current 'kitchen sink' trend of valorizing provincial speech.

In rehearsal Gaskill's practice differed from Browne's in accordance with their different theatrical ideologies. Jaques explains that those who had been in previous productions in the Museum Gardens were 'used to working toward carrying the audience with them,' but now they had to master the Brechtian 'expository approach.'[83] In an interview with Jaques, Gaskill explained that his most difficult task was retraining the loyal mystery play 'crowds,' who had been accustomed to 'close direction ... where to stand, when to move ... when to shout, what gestures to make ... what reactions to have': Gaskill did not want them to shout '"Crucify! Crucify"' in unison, but to 'mutter to themselves in their indecision.'[84]

The inspiration for the costuming of the 1963 production came, in true Brechtian fashion, from the frenetic detail of the peasant paintings of the sixteenth-century German artist Peter Brueghel the Elder. Gaskill and Stubbs boldly abandoned the accumulated mystery play wardrobe in 1963, using the old costumes 'only as undergarments to add bulk,' while their new costumes had a '"chunky look"' that suggested the simplicity of the medieval wardrobes of 'everyday workmen.'[85] Alan Dobie played Christ as a man of the people in a short scarlet medieval-style tunic, while Ian McShane's Satan wore a similar black tunic to accentuate the good versus evil conflict.[86] But while the costume was clearly medieval-style, Vivian Brooks, the *Yorkshire Evening Press* reviewer, was impressed with something approaching modernity in the interpretation of these roles, with Satan receiving a special mention as 'a brash, not over-intelligent smart-alec corner-boy … his manner that of to-day's more corrupt teenage "pop" idols.'[87]

Interpreting the mysteries of the Middle Ages as 'Theatre of the People,' Gaskill wanted to 'create a kind of naivete in the look of it.'[88] Desmond Pratt for the *Yorkshire Post* noted this naive look, comparing Gaskill favourably with the religiously inspired Browne productions and with Giles's 'over-elaborate' efforts. [89] The 1963 production, said this reviewer, was 'the purest of the lot,' and he praised Gaskill's attempts to recreate the 'rough accents' of the original guild presenters, their 'inexperienced stage techniques,' and their 'warm-hearted crudities.' But while such 'crudities' might have appealed to drama critics, they were not necessarily to the taste of the York traditionalists.

One who definitely did not approve was Purvis. He may have come to the Gaskill production with an open mind, as he had advised others to do, but wiser after the event, he again wrote to the Festival Society board.[90] He began with restrained praise, giving the director credit for approaching the problems of presenting a medieval play 'intelligently, and up to a point competently according to his previous experience.' He noted that the aim was 'to achieve a treatment as nearly as possible that of the mediaeval stage,' the result of which was that the 'crowd movements' and the 'spectacle' were cut so as to 'concentrate on the realism of the Plays themselves'; in so doing, Purvis conceded, Gaskill had achieved 'some remarkable effects.' But he considered that 'intelligent spectators' were divided: some were 'impressed profoundly' while others were 'shocked.' He, clearly, was not impressed and duly listed a number of 'irritating details':

- the quite unnecessarily ugly masks, which defeated an interesting experiment
- the ridiculous treatment of the Raising of Lazarus
- the over-elaboration of scenery, as in the Harrowing of Hell
- the refusal to recognise the presence of the background of the Abbey walls.

Purvis also identified 'two deeper and fundamental weaknesses': the 'feeble' handling of the 'reduced crowd,' and the '"throw away" manner of treating the words of the Plays.' To his alarm, he detected a 'refusal to allow any spiritual or religious quality' resulting from the fact that neither the director nor his actors seemed able 'to rise above the idea that this was another piece of Brecht.'

But Purvis had some constructive advice to offer and listed the qualities to be demanded in any future director:

- the right spiritual approach
- the ability to get professional and amateurs to work together in harmony
- a readiness to cast local amateurs for parts of some importance, and to invite the widest possible local co-operation
- a readiness to return to the spectacular by a greater use of crowds, and to use the possibilities of the Abbey ruins, keeping the stage settings to the simplest.

Believing that none but the best should come to York, he added that a director should preferably have a 'name,' but stressed that it was not 'necessary or even desirable' that this 'name' had been made with 'modern plays.' Purvis's pronouncements would certainly have allowed the board to build up an identikit picture of his preferred director for the 1966 festival and to recognize him immediately as Martin Browne.

Browne's 'Theatre of Cruelty,' 1966

Artistic director Hess and the board of the York Festival Society had been, officially at least, seeking novelty, but it was clear that any attempt to institute new formulae in the Museum Gardens was dangerous. In 1963 conservative mystery play devotees like Purvis saw Brechtian approaches as a threat to the continuation of the local festivals and as an insult to the integrity of the ancient drama. Theatrical experimentation in York was therefore curtailed and in 1966, as John Elliott reflected with some cynicism, 'Martin Browne was brought back with a mandate to restore the mystery plays to their original purity.'[91]

Browne returned declaring his own intention to present 'Theatre of Cruelty.' He had been 'persuaded by church authorities to temper' the Crucifixion scene in 1951, but explained to Dorothy Bacon of *Life International* that because of the 'recent developments in "the theater of cruelty" ... he decided that audiences of the mid-1960s could take anything.'[92] Ever a master of publicity, he saw value in associating the mysteries with the recent interest in Artaud's theories sparked by Peter Brook and

Charles Marowitz, whose opening season of experimental theatre with the Royal Shakespeare Company in 1963–4 was itself entitled 'The Theatre of Cruelty.'

Some did not find Browne cruel enough. Canadian scholar Alexandra Johnston, for example, described the 1966 production as 'colourless and pretentiously successful.'[93] In her view, 'the passion sequence was all but ruined' because the 'flagellation was carried on off stage' and the stretching and nailing of Christ on the cross was, as in his previous productions, omitted; thus, said Johnston, the 'minds of the audience were distracted from the major point of contemplation' in the original mysteries, that is, from the contemplation of the agony of Christ.[94]

Browne's 'Passion' sequence may well have been overly sanitized for scholars in the audience in 1966 and the vogue for 'Theatre of Cruelty' in the professional domain would certainly have prepared experienced theatregoers for a more visually forthright treatment of the events leading up to Christ's death on the cross. In 1966, as mentioned in chapters 2 and 3, the ban on the representation of the deity on the professional stage was lifted, and with the mysteries now part of twentieth-century cultural memory, directors were free, at least in theory, to experiment. Browne's reticence in the treatment of the Passion can, perhaps, be put down to his personal sense of religious decorum, and perhaps, be put down to his personal sense of religious decorum, and perhaps equally to what he perceived as the sense of decorum of the York mystery play community. With a conservative local cast welcoming him back and an audience that potentially included considerable numbers of conservative Christians, he may have chosen what he saw as the safer road to Calvary.[95]

5 Theatre of the People

The mysteries of medieval York were fundamentally 'Theatre of the People,' although not in the sense of 'naive' working-class theatre as William Gaskill and others have imagined them. Gaskill's Brechtian approach to the plays in 1963 focused on the idea of an underlying opposition between the poor and their rulers; Sister Bernarda Jaques comments that the director 'traced this strong dichotomy in whatever dealings Christ and his disciples had with authority whether it were political or religious.'[1] But in the Middle Ages, the guilds presenting the plays on Corpus Christi Day were not operating from beneath; as discussed in chapter 1, they were elite associations of people working in the same craft, not 'workers' in the modern sense of employees joined together for protection against their bosses, but masters and their employees joined together to protect the reputation of their trade and the exclusivity and success of its exercise locally. This is not to say that antiauthoritarian comment would have been completely unthinkable in the performance of the original mysteries, but simply that it is unlikely to have supplanted the main agenda, which was to honour God and to bring honour to York and to the guilds themselves.

The medieval mysteries were, nevertheless, 'Theatre of the People' in other very powerful senses. The scriptwriters were probably locally based; the productions were mounted under the auspices of the local council with finance and administration provided by the local guilds; the actors were most likely all local men, and while there is evidence that some actors were paid to perform, it appears that they were essentially 'amateur' and that acting was incidental rather than central to their earning capacity.[2] Most important, the performance space was the city streets, the living and working arena that normally hosted the drama of everyday life, and the audience could be anyone and everyone, regardless of citizenship or social status and without necessarily making any payment for the privilege of attendance. These plays belonged to York and its people in special ways, but in 1951 there were substantial changes that put them at a remove from their traditional owners: outside professionals rather than local amateurs took many of the major roles both on- and offstage, a fixed setting was constructed in the Museum Gardens, and an admission fee was charged. In the four productions between 1969 and 1980, however, there were some further moves towards a 'Theatre of the People' beyond those already made by Gaskill, although none of them fitted the plays back to their medieval profile.

Amateur Theatre Groups

Meg Twycross observes that the scripts of the individual episodes of the mysteries were 'written for the resources of an amateur dramatic society.'[3] Although there were no such societies in the Middle Ages, this is a telling observation in the context of this study. As mentioned in chapters 2 and 3, amateur theatre groups were the mainstay of the York mysteries in the 1950s. The members of these groups were, as David Mills has described them, 'primarily representatives of the middle-class business and professional community,'[4] and as such they shared some common ground with the medieval guilds, those elite groups of craftsmen that presented the mysteries originally; the modern theatre groups were bonded by their social status and common interest in performance rather than a sense of social status in combination with occupational status and the obligations and advantages that went with it that held the medieval craftsmen together. In addition the amateur theatre groups of the 1950s had an infrastructure similar to that of the guilds of medieval York: they had some form of internal management and many of them maintained a collection of costumes and properties.

There are a number of other ways in which the performance of medieval mysteries is comparable to the performance of the one-act plays that were the familiar fare of amateur theatre festivals and competitions in post-war Britain. Indeed, there was an awareness of such comparisons in the early 1950s, when the medieval guild players were envisaged as being engaged in healthy competition with one another like the amateurs of modern times.[5] According to Glynne Wickham, the amateur movement had at that time 'reached proportions comparable with the Guild drama of the Middle Ages' and by virtue of their sheer numbers, the amateurs were worthy of recognition from scholars for their contributions to 'the contemporary [theatre] scene.'[6]

In 1951 E. Martin Browne, as director of the British Drama League, was justly proud of the amateurs who made up the majority of the League's membership, stating that 'for a great many people' in the country, they provided the 'only contact with the living theatre' and had become 'an integral part of British life.'[7] Nonetheless Browne insisted on what Ann Jellicoe later referred to in her magisterial work on community theatre as a 'professional core.'[8] While he noted in 1951 that thirty years on from the initial formation of the League the amateurs were now 'choosing, on the whole, better plays, and doing, on the whole, better productions,' he also believed that there was little noticeable improvement in their acting skills.[9] To this somewhat alarming criticism he added the qualifier that the 'best work of amateurs has been concerned with things of which they have first-hand knowledge.'[10] In this he anticipated the rise of the community theatre movement in the 1970s and 1980s, recognizing that amateurs could show their true strengths in regional, community-based theatre, presenting plays that were grounded in the history of their local area.

The Amateur Theatre Groups in York

When Browne and the York Festival Society began to plan for the first Museum Gardens production, they relied heavily on the local amateurs, not precisely as the city council had relied on the medieval guilds, but to provide unpaid actors for the supporting roles, willing extras for the crowd scenes, and experienced behind-the-scenes workers. There are two important differences between the association of the medieval guilds of York with the original mysteries and that of the modern amateur dramatic societies with the revivals. The medieval guilds, either alone or as a modest consortium, were clearly linked as a group to their own particular episode in the play, whereas members of the modern drama groups, contributing to a now seamlessly scripted play, were dispersed throughout the combined company of the Museum Gardens cast, thus losing the identity of their particular group, a loss that contrasts markedly to the visibility of the individual groups in the more recent wagon plays (see appendix 3, D, E, and F). Furthermore, the medieval guilds, particularly through their representation on the 'the council of Forty-Eight,' were 'always consulted in matters affecting the play of Corpus Christi,'[11] but in the mid-twentieth century, the local drama groups were kept at a distance on matters of organization and policy.

An Amateur Director for the Mysteries: Edward Taylor

Although it resulted from a cost-cutting drive rather than a deliberate decision to experiment with 'Theatre of the People,' the appointment of local amateur director Edward Taylor to assume the Browne mantle for the 1969 production was a significant moment for the York mysteries. Despite the fact that the mysteries always more than covered their own costs, there was increasing concern in the 1960s about the expense of the York Festival, particularly in the wake of a £14,653 deficit in 1966. These were difficult economic times that saw the devaluation of the pound in 1967: cost-cutting in York was inevitable. As their medieval counterparts had turned to the guilds to subsidize the Corpus Christi celebrations in the Middle Ages, so too the city council of the late-1960s looked to the amateur theatre groups for an increased contribution of voluntary labour to reduce expenses of the festival as a whole.

By the time of his appointment, Taylor had been working for a greater say in the York mysteries for well over a decade. As mentioned in chapter 3, there had been rumblings in the amateur ranks from the very beginning, and when it became evident that the York Festivals would continue with the mysteries as their principal feature, the local amateurs made a move to improve their position in 1954, gaining agreement from the Festival Society to an advisory board consisting of members of the drama groups to work under Browne's authority; Taylor was a member of this board. But even this was not enough and the local amateurs were not entirely satisfied. On 1 May 1958 discussions were held between John Styan, then a staff tutor in Literature and Drama in the Department of Adult Education at the University of Hull and chairman of the local branch of the British Drama League, and Taylor, their secretary, on the one hand, and Hans Hess accompanied by the York Festival Society's chairman, vice-chairman, and secretary, on the other. Styan and Taylor made 'various criticisms of past Festivals and ... requested representation ... on the [Festival Society] Board.'[12] This request was denied, although the board replied politely that they would be pleased to 'receive any suggestions which the League might have to make from time to time on Festival matters.' The League then set up a 'Mystery Plays Ad Hoc Committee' comprising representatives from local groups whose members were interested in performing in the mysteries. The battle lines were drawn. The board informed the committee in no uncertain terms that, while willing to contemplate for audition any names that were sent to them, they 'must reserve the right to recruit for the Mystery Plays from any source they consider[ed] fit.'[13]

The difficulties experienced by Hess in securing a director for the 1960 Museum Gardens production were clearly common knowledge in York and the amateurs seized on the situation as an opportunity to advance their cause. In a 'private letter' to the board it was suggested that Styan be engaged to direct the 1960 production.[14] At this time the first of many books published during Styan's distinguished academic career as a theatre historian and theorist, *The Elements of Drama* (1960), was in progress. Styan, like Glynne Wickham in Bristol, was an early champion of the notion that plays should be understood through performance rather than through silent reading and private study, the traditional method preferred by Hardin Craig and others at the time. Had Styan been appointed, York would have chosen the scholarly path that had been proposed by Hess as an alternative to 'first-rate showmanship' in his outline plan for the 1960 festival,[15] and a healthy collaboration between the amateur movement and academic expertise might have been achieved. But by the time the letter reached the board, David Giles had already accepted the post.

In September 1959, James Britten, who had taken over as local secretary of the League from Taylor, now their chairman, reminded the board of the existence of the Ad Hoc Committee, adding that this group was determined to submit names of potential actors and offer suggestions on the conduct of the festival.[16] The list of societies represented on this committee was formidable:

Nunthorpe and Mill Mount Amateur Dramatic Society
St John's College
York Settlement Community Players
York Railway Institute Players
York City Townswomen's Guild
Dringhouses Townswomen's Guild
Heworth Townswomen's Guild
Acomb Townswomen's Guild
Hull Road Townswomen's Guild
The Women's Institutes
Strensall Evening Institute Players
York Co-operative Drama Group
Acomb Community Players
The Workers' Educational Association

Not in the least intimidated, the board replied as before: the existence of the committee was noted but the rights of the board were unassailable.[17]

Unpleasantness was still in the air early in 1960. Hess wrote to T.C. Benfield, the town clerk and secretary of the York Festival Society, warning that a 'boycott organised by the local branch of the British Drama League' was having an impact on planning for the mystery plays and hence for the festival; he suggested that 'one might give serious consideration to whether we should take out an injunction against them restraining them from misrepresenting themselves as spokesmen for the York Festival Society.'[18] Benfield replied that he would need 'some very definite evidence of interference' and hoped that Hess would find that his 'fears [were] unfounded.'[19] Apparently he did, as no action ensued.

When the decision was made to bring Browne back for his fourth mystery play season, the board was treading warily with the local amateurs, notifying them of the plans for 1966 well in advance of arrangements for their own productions for that year.[20] This courtesy may have been an effort to mitigate the effects of another disappointment over the rejection of a proposal that the various local groups be invited to 'produce one of the Plays from the York Cycle, with a Principal Producer' as coordinator.[21] Browne made it plain that he preferred to exercise the same level of authority he had enjoyed in the earlier Museum Gardens mysteries and that this suggestion was quite unacceptable to him. He had previous experience in working with subdirectors for the 1934 pageant play of *The Rock*, T.S. Eliot's first attempt to write for the theatre.[22] He treated Christopher Fry's pageant play, *Thursday's Child* (1939), in a similar manner, dividing the episodes between a number of directors, 'monitor[ing] their rehearsals and memorization, and finally coordinat[ing] their work at the [Royal Albert] Hall just prior to the performances.'[23] These experiences were, clearly, not something that Browne wished to repeat in York; besides, the formula he had arrived at in 1951 had proven its worth there. A chance for 'Theatre of the People,' for a community play with individual episodes under the control of separate groups, something approaching the guild system of pageant sponsorship of the Middle Ages, was thus passed up. If Browne had accepted the proposal the result may have reflected the medieval productions that can be envisaged from the documentation of the period, uneven not only as dramatic writing but also in terms of practical execution. Such unevenness, however authentic it may have been, would not have suited the seamless whole that had been invented for the Museum Gardens or the polished performances that Browne hoped to extract from his mystery play casts.

The Edward Taylor Productions, 1969 and 1973

The local amateurs had to wait to come into their own until Taylor was appointed for the 1969 and 1973 festivals. He was by profession a 'legal executive with a York firm of solicitors.'[24] He had been directing amateurs in the city for many years, had founded the York Co-operative Players, and between 1957 and 1966 he was in charge of *The Living Past*, a historical piece regularly staged at the Castle Museum. He served the city well as the director of all its major theatrical events between 1969 and 1973. As well as the two mystery play productions, he also directed a revised version of Louis Napoleon Parker's *York Historic Pageant* of 1909 for the celebration of 1900 years of settlement in 1971.[25]

Taylor's most important variation of the Browne formula was to make the mysteries an all-amateur event for 1969. He assembled an amateur cast, an idea that had been canvassed a number of times since 1951, enlisted the aid of an amateur set designer, Patrick Olsen, 'a young artist employed as a window-dresser' by the York Co-operative Society,[26] and took on the task of costume design himself. His sole paid professional was the lighting designer, Percy Corry from the Strand Electric Company, who had worked on previous productions in the Museum Gardens. Although not all of the amateur actors were based in York, and, as had been the case with previous festival casts, some had worked on the professional stage, this was a strong gesture towards 'Theatre of the People.'[27] It was announced triumphantly in *The Times* as a 'return to the medieval tradition of community participation.'[28]

Yet even Taylor's faith in his amateurs was not rock solid. He took the precaution of having three actors in the role of Christ, rotating them as God the Father and Judas. Like Browne, he was concerned with the stamina of actors with day-jobs during a long rehearsal and performance run. His Christs were all experienced amateurs: Peter Blanshard, a civil servant from Poppleton and a member of the Settlement Players; Gerald Lomas, a drama teacher from Pudsey and a member of the Leeds Proscenium Players; and John White, a director of an interior decorating firm in York, who had performed in the Museum Gardens as Adam in 1957 and Gabriel in 1960.

There was theatrical sense in having the actors play two persons of the Trinity as well as Judas in that they could explore the central role of Christ through their experience of it from the perspective of other pivotal characters. In addition, seeing others play the role could allow them to reconsider their own interpretation. In terms of community there was also a sense of fairness because this decision 'obviated the necessity of an understudy who would probably never get a chance' to play the central role.[29] Jaques assesses the strengths and weaknesses of the three Christs.[30] She explains that John White 'suffered as God as well as man' and was 'especially strong in ... the Garden of Gethsemane, the buffeting, the nailing, and ... the carrying of the cross' but was at his 'weakest in the scenes with Satan ... the harrowing of hell, and ... the last judgment, finding it difficult to become a terrible figure of righteous wrath.' Peter Blanshard on the other hand 'was better in scenes which required towering moral strength and personal magnetism such as the baptism ... the reception by the burghers of Jerusalem, the harrowing ... and the last judgment,' but he lacked both White's 'gentleness in the scenes of the miracles and the woman taken in adultery, and his compassion toward Magdalene ... Peter and Thomas, and even Judas.' Finally Gerald Lomas was 'consistently compassionate and dedicated ... perhaps too pensive and unaggressive to stand up to Satan and the High Priests at the proper times.' Jaques's personal preference seems to have been for White, who later, with the encouragement of the mystery play director in 1980, Patrick Garland, became a professional actor, using the stage name Richard Conway.

In many respects both Taylor productions were imitations of Browne's work. John Elliott noted in his review of the 1973 mysteries that the performance was similar to those under Browne's direction: 'slow-paced, reverent, dignified, and slightly archaic,' with Taylor himself admitting that 'neither the city council nor the local public would tolerate any major departures from past practice.'[31] This adherence to a successful modern pattern rather than taking risks and, particularly, attempting to replicate medieval practice troubled medieval scholars. Kevin Roddy, for example, commenting on the University of Bristol Drama Department's original staging experiment with the Cornish *Ordinalia* at the Piran Round in 1969, went so far as to suggest that York could have afforded to 'shut off the walled city to traffic on consecutive Sundays' and experiment with a wagon performance 'not just to please the whims of scholars, but because the script seems intimately and essentially bound to a sequential, individualized procession of stages.'[32] The innovation of wagon performance on 'consecutive Sundays' that Roddy yearned for was not to came into force until 2002, but even then York did not close its gates.

Taylor's first Museum Gardens production was staged in the year after the abolition of stage censorship. Actors in the professional theatre were celebrating this new-found freedom by throwing off their clothes, even where, as in John Arden's *Harrold Muggins is a Martyr* (1968), nudity 'was incidental, almost offhand,'[33] but this would not do for the York mysteries, despite the fact that nudity was essential to the narrative. According to Elliott, the amateurs playing Adam and Eve told Taylor that they would be willing to play naked but he declined their offer.[34] When Adam and Eve finally did appear without clothing in Garland's Museum Gardens mysteries of 1980, their boldness went almost unnoticed, largely because their nudity was cut after the first night. Ned Chaillet, who attended the first performance, commented in *The Times* that there would have to be cuts to the production, which ran for over four hours, although he did not seem to think that the nudity scene would be one of them.[35] But by the second night Adam and Eve were modestly clad in nudity costumes and the 'white tights [that] reminded one of a cross between Victorian bathers and contemporary joggers' were held up to ridicule in the *Solicitors' Journal*.[36] According to the *Yorkshire Post* 'hardly anyone noticed' the nude scene on the first night, but 'some of the older members of the cast did – and were shocked', including Betty Doig, a mystery play veteran and 'mother of seven children,' who agreed with others that this was simply inappropriate for the York mysteries.[37]

In 1969 Taylor and Olsen embraced the Museum Gardens ruins more fervently than they had been embraced before. All eight of the arches of the nave were used along with the remains of the towers at both ends, and the polystyrene set was painted to blend with the abbey walls. The stage was bigger than ever, resulting in problems with sight lines, especially for the scenes that were presented at ground level. Taylor also went overboard with his costumes, which he based on Tuscan paintings. In his efforts to create an impressive spectacle, however, he exposed himself to several criticisms: the costumes had no over-all scheme; the effect was too much a 'conglomeration of flashing colours' on the stage that made it difficult to focus on the main characters; [38] and the members of the crowds, divested of their peasant costumes and dressed above their station, were too prominent. This delight in the spectacular was combined with Taylor's 'deliberate levelling off of the performance of the actors so that there were no outstanding stars,'[39] a form of 'Theatre of the People' where everyone was equal.

Because the mysteries were now firmly established as part of the academic study of theatre, Taylor attracted foreign scholars as volunteers in both his productions. His assistant stage director in 1969 was Meg Goin, an Assistant Professor of English at Keuka College, New York, who offered her services while she was on study leave in Britain to observe 'both professional and amateur theatre.'[40] In 1973 Reiner Sauer, a graduate student at the University of Toronto, who was particularly interested in the medieval aspect of the York mysteries, filled the associate director's position in the Museum Gardens production and also directed the 'Exodus' as the wagon play. These unpaid outsiders were welcomed into the York community.

Professionals for the Second Taylor Production

For his second production Taylor felt the need to return to the practice of using professionals: Alison Chitty as his designer, and a professional actor to play Christ. John Stuart Anderson, a specialist in church drama, took the central role and underlined the religiosity of the plays by delivering his lines with a 'chant-like intonation,' which was in Elliott's view 'in keeping with the essentially Pre-Raphaelite design.'[41] Anderson was apparently delighted with the role, declaring that playing 'the Christus' was the 'crown of [his] career.'[42]

The newly commissioned script by Howard Davies retained as much as possible of the original language in 1973, but this, added to the fact that the actors, as in Browne's day, seemed to be trying to 'hide any regional origins' by speaking in 'the most golden-tongued drama school English,' made the spoken text 'difficult to listen to and to follow.'[43] Academic commentators were unimpressed by the changes. Stanley Kahrl was especially outraged that there appeared to be a 'determination of a few families in York to ensure that the York cycle shall continue much as it has been done in the past,' but he did confess that this very feature was an 'instructive analogue with the guilds of the Middle Ages.'[44] Although he did not approve of what he saw in the mysteries, Kahrl recognized in their very defects some of the features of the ancient 'Theatre of the People.'

The mysteries in York were and are 'Theatre of the People' and, for better or worse, families are essential to them. The high-profile Dench family, Judi, Olave, and Reginald, and the Heppell family have been mentioned in previous chapters. Betty Doig, who preferred that Adam and Eve should be decently attired in 1980, played Martha in that year, bringing with her two other Doigs for the crowd scenes. In the previous production of 1976, Mrs Doig had played Mary the Mother, and five members of her family helped to swell the crowd, along with many other family groups, including Diana Thomson and three Thomson children (Alastair [age 2], Angus [age 6], and Rachel [age 7]; see plate 4). Outsiders may see problems when some 'families' appear to be overly dominant, but they are a necessary and healthy ingredient for community theatre.

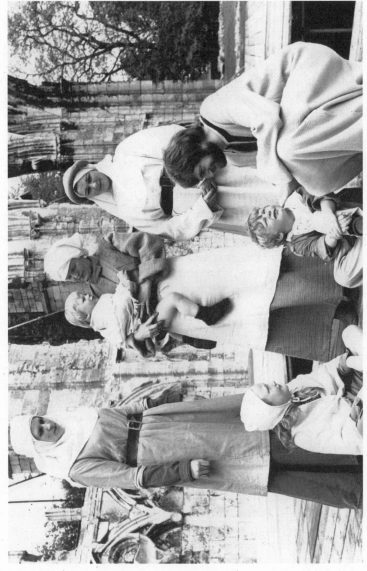

Plate 4. 'Christ' chats to members of the crowd on the set, Museum Gardens, 1976. David Bradley (Christ) with Diana Thomson (standing centre) and three Thomson children (from left Rachel, Alastair, and Angus).

Calls for Change

When the artistic director of the 1973 festival, Gavin Henderson, submitted his report after the event in August of that year, he expressed concern that, although they still paid for themselves, there appeared to be a waning of interest in the mysteries,[45] anticipating the Arts Council's comments about the 'over-exposure' of the plays after the 1976 festival. In Henderson's view there should be either less frequent productions or major revisions to the existing formula. His report was given coverage in the press as he put out a call for change in October 1973, not for 'a William Gaskill, or a BBC Omnibus, approach, but [for] some new ideas.'[46]

Enthusiasts in the local community rose to the challenge. Professor Wilfrid Mellers of the University of York, as mentioned in chapter 2, suggested a new script with musical 'accompaniment by Peter Maxwell Davies'; and freelance theatre director Richard Digby Day thought that the first step should be to find a new performance site, perhaps Dean's Park or the Minster, or to try out wagon productions, an alternative that he was later to contribute to with considerable credit.[47] When Browne was approached for his views, he reiterated a version of the advice about structural change he had given in 1966, that the 'cycle could be split into ... three parts, each of which could be treated in more detail ... with a condensed version only every twelfth year.'[48] Each of these suggestions was in its own way prophetic, foreshadowing the new scripts by Liz Lochhead (1992/1996) and Mike Poulton (2000), the move into the Minster, the consolidation of the multiple-wagon tradition, and the currently emerging pattern of wagon plays every four years and a condensed cycle every ten or twelve.

There were numerous factors affecting the mysteries in York and perceptions of the need for change in the 1970s. New models for sacred theatre had emerged after the lifting of the censorship laws; the establishment luminaries of the religious drama movement, such as T.S. Eliot, Christopher Fry, and Dorothy L. Sayers, whose work had featured in the Festival of Britain year, were no longer dominant.[49] Religious theatre was going wild. On the other side of the Atlantic the genre of the rock opera, particularly *Godspell* and *Jesus Christ Superstar*, both of which came to London (in 1971 and 1972 respectively) demonstrated that religion could communicate successfully to the masses outside the safe confines of an arts (or religious) festival. In making biblical narrative widely popular, rock opera itself was a form of 'Theatre of the People,' and the mystery play director for Chester in

1973, James Roose-Evans, founder of the Hampstead Theatre Club, experimented with the rock-opera format in an attempt to capitalize on the current theatrical fashion. Roose-Evans was almost outrageously adventurous: he abandoned the customary outdoor mystery play setting against the walls of Chester Cathedral and took his production 'indoors' under the canvas of a huge circus tent. His actors shed medieval garb in favour of contemporary costume, the 'original dialogue' was replaced by 'mime and Biblical narrative,' and the 'addition of a potpourri of popular songs succeeded in modernizing the medieval cycle almost beyond recognition.'[50] In this context Taylor's mysteries were looking more than a little old-fashioned.

Other Models for 'Theatre of the People'

Following Taylor's productions, other models of mystery plays as 'Theatre of the People' were provided by the work of directors in academic circles, community theatre, and on the professional stage. Jane Oakshott's work in community theatre, with the outstanding success of her wagon production of the York cycle at the University of Leeds in 1975, showed the value of responding to the original staging conditions of the plays. Oakshott's medieval-dress production was provided as an open-access outdoor entertainment. It conjured up medieval 'Theatre of the People,' creating the spirit of community festival by setting the wagon performances within a medieval fair, a secular/commercial festival rather than a religious one, and offering a play-within-a-play with the audience as part of the event as they attended the fair. Slightly further afield in an indoor experiment at the University of Lancaster, Meg Twycross tested the dynamics of street performance with her York 'Resurrection' wagon in 1977. This was a major investigation of the interaction of audience and actors in the processional performance mode. In the same year the professional theatre appropriated and reinterpreted large sections of the York cycle in Bill Bryden's National Theatre production of Tony Harrison's *Passion* (1977), the first of his *Mysteries*, aptly termed by Sarah Beckwith 'workerist theatre.'[51] This production encouraged the attractive myth of the ancient guilds as working-class institutions and remade medieval 'Theatre of the People' in the image of a modern construct, particularly suited to the political and social conditions of 1970s Britain that had been coloured by two memorable national miners' strikes in recent years. In 1976 and 1980, the York Museum Gardens mysteries responded to these new models.

The Jane Howell Production, 1976

Jane Howell, who was appointed as director for the 1976 production, had worked for William Gaskill at the Royal Court Theatre in London for some years; she had also 'worked with amateurs, especially children' and understood 'the techniques of directing people with no background of professional theatre.'[52] Phillip Gill, the administrator of the York Festival for 1976, announced pointedly that although there was to be a 'professional production team' with 'a few professional actors, the cast will still be 95 per cent amateurs.'[53] This was still, officially, to be 'Theatre of the People' and care was taken to encourage the community to accept the four professional actors as honorary locals. David Bradley (see plate 4), who played Christ (and also a pair of legs on the comic dragon that swallowed Lucifer in the scene of his fall), was eminently acceptable, being York born and having appeared in the 1960 Museum Gardens production as Second Knight in the 'Agony in the Garden and the Betrayal' episode. David Hill (Archangel Michael/Pilate) was accorded local status by sleight-of-hand because he had appeared in the production of Pirandello's *When One is Somebody* at the Theatre Royal in the 1969 Festival. Paul Jesson (Shepherd/Judas/Herod's Knight) had lived in York for a time and his wife had taught at the Mount School, and that meant that only Raymond Platt (Satan/Annas), suitably perhaps given his roles, could not be reinvented as a York man.

The 'fairground atmosphere' of the Leeds production inspired Howell's mysteries, and, as Oakshott had done, she stressed the community aspects of the plays.[54] Again following Oakshott's lead, Howell included wagons on the Museum Gardens set, using them for the stable in the 'Nativity' and to represent Herod's palace and Pilate's house. This was a deliberate move back to the Middle Ages; by presenting her audience with something strange, Howell hoped to surprise those watching the action in front of the familiar abbey ruins into considering what it might have been like to be part of the medieval theatre in the streets. Howell also used live animals on her set: horses, sheep, donkeys, and dogs. The animals were said to give a touch of biblical 'verisimilitude' and they also added to the fun and confusion of the fair.[55] Then there were brass bands to further signal 'Theatre of the People': the Rowntree Mackintosh Works Band, the York Citadel Salvation Army Band, and the York Railway Institute Band.[56] This was a departure from the medieval-style music of previous productions and celebrated the long history and great popularity of brass bands in York.[57] Besides the brass bands, bound to be favoured by the locals, there was sexy ragtime music used in the Pilate-Percula scenes.

Musical director Alan Gout took an innovative and upbeat approach, possibly inspired by the contemporary biblical rock operas and by the 'sprinkling of popular songs chosen to lighten the action' in the 1973 mysteries in Chester.[58]

Howell moved away from the notion of 'a formal religious pageant performed on levels, or rostrums' of the kind presented by Taylor, and, when she spoke to the press, she was also firm, like Gaskill, on the fact that the mysteries had been written for 'Yorkshire voices';[59] consequently the only BBC English was that of the angels. The fairground motif also meant that she gave spectacle a high priority and reporter Michael Chaddock pushed this line in the local paper: 'spectacle first, drama second, religion and poetry neck and neck, but quite plainly among the also-rans.'[60] This reporter was not impressed by the 'quaint, almost apologetic retreat to the equivalents of medieval wagons for a handful of the individual plays,' but was delighted with the anachronisms of the 'jaunty overture reminiscent of an Edwardian Sunday afternoon' coupled with composer Edward Gregson's 'specially composed and usually reverent music,' the 'fairy-tale witches, pointed hats and all' in the 'Harrowing of Hell' episode, and the 'Chinese dragon' of the 'Fall of Lucifer.' These were clearly not 'medieval' elements but they allowed medieval 'Theatre of the People' to fit playfully with recognizably modern constructs, making it a theatre for contemporary people rather than an historical re-enactment.

Howell's designer, Hayden Griffin, was also determined to bring 'the audience nearer to the action' as Giles and Gaskill had done in their productions.[61] When the set design was unveiled, readers of the local paper were encouraged to observe and appreciate his attempts to achieve this: 'the tiers of seats leading directly from the stage will allow close communication between the actors and audience ... [and] help recreate the informal atmosphere of the original medieval production.'[62] The set was likely to win favour locally because, as the *Yorkshire Gazette* reviewer commented, it did not 'compete with the simple elegance of the curving stone arches of the Abbey ruins, which form[ed] such a perfect backdrop, so [the] starkly bare wooden platform [was] in marked contrast, with its twin sunken areas, one filled with water whose reflection flickered on the walls, the other with sand.'[63] This reviewer was impressed by the 'greater identification between the audience and players' that resulted from the seating plan and was further encouraged by community singing and the deployment of the onstage crowd as 'genuine family groups.'

Although the iconic splendour of the ruins shone through in Howell's production and the 'Theatre of the People' was evoked in various ways, the locals were divided in their reactions. While some complained about a lack of religiosity and dignity, there were plenty of supporters, including one of the three clergymen taking part in the production, the Rev. David Johnson, who played God the Father and wrote to the press defending the production as 'a vivid experience for audience and actors alike, of the Gospel of God's love for men.'[64] The drama critics were likewise divided. John Barber, for the *Daily Telegraph*, complained that the production reflected the 'dedication of a city' but that 'in her anxiety to avoid dullness, Miss Howell has diminished the drama' and that the whole was 'secular in tone' with 'no burning conviction in the Bible stories.'[65] Ian Stewart, for *Country Life*, declared that Howell's production should be remembered for 'its revelation of the plays as a communal experience shared by actors and audience, for its bold use of music for brass band ... and carols in which everyone could join' and he also commented that as 'spectacle ... Howell's production was as fine as any [we] have seen.'[66] Robin Thornber, for the *Guardian*, preferred the previous productions, which were 'ritually restaged' and offered 'a socially, culturally, and religiously respectable way of spending a pleasant summer's evening ... and attracting visitors to the city.'[67] He was somewhat scathing about the Howell production, describing it as 'like a teeming landscape by Breughel or Bosch or ... like a big collage on the wall of an infants' school'; in his view, the story was 'swamped by the spectacle,' although he ultimately blamed the Purvis text, 'which has more of the nineteenth century's notions of cardboard pageantry than fourteenth-century vitality or twentieth-century lucidity.' He suggested that if the plays were to be an 'international event ... the festival authorities might start wondering how to recapture some of the original life, purpose and meaning.' He advocated the commissioning of 'a fresh interpretation of the text,' and suggested 'farming out each episode to a different company, either fringe theatre groups, students or local amateur societies' to avoid the 'very present danger of the event ossifying into an atavistic amateur dramatic jamboree or a county set social occasion.' These suggestions for the future and for change were another way of urging 'Theatre of the People,' and reiterated suggestions that had been made, and rejected, in the past.

Howell had promised that there would be no emulation of previous productions in her work, and she most certainly kept that promise. There were many innovations. Adam and Eve, for example, emerged from a sandpit and the shepherds encouraged the audience to join in the community singing, approaches that were seen again in the later professional production of Tony Harrison's *Mysteries*. Howell wanted to achieve the

essence of performance within the community that had been one of the
hallmarks of the original production mode, to 'go back, as far as possible
on a static stage, to the original conception.'[68] She re-cut the Purvis text to
suit her own tastes, adding 'fragments from the Cain and Abel scene and
the Last Supper' but excluding the 'Last Judgment' because she thought it
inappropriate in the modern context and 'personally could not support
such an arbitrary fashion of dividing people into good and bad,'[69] a rejection of the 'Judgment' as the grand finale that may have been inspired by
the Chester mysteries of 1973, which 'ended ecumenically with the
descent of the Holy Spirit and the singing of a Shaker hymn.'[70] Howell's
production closed with a triumphal release of balloons for the 'Ascension.' John Peter, the *Sunday Times* reviewer, wrote that this was 'one of
the most exhilarating presentations of any of the great mystery cycles [he
had] ever seen' even though Howell had given 'the plays a celebratory
ending which they were not meant to have.'[71]

1980: A People's Festival

The artistic director for the York Festival for 1980, Richard Gregson-
Williams, was determined to create a people's festival, and Councillor Richard
Oxtoby, chairman of the York Festival and Mystery Plays board, claimed in
the local paper's *Festival Guide* that in this year 'greater efforts' had been
made 'to broaden the appeal' and make this 'genuinely a festival of the
people, by the people and for the people.'[72] In the planning stages in 1979
Gregson-Williams called for suggestions from local organizations, targeting
groups that might have felt they had been 'for too long ignored,' something
that was not to be the case in this festival, which was to 'arise from within
the community.'[73]

   For the first time, the Festival board was to have 'a grass-roots representative' among its members; accordingly, the chairman of the city
branch of the Working Men's Club and Institute Union sat on the board
alongside more traditional non-council members, the dean of York, the
vice chancellor of the University of York, and the chairman of the Theatre
Royal.[74] York had come a long way since the Hess years when even the
local drama groups, on whom the festival depended so heavily, were
denied representation on its governing body. The mysteries were to be
'Theatre of the People' in a festival that was declared a 'People's Festival.'

   The spirit of a people's festival shaped director Patrick Garland's mystery play production and the publicity that accompanied it. This was particularly evident in Yorkshire Television's feature on the plays for their

arts program *Calendar Carousel*, where the focus was not on one of the local players but on Brian Glover, who had appeared in the BBC television series of the Chester mysteries (1976) and in Harrison's *Passion* (1977).[75] He was to play God the Father in the revised and expanded version of Harrison's work, the *Mysteries*, in the Assembly Hall at the 1980 Edinburgh Festival. Glover was a highly visible working-class mystery play star and he was thus deemed a suitable, albeit non-local, ambassador for York in 1980. He was filmed in the role of the mounted Herald reading the proclamation of the York plays. Christopher Timothy, who played Christ for Garland, was interviewed, along with a number of the other leading players, and in an effort to suggest the medieval performance context, viewers were given a visual tour through the streets along the route of the original wagons.[76]

The Patrick Garland Production, 1980

Many felt that Garland's production lacked religiosity, but he did win a number of fans. One visitor from Berkshire wrote to the *Yorkshire Evening Press* to comment on the festival as a whole and to give special praise to the mysteries, comparing them favourably with the Oberammergau Passion Play performance he had seen in May of the same year; he particularly noted the way that the York mysteries balanced humour in the 'early plays' with the 'later solemnity' of the 'Crucifixion.'[77] The *Daily Telegraph* reviewer approved of Timothy as Christ and absolved him of all 'fake religiosity' in his interpretation of the role of Christ as a man of the people, 'who laughs and claps when he pulls off the cure of the lame man.'[78] Lucy Hughes-Hallett, for *Now!* magazine, praised the 'sense of community' in the production, commenting that 'if the religious content has lost some of its force for both cast and audience the sense of community is still strong.'[79] For this reviewer, at least, the community bond was more important than an aura of religiosity.

Following Howell, Garland retained the live animals, the brass bands, and much of the musical score. The sing-along with the shepherds was not repeated, but the audience was encouraged to join the onstage community in the singing of Blake's 'Jerusalem' at the end of the 'Entry into Jerusalem' episode, just before interval, and Psalm 100, 'All people that on earth do dwell,' to close the performance after the partially reinstated 'Last Judgment.' The words of these hymns were printed in the program; they may not have been familiar to all members of the audience, but there would have been sufficient cultural recognition to bring the biblical narrative into 'England's green and pleasant land.' The singing of the psalm by the audience and the cast, a tumult of thanksgiving for God's generosity to humanity, was offered as a reminder to the spectators that this was a play that was potentially about them. Not all those congregated to see the mysteries would have been Christian, of course, but as they joined in the grand finale, there was at least scope for them to appreciate what Browne had referred to in 1965 as 'the spirit in which they were written by the medieval playwrights.'[80]

Garland stepped up moves towards a 'Theatre of the People' with some innovations of his own. Under his direction the crowd scenes of the York mysteries took on a different meaning. The crowds were not merely part of the biblical narrative, they also functioned as an onstage audience. Ian Stewart, reviewing the production for *Country Life*, described the way that the crowd 'cheered or hissed the action' as one of Garland's 'most successful devices for suggesting the total and continuing involvement of all concerned.'[81] This crowd not only reacted to the action with the hisses and boos of melodrama, they also partook of it in other ways: during the 'Last Supper,' for example, they brought out 'Thermoses and buns [to] have a bite themselves.'[82]

Not everyone was happy with this treatment of the York crowds. Even among academics, who might have been expected to be pleased with any attempt to change the status of these anachronistic hordes, the reaction was, at best, guarded. Peter Happé, for example, called it a 'pseudo-audience' and felt that the two hundred or so actors in the onstage audience were confusing because 'their real function seemed ... ambivalent, and perhaps they prevented the development of any real relationship between us the real audience and the actors.'[83] Happé was able to compare his much more positive reaction as a member of the audience for Oakshott's Towneley mysteries in the Wakefield shopping precinct in the same year, where the processional mode allowed the audience to become 'part of the dramatic experience without participating in the action.' He also compared the experience for the York audience unfavourably with that of the audience for the promenade productions of Harrison's *Passion* and of the Coventry mysteries in the ruins of the city's bombed cathedral, where the 'impact' of the actors infiltrating the audience was 'powerful theatre, and moving in religious terms.'[84] Happé wrote a similar review for *Research Opportunities in Renaissance Drama* to which he added a comment on the text for York, noting that despite some excellent acting, especially by Christopher Timothy, 'the text had been so heavily cut that there was often little sense of development in individual scenes, and some of the actors had trouble with the feeling and content of their lines.'[85]

The cuts to the text worried Happé, but the additional dialogue that David Buck had written for the production enraged Elliott. At the beginning of the play, Christopher Timothy (Christ) delivered some lines to the audience as Nick the Carpenter and Larry Coles (3rd Burgess/Malcus/Joseph of Arimathea) spoke as Lambert the Joiner after the interval:

Lambert the Joiner:
Unpractised in the Players' arts
Are these our actors, stammering their parts.
Clumsy of gesture, rough and rude of voice;
Forgive their faults; indeed you have no choice.[86]

Elliott found this dialogue insulting, perpetuating the 'absurd idea' that medieval actors were as bumbling and incompetent as the 'rude mechanicals' of Shakespeare's *Midsummer Night's Dream*. As always, Elliott's commentary concluded with an attack on the York productions, suggesting that they needed to find a proper blend of 'game and earnest' and could learn from Oakshott's mysteries in Wakefield 'where the medieval festive atmosphere was implicit in the mode of performance rather than sententiously written into a script.'

Christopher Timothy's Nick the Carpenter did please one local reviewer, who saw him as 'a craftsman "anchor-man" to convey to the 20th century audience, in jokey conversation with a 14th century one, the roles the various guilds and individuals had on the day.'[87] As a tribute to the plays as a local product, Timothy's Nick spoke broad Yorkshire, allowing the audience 'time to sever any lingering mental links with the TV vet and Flaxborough's Sgt Love before his dignified and authoritative appearance as Christ.' Another reviewer regarded this as 'a bold stroke by Mr Garland [that] set the tone of joyful celebration at the outset.'[88] This 'jokey' atmosphere was fostered in the scene of the washing of the disciples' feet. Like other mere mortals, the disciples proved to be ticklish and Robert Cushman, the *Observer* critic, declared it Garland's 'best production-touch,'[89] although the local reviewer was less than impressed by what appeared more like 'a rugger team romp in the showers ... than a deeply serious action lesson in humility.'[90]

Perhaps in partial agreement with Howell's aversion for the 'Last Judgment,' Garland curtailed this scene 'after Christ's first speech to the faithful'; the result for some was that 'the great moral lesson' was absent from the plays, and the 'hand-clasping and passing of flowers from cast to audience' did nothing to convey the notion 'that Christians are required to do something active to gain salvation – and that not all of them are going to make it.'[91] Regardless of the truth of this assessment, the flowers and the embracing must also have gone at least some way to underlining the lesson of the importance of the bonds of community that were inherent in the medieval mysteries as well as suggesting the practices of some modern church communities.

By the end of the mystery play season in 1980 the notion of 'Theatre of the People' was firmly entrenched in British theatrical culture. Several forces had contributed to the achievement of this result. *The Times* theatre critic, Irving Wardle, claimed that when he saw the Bryden/Harrison *Passion* in 1977 he had wondered 'what real connection' there was 'between the fifteenth-century artisans who created these plays' and the modern world, but by 1980, Bryden's subsequent work with the '*Lark Rise* trilogy and Ann Jellicoe's community shows in the West Country' and, most importantly, 'the promenade performances that began with [Harrison's] *Passion*' had 'kept the idea of "people's theatre" alive' for him.[92] 'Theatre of the People,' however, was still little more than an 'idea' for the citizens of York in the 1980s. The amateur theatre groups remained under the control of outside professionals, keeping them in line with the Jellicoe-style community theatre that was enjoying such popularity around the country at that time, but still separating them from their guild counterparts of the Middle Ages.

Theatre in the open air is desperately reliant on the weather, and – as every outdoor event manager knows – the English weather is extremely unreliable. In 1958 E. Martin Browne, by then the veteran of three Museum Gardens productions, extolled the 'ancient magic' of 'acting in the open air,' praising the efforts of 'hundreds of English men and women' who put on plays alfresco and heroically confront the 'hazards' of the climate, risking a drenching and the loss of 'all their labour' in pursuit of the special magic that comes naturally with 'a good evening.'[1]

A perfect midsummer night in the Museum Gardens was indeed spellbinding: the day faded majestically and the sky turned a luminously deep blue behind the ruined arches of the abbey in harmony with the sublime spiritual moment of Christ's Passion. Commentators were dazzled by the theatricality of the natural illumination that enhanced the stage lighting provided by the Strand Electric Company; and they rhapsodized over the appropriateness of the unscripted birdsong that occasionally complemented the music specially written for the occasion – the triumphant notes of a blackbird at the 'Crucifixion' or the hooting of an owl as the 'Last Judgment' drew near.[2] Realistically, though, those who came to York would have been wise to emulate the clear-eyed practicality of Dorothy L. Sayers, who arrived sensibly equipped with 'fur coats, thick boots, rugs, anti-midge cream, and ... an air cushion, so as to be well prepared for all eventualities.'[3]

Problems with the Outdoor Venue

The outdoor venue had major problems: cold, wind, and the cancellation of wet-weather performances without compensation to ticket holders. But despite these considerations and the added annoyance of inappropriate background noise from road traffic, aircraft, and the trains, audiences continued to come and the festival organizers clung tenaciously to the Museum Gardens before finally abandoning them in 1992. This was in the face of the increasing costs of erecting the seating-stands and set, and the continued callousness of the elements, at their most callous, perhaps, when rain forced the cancellation of the performance that was to have been attended by Her Majesty, Queen Elizabeth, and the HRH Prince Philip, Duke of Edinburgh in 1957.[4]

In the lead-up to the 1951 revival the York Festival Society agonized over the prospect of rain. Should they take out insurance against inclement weather, put on additional matinees to make up for cancellations, or allow rained-off audiences to transfer their tickets to another performance?[5] Ultimately the board decided to accept the risk and ticket holders had to take their chances as well. For 1954 Browne suggested that a tape recording of a ninety-minute version of the production could be broadcast over the Minster's sound system to compensate disappointed audiences on the night of rained-off performances.[6] This came to nothing, although it would have had the added advantage of being available for future publicity as well as during future downpours. Other alternatives such as a 'live performance' or 'a reading' in the Minster, or even a filmed version of the plays, were also set aside.[7] Audiences continued to be evicted from their seats and sent home in the rain with little or nothing to show for their money.

Ambient noise was a serious drawback. As Bruce Smith has argued, 'automobile traffic, even at a distance' produces a 'masking effect ... reducing the distance at which sounds of all kinds can be heard' and shrinking the '"acoustic horizon."'[8] Furious at the limitations placed on the mystery play 'horizon,' the artistic director of the 1960 festival, Hans Hess, instructed the secretary of the York Festival board to write to the chief constable asking for assistance in silencing motor traffic and to the general manager of British Railways to protest about the trains.[9] Little could be done, however, and letters of complaint continued to arrive at the festival office. One disgruntled playgoer, irritated by the clamour of the steam trains, quipped that he felt like writing to 'Dr. Beeching and telling him that not only is he setting out to obliterate many of our railway stations but he has succeeded too in almost obliterating the Stations of the Cross.'[10]

But repeated complaints about audibility problems fell on deaf ears. After seeing the 1957 production Charles Mein, who had played one of the Burghers in 1951, suggested the use of microphones.[11] This was, how-ever, a measure that Browne strenuously resisted even when it was urged by the Festival Society board. He remained adamant that ampification could only work at the expense of the immediacy of live performance; microphones, he insisted, created 'a barrier between actor and hearer.'[12] In his concern for direct communication with the audience and his aver-sion for the disembodying of the human voice by means of amplification, Browne was in advance of the Brechtian thinking on theatre that was so influential in the early 1960s in Britain, but this was cold comfort to people in the Museum Gardens stands who were unable to hear the per-formance properly.

Storms of 1984 and 1988

In the summers of 1984 and 1988 some rather alarming meteorological pronouncements issued from the heavens over York. Just one week after the final mystery play performance in 1984 the Minster was struck by lightning and fire broke out in the roof of the south transept causing extensive damage. Some said that this was evidence of divine disapproval of the recent consecration of David Jenkins, the controversial bishop of Durham, who had cast doubts on accepted truths such as the Virgin Birth.[13] But John Elliott, voicing his by then familiar discontent with the York mysteries, remarked that the lightning strike had been 'the ultimate act of dramatic criticism'; this year, he said, it had been obvious yet again that 'even talented directors' from the professional theatre could not 'extricate' themselves from the 'mush' that was 'ingrained in York's atti-tude towards its plays.'[14]

This was the last and the most vitriolic of Elliott's appraisals of the Museum Gardens mysteries, but had he reviewed the 1988 production, he might have scored some good points by referring his readers to the spec-tacular meteorological attack on the Gardens themselves that took place on 30 June. As the audience queued at the gates for admission, the city was engulfed in a severe electrical storm, a tree near the entrance was struck by lightning, the performance was cancelled, and the Gardens were cordoned off. As the tree 'lit up and glowed' and the 'pigeons started dropping ... feathers flying everywhere,' three teenage girls and two policemen standing under it were knocked down, although on arrival at hospital they were, fortunately, pronounced unharmed.[15] This may not have been an act of divine 'dramatic criticism,' but it certainly underlined the negative aspects of outdoor performance.

Dampeners to the York Festival and Mystery Plays

The lightning strikes and the wind and rain that so often dogged the mysteries were literal storms over the Museum Gardens, but there were other kinds of storm clouds threatening. As early as 1976, although 'good weather and good reviews' encouraged the organizers to predict a sell-out run for Jane Howell's production,[16] there were concerns about the future of the festival itself, and later in the same year there were serious discussions about the continuing viability of the traditional mystery play venue. The Yorkshire Philosophical Society, then in joint control of the Gardens with the city council, was worried about degradation of the grounds resulting from the plays and other festival events that were held there. The Gardens subcommittee recommended that investigations be made into alternative sites, declaring the 'festival events and the gardens ... incompatible.'[17] Artistic director for the 1976 festival, Gavin Henderson, stressed that the city had a 'responsibility' to present the mysteries and that 'to avoid that responsibility and to deny people the opportunity to experience a unique heritage would be akin to demolishing the Minster.'[18] At this time the festival administrator, Phillip Gill, was concerned about costs to ratepayers and suggested that the plays could be moved from the 'aesthetically perfect' Gardens and, at least as a 'temporary measure,' staged as a 'smaller scale or alternative type of production on an another site.'[19] But this too would have been regarded as an outrageous act of vandalism in the 1970s, and no action was taken to secure another site or to change the traditional production style.

The rumblings continued into 1977. Labour councillor Ken Cooper proposed a referendum to determine whether ratepayers really wanted to continue supporting the York Festival, an event that he claimed was 'becoming a "tourist jamboree."'[20] This idea was quashed, but there were tempests in the council chambers with Councillor Steve Galloway (Liberal) calling, also unsuccessfully, for the festival to be run as a 'more "popular event primarily for the citizens of York."' Galloway reexamined the accounts to argue that the 1976 mysteries actually lost £11,000, although previous assessments had shown that the ticket sales almost covered costs and with the addition of 'other income ... the plays made a profit';[21] ultimately the majority agreed with Councillor Jack Wood, chairman of the Recreation and Amenities (Festival and Entertainments) Subcommittee, who maintained that the continuation of the plays as the main event was essential.

The 1980 festival went ahead, but dark clouds were lowering and by February 1981 financial support for a 1984 festival was by no means assured;

reports in the local paper complained that the city council was undecided about allocating funds to the event, although the Arts Council of Great Britain was considering doing so even if the local authority would not.[22] By August the matter was settled: there was to be a festival in 1984 and the council would contribute £90,000 towards it.[23] But this decision was not reached without further stormy debate. Councillor Cooper complained once again 'that the council was blindly subsidizing highbrow entertainment for the sole benefit of tourists, hoteliers and local caterers,' while Councillor Galloway also held his ground, asserting that he was 'prepared to give the Festival another try but ... wanted more sponsorship, more popular events and some sort of booking priority and discount prices' for locals.

Even when the mysteries were underway in 1984 it was not all clear skies. The players were resolute and continued on through the rain on several occasions, but the discomfort was so great that one of the performers, Peter Jackson (Satan), wrote to Delma Tomlin, the festival administrator, with some suggestions for making a 'marvellous experience ... more marvellous in future years.'[24] Jackson had concerns about several aspects of the production, including the audition process, the rehearsals, and the lack of discipline in the backstage area. He praised Tomlin for her 'labours in making this a hugely successful Festival,' but he was also concerned about the weather and asked that 'some policy' be put in place to secure the comfort of the actors:

> The audience must be the first consideration but many of us felt that it was unreasonable to expect us to carry on for 1½ hours in almost continuous rain especially bearing in mind the almost non-existent drying facilities.

But the rain in 1984 was the least of York's worries. Even before the festival opened the Arts Council gave notice that it would not provide financial support for any future events of this kind in the city. *The Glory of the Garden*, the Arts Council's 'strategy for a decade,' showered no glory on the Museum Gardens, but announced the withdrawal of its traditional subsidy of £70,000 to take effect on 1 April 1985.[25] Richard Gregson-Williams, the York Festival director, deplored this decision, claiming that his festival included 'probably the most important presentation of a cycle of Mystery Plays in the country (this year attracting audiences just short of 40,000 people and playing to virtually 100% capacity).'[26] In a letter to Richard Lawrence of the Arts Council, Gregson-Williams complained that the timing of the announcement had cost the city funding for the current festival, with potential sponsors being frightened off by the Council's action. Now that the national body had abandoned the York project, others, he said, were extremely wary about making donations. He drew attention to the 'uniquely fierce pride' of the people of York in the 'Festival as a whole, and most particularly in the Mystery Plays' that were 'part of the cultural life of the region.'[27] In his strongly worded appeal against the Arts Council's decision, he pointed out, again as a matter of pride, the complexities and costs of organizing the Museum Gardens performances:

> huge problems, artistic, logistic, financial, of staging the Plays with a cast of hundreds in a specially built auditorium seating 1500 a night for twenty five performances ... the effort that goes into providing a rota of 1000 stewards, 40 technical staff, hundreds of costumes and countless other people solving the problems of party visits, wheelchairs, Box Office etc.

This appeal on the grounds of the difficulties and costs associated with the production was unlikely to impress, indeed to highlight such factors might even have been interpreted as an endorsement of the wisdom of the Arts Council's decision. If there were such great 'problems,' why did York persist with the 1951 format rather than finding a more cost-effective method of presenting their plays? Worse still, expenses were on the rise. The provisional amounts for the 1988 production totalled £93,610, including £60,000 allowed for the seating-stand and lighting towers.[28] Since the seating, the set, and the lighting and sound equipment had to be reinvented with each production and health and safety regulations were increasingly stringent, costs were likely to continue their upward spiral as the years went by unless some significant changes were made.

The Toby Robertson Production, 1984

In 1984, the mystery play director Toby Robertson expressed misgivings about the traditional staging methods, although he did not go so far as to suggest a move indoors out of the weather or even out of the Gardens themselves. He was, however, toying with the idea of a promenade performance, a format that had proven successful in 1980 in the community mystery plays in Wakefield (dir. Jane Oakshott) and Coventry (dir. Ed Thomason) and in Bill Bryden's professional production of Tony Harrison's mystery play adaptation for the National Theatre.[29] An audience promenade in York, although he reluctantly declared it to be impossible when interviewed for *The Times*, would, in his view, have captured something of the feel of the original processional performance mode of the Middle Ages:

Dotted all round the abbey, all over the Museum Gardens – instead of moving the carts we could have moved the audience. But too many of the audience would be faithful old ladies, too old to move.[30]

The thought of complaints from 'old ladies' was, apparently, enough to deter Robertson in 1984, and he dutifully placed his mysteries against the abbey ruins according to custom. But because he considered the playing area too large, its sheer size causing 'audibility problems,' the designer, Franco Colacecchia, devised a much smaller stage than usual, only thirty feet wide, with the audience ranged around it in a semicircular fashion in sympathy with the more intimate theatre of the medieval streets.[31] Ironically, the reduced stage area caused its own problems, and a number of people in the highest priced seats were unable to see large parts of the action; audibility was actually decreased despite the greater proximity of the audience to the stage because the 'plastic sheeting which screened the stage floodlighting and sound equipment from the weather' was whipped into a 'thunderous rattling by the wind, so that the actors could not be heard properly.'[32]

Robertson went to work on the script and reconsidered the selection of episodes from the J.S. Purvis text. The Old Testament sequence, which successive directors had gradually expanded from the 1951 format, was cut back to the bare bones again, with only the first three episodes from the Creation sequence represented. This left scope to incorporate extracts from a number of other episodes not played in previous revivals (see table 2). The result was an emphasis on the Virgin Mary that had not been seen in the mysteries since the sixteenth century, thus reversing the Protestant leanings that had offended some scholars in the past. The Gospel of St Luke served as a guide for the content of the New Testament sequence and Robertson developed the Doctor in the 'Annunciation' episode as a chorus figure, giving him an invented dialogue to introduce the individual episodes.[33] The purpose of this, he said in the program notes, was deliberately to remove the seamless flow of previous productions and to introduce breaks to show the 'individual quality of each play,' allowing his production to 'stop and start following the pattern of the arrival and departure of each pageant wagon.' The Chorus, played by Father Hugh Curristan, who appeared in modern dress, explained what was to follow. His costume and his function as a mediator between the audience and the play were certainly medieval in spirit, but there was disapproval even among those of scholarly inclination. Elliott dismissed the Chorus as a 'chummy narrator,' who was both 'superfluous' and 'distracting' and gave the 'impression of an embarrassed time-traveler who had suddenly found himself the host of a game-show.'[34]

Table 2
Episodes represented in the 1951 and 1984 Museum Gardens mysteries

Title of episode	1951 Browne	1984 Robertson
The Fall of the Angels	x	x
The Creation		x
The Creation of Adam and Eve	x	x
Adam and Eve in Eden	x	
The Fall of Man	x	
The Annunciation and the Visitation	x	x
Joseph's Trouble about Mary	x	x
The Nativity	x	
The Shepherds	x	x
Coming of the Three Kings, the Adoration	x	
The Purification		x
The Flight into Egypt	x	
Christ and the Doctors		x
The Baptism	x	x
The Temptation	x	x
The Woman Taken in Adultery/ The Raising of Lazarus	x	
The Entry into Jerusalem	x	x
INTERVAL		
The Conspiracy	x	x
The Last Supper		x
The Agony in the Garden and the Betrayal	x	x
Christ before Annas and Caiaphas	x	
Christ before Pilate 1: The Dream of Pilate's Wife	x	
The Remorse of Judas*	x	x
INTERVAL		
Christ before Herod*		x
Christ before Pilate 2: The Judgement	x	x
The Road to Calvary	x	x
The Crucifixion	x	x
The Death of Christ	x	x
The Harrowing of Hell	x	x
The Resurrection	x	x

Table 2
Episodes represented in the 1951 and 1984 Museum Gardens mysteries (*continued*)

Title of episode	1951 Browne	1984 Robertson
Christ's Appearance to Mary Magdalene	x	x
The Incredulity of Thomas	x	x
The Ascension	x	x
Pentecost		
The Death of the Virgin		
The Assumption of the Virgin		x
The Last Judgment	x	x
The Coronation of the Virgin**		x

* The manuscript order of the 'Remorse of Judas and 'Christ before Herod' was reversed.
** The later fragment of the 'Coronation of the Virgin,' described in the program as 'A Father taking leave of his Son'.

Robertson was unhappy with the large-scale abridgement of the original cycle necessary to fit it into a single evening's entertainment. Mindful of the success of the two-part/two-night National Theatre mystery play production of 1980 (Harrison's *Nativity* and *Passion*), he considered the possibility of the same approach for York. However, as he had done when he contemplated the hypothetical objections of 'old ladies' to promenading, he abandoned the thought of a two-night structure for fear of offending people who 'don't like the idea of seeing any of it without the Crucifixion.'[35] Tradition won out over experimentation once again.

Even though York did not adopt the promenade mode or a two-part structure, the influence of Bryden's production of Harrison's mystery plays was evident in the Museum Gardens in 1984. This was particularly visible in Robertson's use of a hydraulic lift, an imitation of the fork-lift truck that brought God on stage in the Bryden/Harrison 'Creation' sequence. The scholars and members of the press were horrified. Elliott found the 'gleaming hydraulic elevator' distasteful and inefficient;[36] Irving Wardle wrote scathingly in *The Times* that when Mary and Christ approached the lift to ascend to heaven, they looked as if they were 'boarding a No. 19 bus.'[37] *The Sunday Times* reviewer, John Peter, concluded that Robertson's production was 'a brave experiment' that failed, declaring that it was 'not really religious and not in the least harrowing.'[38]

Local traditionalists were, it seems, not alone in resisting change. Michael Coventry for *The Financial Times* thought that the 1984 set was 'a scenic impertinence in front of the ruined arches' and longed for a panoramic view of the full expanse of the remains of the abbey.[39] Wardle recalled his experience of earlier revivals and yearned for a 'good crowd shout,' while Peter felt the loss of the episodes that had been omitted in this production and regretted all the additions other than the 'Trial before Herod.' Simon Ward as Christ, fresh from his success in *The Young Winston*, was the only professionally paid actor in the cast, but he did not please these critics either, although the local amateurs, Keith Jefferson, a black God the Father (and Herod), and Harry Bridge as Joseph were much admired. Despite the cold weather in 1984 and the less than rapturous reviews in the newspapers, however, the festival audiences kept coming.

The Steven Pimlott Production, 1988

There were signs that at least some of the reviewers' complaints in 1984 would be addressed for 1988. When Steven Pimlott was appointed as director, advance publicity promised splendid crowd scenes and religious reverence. Jude Kelly, the artistic director of the festival, emphasized Pimlott's 'considerable reputation in the field of opera and theatre' as well as his experience 'with large numbers of people in choruses' and his 'sympathy with the Christian message of the Plays.'[40] Perhaps to counter the minimal impact of Simon Ward in the central role in 1984, local publicity, as it had often done before, focused on the quest for a Christ.

Pimlott conceded that York's star player 'did not have to be a professional actor,' thus challenging the local community to produce a suitable aspirant from among their own ranks, while appealing to local pride in another way, Kelly confessed that 'top names' were under consideration, including 'heart-throb actor Jeremy Irons.'[41] Irons had achieved star status in 1984 in the *Brideshead Revisited* miniseries (dir. Charles Sturridge and Michael Lindsay-Hogg) and *The French Lieutenant's Woman* (dir. Karel Reisz), while in 1986, he had played an eighteenth-century Jesuit priest in *The Mission* (dir. Roland Joffe); he was thus a most desirable candidate for the starring role in York.

York was aiming high and Kelly had been pursuing Irons for some time. She had met with him in Stratford in mid-1987 and wrote in August that year to urge him to consider the idea seriously: if he took the role, she claimed, she was certain that 'the Plays would be filmed and marketed abroad' and his 'reputation as a classical actor' would be enhanced.[42] Irons read the selections from the script that Kelly sent him, but although he was interested in the 'challenge' he was unable to commit himself to 'ten weeks in the middle of the summer' at that point.[43] In the end, another star was engaged, Victor Banerjee (see plate 5), who, although he had never performed in the United Kingdom before, was then well known for his role as Dr Aziz in the 1984 film of *A Passage to India* (dir. David Lean). Banerjee was hailed as 'the Mystery Plays' first coloured Christ,'[44] following comfortably in the footsteps of Jefferson, whose God had been so much admired in 1984. Although Banerjee was a Hindu, the publicity surrounding him cemented his credentials by announcing that he had been 'educated by Irish Missionary brothers, who not only gave him a thorough knowledge of the Christian scriptures, but also a deep love of English and European literature.'[45] Banerjee was, then, an honorary Christian English gentleman as well as a politically correct representative of racial 'others.'

The papers were also interested in the casting of the role of the Virgin and dwelt on the young women who had appeared as Mary before going on to stardom. Mary Ure (1951) and Judi Dench (1957) were the shining examples of the trend, but other Maries had also been on the professional stage: Jean Buckle (1954), Loretta Ward (1966), Teresa Forbes-Adam (1969), and Penn Charles (1980). This was again a matter of local pride and, accordingly, the *Yorkshire Evening Press* ran stories on the issue when the announcement was made that Sue Parkinson, an occupational therapist at St Mary's Hospital, Scarborough, had been chosen for the role in 1988.[46] But while the choice of Banerjee and Parkinson was pleasing rather than controversial, the casting of a thirteen-year-old schoolboy, John Lacy-Colson, as God caused some major squalls.[47] Father Curristan, the religious advisor to the production, wrote to Pimlott to pledge his support for this 'challenging and exciting decision' and to prepare the director for possible 'opposition from the traditionalists.'[48]

On cue, as Curristan had warned, there were negative reactions from a number of local people. Ursula Groom, then chair of the Friends of the York Mystery Plays and Festival, was 'especially' worried about the casting of a child as God as well as the plans for 'modern dress, and uniforms to be worn by soldiers and guards'; in this she was representing not so much the Friends but the 'people of this ancient city, of all ages and many political persuasions' who had expressed to her their 'great concern about "OUR PLAYS."'[49]

Another correspondent who was closely associated with the established mystery play traditions in York was Stewart Lack, whose dedication and energy had been invaluable in the development of the single-wagon play

Plate 5. Three 'Christs' at rehearsal, Museum Gardens, 1988. Victor Banerjee (adult Christ) can't still the storm of tears from eight-month-old Robert Leake (Christ child) while Martin Harman (15), who plays the role of Christ at age twelve in the scene with the Doctors in the Temple (and the Angel at the Tomb), manages to smile for the camera.

tradition to be discussed in chapter 8. Lack, a schoolmaster, with many years' acquaintance with the young, was decidedly opposed to the idea of 'schoolboys ... to play God and Lucifer – to demonstrate the goodness and innocence of man before the Fall.'[50] Was this, he asked, a 'sensational gimmick that will assure one's name is remembered?' He wished Pimlott all the best, but could not refrain from offering his own opinion, based on long experience in his profession, that 'schoolboys are not renowned for goodness and innocence' nor could they carry the 'weighty import of the parts.' He was 'not against innovation,' he insisted, but felt that the standard of the productions had 'consistently fallen since 1973.'

There were, clearly, many tensions in the city during the 1988 festival, and in an announcement that paralleled the fears entertained by Hess in 1960 about the activities of the local branch of the British Drama League, Kelly alleged that the Friends had been spreading rumours about the mystery play production that had resulted in 'slow ticket sales at the start.'[51] While some of the Friends had been 'wonderful,' she said, others had been considerably less than supportive. Such gossip, of course, was excellent publicity.

On the final night of the production, however, there was an incident that caused another flurry of objections. In the scene of debauchery before the 'Flood,' a 'simulated sex scene ... reached a startling level of realism due to "high spirits" among the cast.'[52] Most of the audience could not see the offending couple, who were obscured by the cross, but traditionalists were predictably upset. It was twenty years since the abolition of stage censorship, and professional theatre practitioners had no qualms about confronting audiences with scenes of this kind, but it was a different matter for the York amateurs, especially in the context of the mysteries that, for many, still required the decorum that Browne expected of his Museum Gardens casts in the 1950s.

There were mixed reactions to the 1988 production. Eighty-five-year-old Laura Grayson, who had seen the mysteries in the Museum Gardens in five festivals, thought that the whole production looked like a '"Fringe" show' or a 'pantomime,' despite approving of Banerjee as Christ and the line of blue umbrellas for the 'Flood' that had been inspired by the Bryden/Harrison Nativity.[53] Claire Field, seeing the plays for the first time, was enchanted with the 'mixture of modern and medieval costumes' and the youthful God, hailing him as 'surely a Jesus of the future.'[54] The Times reviewer, Jeremy Kingston, was positive. He praised Lacy-Colson's God for his 'ageless power' and Banerjee's Christ for his 'intelligence and grace'; the umbrellas rated an honourable mention again, and 'Joseph's Trouble' was well received along with the finale to the 'Slaughter of the Innocents,' the death of Herod's son, a borrowing from the Chester cycle.[55] The medieval-style anachronism of updating the Jewish priests, Annas and Caiaphas, as Christian bishops was, however, lost on this reviewer, although Heather Neill for the *Times Educational Supplement* was more receptive to such touches, delighting in 'John the Baptist's converts ... like born again Christians, Pilate ... a mounted colonial grandee, [and] the merchandise in the temple ... reminiscent of that on sale at any cathedral shop.'[56] Neill also stressed that 'Christianity [was] firmly at the centre of the 1988 production,' noting the typological use of the 'rough wooden cross' that represented the Tree of Knowledge and later overshadowed the 'Sacrifice of Isaac.' Robin Thornber in the *Guardian* was impressed by the crowd that was used in what he described as 'a painterly way, like figures in a Breughel landscape.'[57] Some commentators, clearly, were struck by the modernity of the 1988 mysteries, while others delighted in impressions of the distant past.

Thornber felt that with this production the York mysteries were finally 'getting there'; they were at last presenting festival audiences with 'something you might enjoy rather than something that's good for the soul.' But Thornber's review was equivocal. He complained that there was 'still an air of worthy amateurism around the edges,' but as if hedging his bets, he also asserted that 'too much commercialism would spoil the atmosphere.' This conflict between 'amateurism,' which would bring the plays into line with the notion of medieval 'Theatre of the People,' and 'commercialism,' which would make them more like the modern professional productions of the Bryden/Harrison type, was an issue for York. The report prepared by Scapegoat, the aptly named production company employed for the 1988 festival, framed the central problem as a question of who was really in charge, outside professionals or local amateurs:

> The main problem is one of definition; it has to be decided whether the Mystery Plays are a professional production with an amateur cast or an amateur production with professional management.[58]

Ten years later, wagon play director Jane Oakshott, whose work is discussed in chapter 8, brought a scholarly interest as well as her training as a theatre professional to the York mysteries and refocused the issue after her street production in 1998. She insisted that the use of outsiders had been a major problem for the York revivals and that the local guilds should trust to the management and theatrical skills of insiders and become the stewards of an ongoing mystery play tradition in their own right.[59] She looked to the medieval past and the ancestral structures that had supported the plays in the Middle Ages and to a future in which a stable infrastructure provided by the modern guilds would advance the tradition as a more inclusive community project than it had been in its previous manifestations.

In 1988 there was, potentially, another contest over the playing of the York mysteries, this time between local enthusiasts for the abridged mystery play format and an outside academic community concerned that the locals, devoted as they were to the abbey ruins site, were not interested in replicating original performance conditions. The contest was brought into sharp relief in 1988 when Meg Twycross from the University of Lancaster brought in a team of academic wagon players to join the local Lords of Misrule, the drama group of the Centre for Medieval Studies at the University of York, in a more 'authentic' re-enactment on part of the medieval pageant route in the streets, to be elaborated on in chapter 8. This was an outwardly friendly contest. Strictly speaking the Pimlott and Twycross productions were not in competition at all and Twycross contributed an account of the original staging conventions to the program notes for the Museum Gardens plays. But academic reviewers remained unhappy about the fixed-place tradition. David Mills, for example, commenting on the 1988 Museum Gardens mysteries, claimed, as Elliott had done before him, that the ingrained Museum Gardens revival traditions were a 'millstone' for directors, even though he conceded that Pimlott had introduced some innovations like the 'child–God' that 'seemed gimmicky in prospect,' but 'in practice ... proved a powerful invention.'[60]

Margaret Sheehy: Changes in the Wind for 1992

There will always be room for conflict in the mystery play community, and the conflict between academic purists and theatre practitioners is likely to remain one of them. Reginald Hill derives comedy from this scenario in his Dalziel and Pascoe novel *Bones and Silence* (1990),[61] where his mystery play director gives a severe put down to her tame 'university medievalist' when he objects to her departures from authenticity:

> Shit, man! This show's for your person-in-the-street. Ask yourself, do they want it authentic, or do they want it *fun*? (50)

But when authenticity and contemporary theatre practice actually coincided in York during Margaret Sheehy's controversial tenure as artistic director of the 1992 festival, conflict became much more public than it had been in previous years. The newspapers were full of debates and uncertainties, first about Sheehy's proposals for change in the Museum Gardens and later about her strained relationships with the York Festival board. Affronts and accusations were bandied about in the press and the festival producer, Kevin West, and Sheehy herself both eventually left the project. Looking back in 1993, after the board had been wound up and the future of the mysteries was looking grim, an editorial in the *Yorkshire Evening Press* complained that the festival had 'expired through sheer incompetence'; everyone and everything was blamed, the difficulties of winning sponsorship, the lack of planning, the Labour-controlled council and its 'muddled vision' and 'distrust of "elitism,"' the Festival board and its chairman, Councillor Ken King, and by implication, both West and Sheehy.[62]

Right up to her dismissal in November 1991, Sheehy championed a promenade production of two three-hour mystery plays over two nights. These were radical changes to the age-old format established in 1951, and ones that had in fact been considered but, wisely it seems, abandoned by Robertson in 1984. But while her plans for the mysteries did not come into effect and the festival was left in considerable disarray following what was referred to in the *Press* as the 'Sheehy saga,' she should be given credit for the stand she took on the issue of promenading, her commitment to the idea of 'Theatre of the People,' and her engagement of renowned Scottish poet, Liz Lochhead, the first professional writer to work on a script for the mystery play revivals.

Promenade Production

There were several respectable precedents for Sheehy's approaches. Medieval Chester, for example, had opted for a three-day processional production, and there had been modern promenades in Leeds, Wakefield, and Coventry, and closer to home, a two-part production of an adaptation of the Towneley mysteries scripted by Liverpool poet, Adrian Henri, for Wakefield's centenary celebrations in 1988. Henri's mysteries were performed as an audience promenade over two nights 'on alternate weekday evenings, and end-to-end at weekends.'[63] The script was custom-designed for the ruins of Pontefract Castle; each night's performance ran for two hours; there were various modern touches, such as the use of a tractor in the 'Cain and Abel' episode and an eclectic selection of music, from medieval favourites, the *Magnificat*, *Stabat Mater*, and *Dies Irae*, to the modern Negro spiritual, 'Go Down Moses.' Sheehy and Lochhead had a similar vision for York's Museum Gardens.

Theatre of the People

The 1992 festival aimed to set new standards. West, appointed as festival producer, wrote to a number of graphic design firms early in 1991 calling for submissions for a new 'corporate image' that would reflect what was to be 'a celebration by and for local people.'[64] The 1988 York Festival had overspent by more than £80,000 and Sheehy proposed to save something in the vicinity of that amount by staging the mysteries as a promenade and eliminating the expense of the seating-stand and the traditional large-scale set in front of the ruined arches of the abbey. She was in sympathy with the Labour council's move to a more truly 'community' festival, stressing community involvement and urging that the mysteries adopt a presentation style 'closer to the original and more appropriate to the text.'[65]

Sheehy envisaged the plays being 'rehearsed in clusters in different centres,' thus approximating the medieval guild system of preparing for their separate contributions to the mysteries. The clusters were to be 'merged into the larger community in performance,' a variation on the notion of subdirectors working on various sequences of the mysteries that Browne had rejected in 1966. Simultaneous rehearsals for the various individual groups were to be facilitated by the appointment of two professional directors, Ian Forrest and Sheehy herself, who, in her enthusiasm for the project, took on the onerous task of codirector of the mysteries in addition to her already demanding position as artistic director of the festival.

In her initial proposal, Sheehy was careful not to alarm the traditionalists and insisted that her 'promenade production' would 'acknowledge and feature rather than obscure the beauty and uniqueness of the Gardens and the Abbey ruins.' The audience (of around 1500) would 'move around 6–7 "stations" guided by stewards in controlled moves'; they would be 'seated on the grass (on cushions) or standing' and a 'reasonable number (50–100) of seats' would be provided at each station for the disabled and the elderly. The sense of community participation would be further enhanced by allowing the audience admission to the Gardens at 6 pm so that they could 'wander about, eat, watch and participate in various informal entertainments provided by community groups' before the main event commenced. This proposal was eventually accepted in principle; Liz Lochhead was secured to prepare the script; and Mary Turner, as associate director, began a series of workshops with local community groups.

Pros and Cons of Promenade

From the outset Sheehy's plans attracted both praise and censure. The *Yorkshire Evening Press* appealed to long-standing perceptions of a predominantly highbrow element in the festival and asked provocatively whether the 'walkabout' production was to be a 'farce for the elite?'[66] Ironically, what Sheehy had envisaged as being a performance by and for the community was being turned into a basis for division in the community, between those who endorsed change and a more pointed acknowledgment of the medieval tradition and those who wished to maintain the 'tradition' of the 1950s. The idea of recreating the 'atmosphere in which the plays were first performed' was good in itself, the *Press* claimed, but there were concerns about practicalities such as wet grass and possible lack of audience concentration resulting from fatigue. Sheehy was quick to respond, accusing those opposed to 'this new promenade-style' of 'trying to preserve "dead" [i.e., 1950s] theatre' and to protest that promenade had been 'done everywhere but not in York.'[67]

There were many others who favoured the idea of a promenade production. Christopher Timothy, who had played Christ in 1980, applauded the notion of the 'walkabout' that would 'return the plays to their original, medieval roots,' despite the fact that it would be 'harder work to set up and to rehearse' and the audience 'may get wet [and] tired'; and Jude Kelly, the artistic director of the previous festival 'hailed the proposed new-style performance as "exciting and challenging."'[68] Edna Ward, representing the Friends of the York Festival, offered authoritative local support when she agreed that the costs of the 'expensive seating to which we have grown accustomed' must be accepted and that what was important was that the plays 'survive, ideally within the historic setting of the Museum Gardens' even if they had 'to walk them through the economic recession.'[69] There was also scholarly endorsement of the promenade from Twycross, who had plans underway to bring her second wagon production to York in 1992 and wrote to the local newspaper to say that the proposed two-night promenade was 'an imaginative and honest attempt to get back to the spirit of the original 15th-century Mystery Plays.'[70] For Twycross, the promenade was a chance to break away from the 'monolithic' fixed-place tradition established by Browne and 'reach out and touch' the audience in a way that the conventional Museum Gardens productions, in her view, could not. Even after Sheehy's departure and the forced transfer of the production to the Theatre Royal, there was support from her former codirector, Forrest, who took over the mysteries in their new indoor configuration but lamented the 'missed opportunity' of the promenade production, which he believed could have worked.[71]

Liz Lochhead's Script

Lochhead's script for the York mysteries of 1992 was a creative adaptation based on the complete edition by Purvis but departing from the pseudo-translation method he had adopted in the 1950s. Her treatment of the text, moving the action forward through swift transitions, sometimes facilitated by music, allowed for condensation and also for expansion where the original text was faulty. The original text is incomplete in, for example, the Cain and Abel episode, and so Lochhead added a ballad, 'The Sin Song' to supply the narrative. Songs as transitional narrative to move the action along had been a feature of the Bryden/Harrison mystery plays and of Henri's *Wakefield Mysteries*, and Lochhead capitalized on the audience acceptance of the convention. While she was sympathetic to the medieval text, she brought the creative writer's licence to bear on it rather than the historian's determination to adhere as closely as possible to words and music as set down in the fifteenth century.

Lochhead outlined her approach in a letter accepting the commission:

> I would be scripting, out of the extant text, a play (or two plays) which were about a community-performing-the-mystery plays, rather than smoothing and eliding the text into a play *about* Adam & Eve, and Jesus etc. ... like the original experience in some senses.[72]

The two-night structure was essential, she felt, to free this year's production from the strictures of the past:

> Unless we have the time allowed by two productions, then it is difficult to make the plays radically different, (except in their staging which, of course, is going to be an enormous departure from the ossifying structures the plays are heir to) ... Yes, everybody want [sic] to see the crucifixion, granted. However there *might* be a way of ending one play with same (or at least the resurrection) then beginning the next play with a fuller, although overlapping, version of the crucifixion and going on to the Judgement.

Production over two nights had already been successful for local mystery play revivals in Chester and Sheehy discussed her plans with Michael

Williams, administrator of the Chester Mysteries for 1992. He was supportive of the idea of splitting the York production as Chester had done in 1987 when the decision was taken to 'move nearer to the original intention of the cycle':

> A new adaptation was commissioned and the majority of the plays (18) were performed over three performances. The result was a success, new life was breathed into them ... tickets were even being sold on the black market ... [and] a substantial number of the audience wished to see all three performances.[73]

The Chester production of 1987 added a veneer of authenticity with the three-part structure imitating the medieval practice in that city and, in imitation of the apportioning of the episodes of the cycle to the guilds, used separate groups to perform 'the separate plays with the whole tied together by a small number of professional actors.' But Mills was convinced that the generalist audience on the Cathedral Green in 1987 would not for a moment have believed that what they saw 'bore the remotest relationship to the performances' seen by the citizens of Chester in medieval and early modern times.[74] He was, moreover, also convinced that an '"authentic" production' would not have worked for a modern audience and was pleased that the Chester revivals were 'constantly being reinvented and revivified as the needs and expectations of their communities change, and their significance shifts as the spectrum of traditional activities in which they stand changes with the introduction of new kinds of activity into the community.' An influential part of the community in York was resistant to change – or at least change from the pattern set in the 1950s revivals – but in 1992 they suffered unexpected upheavals that made change unavoidable.

7 Indoor Mysteries

Bill Anderson, commenting in the *Stage*, described the 1988 mysteries as 'Pimlott's masterpiece,' declaring that the only thing 'needed to seal perfection' was an 'extra 15 degrees rise in temperature.'[1] Temperatures and tempers were indeed rising as preparations got underway for the 1992 production, but when summer finally arrived, the warmest for many years, the mysteries and the Museum Gardens had parted company and the Theatre Royal had taken the plays indoors, thus providing the players and their audiences shelter from whatever the weather might bring and mopping up in the aftermath of the storms of controversy. Despite the potential virtues of a two-night promenade in the Museum Gardens for 1992, it was destined not to be.

The Theatre Royal: Pros and Cons of Change

When the organizers of the York Festival of 1976 were looking for ways to cut costs, they considered tapping into the resources of the local theatre. The artistic director, Gavin Henderson, and the festival administrator, Phillip Gill, canvassed opinion on the matter early in 1975, but their suggestion of using the resident professionals at the Royal to orchestrate the Museum Gardens mysteries was not well received by the community. They therefore concluded that this was a measure that could be implemented only as 'a last ditch stand' that 'would not create a happy situation with local amateur involvement' and played it safe by staying with the established custom of importing a 'well-known guest director.'[2]

In 1992, however, circumstances forced a much more radical departure from traditional practice. By the time Margaret Sheehy left York and the idea of a promenade through the Gardens had been abandoned, it was too late to arrange for an old-style abbey ruins production despite the fact that Sheehy's codirector, Ian Forrest, remained in his post. At this time, quite fortuitously, the Theatre Royal, a fine old theatre established in 1769 by a royal patent granted to Tate Wilkinson and itself a treasured institution in York, was emerging from a period of inactivity after an expensive refurbishment.[3] In an arrangement that was advantageous to both the theatre and the organizers of this troubled festival, the management of the Royal agreed to give the mysteries a new home. The controversies surrounding the Sheehy dismissal, deeply troubling as they were, had been good publicity, and the theatre was delighted to play host to a show that was sold out before it opened. The Royal had been the venue for amateur shows for many years and the artistic director, Derek Nicholls, saw potential for even stronger links with the community through the mystery play production. He hoped that when the mysteries came indoors in June they would be a 'catalyst for future community projects' that would be a further welcome boost for the theatre's finances.[4]

When the move indoors was first announced, the local newspapers suggested that this might well be the end of alfresco mysteries in York, but the official word was that the public would be allowed to decide on this after the Theatre Royal experiment was complete. Even before the opening night, however, there were many who prayed that the theatre would be no more than temporary accommodation.

Some elected members of the city council contemplated the move into the theatre with trepidation. Councillor Susan Cooke wrote to fellow councillor Mike Painter to praise the community theatre workshops conducted by the associate director, Mary Turner, but also to express concern that the transfer to the commercial theatre building might counteract the effect of the workshops and diminish the 'community feel which the Plays [had] always enjoyed.'[5] But such fears were unfounded and community involvement remained a central feature of the Theatre Royal project; Turner's workshops continued alongside the preparations for the indoor production, although taking part in these workshops 'no longer guarantee[d] a part in the plays' as had been the case under the Sheehy regime.[6] All such uncertainties were good for ticket sales and the matter was aired with considerable frequency in the media. On Radio 4's *Kaleidoscope* program in April, Councillor Ken King, chairman of the Festival board, explained that it was partly the fear of the weather, but mainly the cost of the seating-stand, the lighting, and sound equipment that had driven the plays indoors.[7]

But mystery play faithfuls had grown accustomed to the time-honoured outdoor site and the traditions that had become attached to it. Features that scholars and directors regarded as drawbacks in the Museum Gardens, die-hard audiences often saw as virtues, and, inevitably, there were negative responses to the change. The proscenium arch of the Theatre Royal was more suited to musical comedy and conventional modern plays than to the epic proportions of the mysteries, despite the stage being extended through to the back wall of the building for the occasion. So mundane a backdrop could scarcely compete with the romantic allure of the ruins of the eleventh-century abbey, and even though the cast was reduced to almost half the usual number, the mysteries gave the impression of being uncomfortably over-sized in their new surroundings.

Those who had seen previous productions missed the aura of medieval antiquity, even regretting, it seems, that they had escaped at last from the vagaries of the weather. Julia Veall, who was appointed as executive director of the festival after Sheehy's departure, had to deal with complaints about the loss of the 'magic' of the outdoor setting as well as outrage that the theatre was 'ugly and cramped and unbearably hot.'[8] The standard reply to such expressions of resentment was that there were two reasons for the decision to go indoors in 1992: the estimated £300,000 that a Museum Gardens event would have cost, and the belief that 'the Theatre had the skills necessary to put on a marvelous production equal to any previous experience.'[9]

Ominously, some prominent community groups were not impressed. The York Civic Trust, whose founding members had been so much involved in the promotion of the city's contribution to the 1951 Festival of Britain, felt that they had been let down by 'a mish-mash of the mediocre' in the 1992 festival and had particularly strong views on the mysteries.[10] In the previous year the Trust had agreed that the 'extremely high cost of erecting scaffolding for the seating, together with the restrictions imposed by the authorities in the interests of public safety, had made the Gardens as a site for the Plays in their original setting completely unpractical.'[11] But, wiser after the event, they were now indignant that they had 'seen no figures to substantiate the claim that it would have cost too much to erect scaffolding for the seating.'[12] Ironically, they had originally welcomed the move to the theatre as 'an imaginative and challenging decision,' though this may have been only because it was 'infinitely preferable to the appalling prospect of conducting a peripatetic wander around the gardens.'[13]

Ian Forrest: A New Director, 1992

Once the decision on the move was final, advance publicity settled into a positive mode. Forrest, now the sole mystery play director, was sorry that the outdoor promenade was not to be, but he was even more determined to capitalize on the advantages of the theatre, which, he said, was 'a very intimate ... space' that had the potential to engender a moving 'shared experience between a huge cast of 150 and a large audience.'[14] Previously in Sheehy's shadow, Forrest was now triumphantly touted as a 'York man' of thirteen years standing, a strong indication that he had at least one of the credentials necessary to make the mysteries a bonding community event.[15] But as well as being a local, he also had appropriate professional expertise. He had originally been appointed as codirector of the mysteries on the basis of his experience with promenade productions, but, happily, he could now be promoted as 'no stranger to the Theatre Royal,' where he had directed repertory productions of Willy Russell's comedy *Stags and Hens* and Walter Greenwood's *The Cure for Love*. Forrest and the venue were thus an appropriate fit with the mysteries in their new configuration.

Searching for a Star

Interest also focused on the appointment of a star to play the central role. Sheehy's original brief included an instruction that 'she must recruit a big name to play Christ,'[16] and, accordingly, she had made up a shortlist of possible candidates. Forrest consulted this list, but the first choice, Robert Lindsay, then widely known to television viewers from his roles as Wolfie Smith in the sitcom *Citizen Smith* and Michael Murray in the Northern drama serial *GBH*, turned down the offer. This was disappointing, but the mystery play organizers had more names to consider: the stars of other television sitcoms and miniseries, Bill Nighy (*The Men's Room*), Jeff Rawle (*Drop the Dead Donkey*), and Nathaniel Parker (*Never Come Back*); James Wilby, who had appeared recently in the film *A Handful of Dust* (1988, dir. Charles Sturridge); and 'the sensation of the Royal Shakespeare Company, African Prince Cyril Nri.'[17] Any of these actors might have brought distinction to the role, but none of them came to York and the part of Christ was eventually filled by Robson Green, who was 'plucked from rising TV stardom' as Jimmy Powell in *Casualty* and Private Tucker in *Soldier, Soldier*.[18]

As it transpired, Green was not a popular Christ. Other television actors before and after him, like Christopher Timothy in 1980 and Ray Stevenson in 2000, made the grade and won the hearts of their audiences and fellow mystery players, but Green was unhappy in the role and confesses that he was relieved to escape at the end of the run and embark on his second series of *Soldier Soldier*:

> I tried to play Jesus as a normal bloke faced with a terrible dilemma, but people didn't want a vulnerable bloke in a T-shirt and jeans. They wanted the all-knowing Jesus in white, flowing robes, long hair and a beard.[19]

Green, a northerner of working-class origins, certainly had the potential to appeal because of the success of the Bill Bryden/Tony Harrison *Mysteries*, especially as Forrest had adopted a number of the features of this show in his Theatre Royal mysteries (see plate 6). But the fascination of the myth of northern working-class roots for the medieval plays engendered by this professional theatre project did not flow through to enhance the reception of Green's portrayal and he was disappointed by the reviews:

> The *Independent* was especially damning: 'I do not know what Robson Green was playing at but it was hard to believe anyone would follow him across the stage let alone Israel.' The local papers agreed, but the *Mail* and the *Guardian* heaped praise on it.[20]

In the past, professional actors had strengthened the confidence of the largely amateur mystery play cast, but Green, at least in his own estimation, was a disappointment to the locals:

> The first night was organized chaos. Everyone was suffering from such terrible stage fright they were queuing up to be sick. We were down to ten disciples ... They were so nervous they couldn't find the tables, chairs, bread or wine, and when I came out for the last supper there was nothing there. They all looked at me expecting a miracle.[21]

Problems at the Royal

There were many problems in 1992 and not all of them can be laid at the feet of this jocular Geordie Jesus. Because of the rushed preparations after the delays caused by the Sheehy controversy and the late switch to the unfamiliar terrain of the indoor venue, the amateurs were under-rehearsed

Plate 6. 'Christ's Appearance to Mary Magdalene,' Theatre Royal, 1992. Robson Green (Christ) as 'Man of the People' with Jenny Burrage-Smith (Mary Magdalene).

and the script that Liz Lochhead had been preparing for a six-hour promenade production to be played over two nights was too long. The first performance ran for five hours; audiences fell asleep; theatre critics were united
in their dismay; Lochhead and Forrest hastened to 'reduce the length
immediately'; and Elizabeth Jones, the executive director of the theatre,
went into damage-control, quickly pointing out that this was all perfectly
'normal' and that 'in 1984 Toby Robertson's [Museum Gardens] production ran for five and a half hours on the first night.'[22] Even when things
went wrong, it seems that the mystery play traditions were being upheld!

Reactions to Change

The building-site set and the twentieth-century costumes that featured in the
1992 production drew adverse criticism from patrons even though several
professional reviewers praised the same ingredients. Released from the constraints of tradition that operated so fiercely in the Museum Gardens, these
new-look mysteries unashamedly and obtrusively combined the past with
the present. Lochhead had moved further away from the medieval text than
any of the previous scriptwriters had dared. The set and costume choices, in
sympathy with the medieval method of projecting the biblical past onto the
present, followed suit to underscore the transfer of the fifteenth-century
mysteries to the contemporary theatrical context. The program cover and
poster devised by the mystery play designer, Martin Johns, made the point of
the seamlessness of the past and present by superimposing photographs of
modern construction workers onto a redrawing of a thirteenth-century manuscript illustration of the building of the Tower of Babel. The people of York,
then and now, were thus portrayed as labouring in this 1992 mystery play
enterprise together, reconstructing the past using modern techniques.

   The work-place motif with modern builders toiling alongside their medieval colleagues had resonances with the setting and the working-class
veneer of the Bryden/Harrison *Mysteries*, and also with the numerous
'ongoing restoration and reconstruction programs' in York in the 1990s,
including the recent renovations at the Theatre Royal itself.[23] For the first
time in the history of the York revivals, the emphasis was not on physical
aspects of the medieval past but on the medieval dramatic technique of
reflecting the here and now: Adam and Eve at last lost their embarrassingly
baggy tights and disported themselves in snug-fitting bicycle gear, Isaac was
a local teenager in 'a York City football kit,' Christ wore boxer shorts at the
Crucifixion, and only Satan was out of date, 'dressed in lycra with the ...
1970s wet-look,'[24] thus rendering him visually as well as morally out of step
with the rest of the cast.

Musical Innovations

One important consequence of the transfer to the enclosed space of the theatre was that it offered an acoustically sympathetic environment for the mystery play music. In the Museum Gardens, as discussed further in appendix 1,
the music that accompanied the productions had wasted its sweetness to a
large extent in the airy expanses of the night; now the music could be heard
properly, but, ironically, for some theatregoers the 1992 music was not only
too modern but also much too loud. John Jansson, Forrest's composer in
York, used music of various styles to suit the varying episodes of the production. Following the example of Andy Roberts, the composer for Adrian
Henri's *Wakefield Mysteries* in 1988, he included a well-known folksong,
'Green Grow the Rushes, O!' as well as traditional medieval music and other
pieces specially composed for the lyrics written by Lochhead. According to
the program notes Jansson saw himself as following what he imagined was
the 'medieval practice' of using the 'best and most recent instruments available'; in harmony with modern times, a 'street band of winds, brass and
drum' accompanied the 'Entry into Jerusalem' episode, a 'suggestion of
heavy metal' backed the 'Harrowing of Hell,' and in situations where he
could not use live music, he 'resort[ed] to electronics.'[25] This was theatre for
York in the 1990s, but the big sound did not please everyone.

The John Doyle Production, 1996

Despite a variety of complaints, the mysteries were destined to remain
indoors for the next production staged in the summer of 1996. The differ-
ence was that in this year the theatre was fully in charge. John Doyle, the
resident artistic director at the Royal, took up the challenge of this second
season of indoor mysteries, thus fulfilling the vision of Henderson and
Gill in 1975 of using the creative talents of the staff of the local theatre.
Once again the indoor venue was a matter for discussion. Traditionalists
were worried that a 'sanitisation' of the plays in the professional theatre
environment meant the loss of the 'gruff emotionalism that an alfresco
stage encourages' while the team at the theatre countered bravely with an
argument for healthy change adapting to the times and claimed that the
plays were a 'developing cultural phenomenon.'[26]

Infrastructure

Much more than the 1950s-style site in the Museum Gardens and the traditional importation of a guest director was lost in 1996: the traditional

administrative involvement of the city council was also absent. The mysteries were now a stand-alone enterprise and the York Festival of the Arts as it was formerly constituted, with the plays as its centrepiece, had ceased to exist. This was a development that was bound to provoke indignation and the local paper made the most of it. A lead article in the *Yorkshire Evening Press* in August 1995 fanned the flames by claiming that the festival had been 'allowed to wither and die' and the 'York City Council must take most of the blame.'[27] The 'mistakes' of the council-controlled Festival board for the 1992 event were listed as 'vast overspending, the appointment of an unsuitable director ... who then had to be sacked, and a policy of staging community events in which no one was interested.' The *Press* was not about to denigrate the Theatre Royal, though, merely to point out that, 'beautiful' as it may be, the theatre could not hope to 'compete with the thrilling backdrop of St Mary's Abbey as the sun slowly sets on a summer's evening.'

Even though there was no official York Festival in 1996 the city council did not leave Doyle's mysteries out in the cold completely but provided some solid financial backing, although the amount of £50,000 was less than the £80,000 that the theatre would have liked. Other sponsors and supporters rallied to the cause, and preparations went ahead in a flurry of publicity focused on a lively debate over the casting of local resident Ruth Ford, a professionally trained actor turned antique dealer, as God (the Father).

Is God a Woman?

Asked his opinion on the propriety of a female God, the Venerable George Austin, one of the archdeacons of York, obligingly opened the discussion by remarking that this was 'political correctness gone silly.'[28] Doyle immediately denied that he had set out to cause controversy but seemed quite happy to encourage an ongoing debate as he threw down the gauntlet to his detractors:

> The criticism we have had from some churchmen seems to be much more to do with their internal politics than our play. It seems that seeing a woman in this role at this particular time is making them ask fundamental questions about their church and their beliefs. It is a sensitive time for the church as it wrestles with its own internal problems over women, and I'm afraid we have touched a nerve somehow with this casting.[29]

Ford was not the only cross-dressing female in the cast; Lorna Dutka was Beelzebub, Sarah Gollins a 'Herod Heavy,' Sarah Harvey the Angel

Gabriel, Tricia Lane a knight, Sue Morris Caiaphas, and Shirley Morton a shepherd, all roles that were usually filled by men. This may have been a reflection of the conventional shortage of male actors in amateur theatre productions that had been a perennial problem for the York mysteries; but it may also have been a cheeky riposte to those who had objected to a woman in the role of God. Doyle certainly kept up the pressure, casting Kate Thomson, who had played the Virgin Mary in the 1992 production, in the role of God's adversary to 'share satanic duties' with Dave Parkinson:[30]

> I'm not saying God is a woman, but God is being played by a woman, and I'm not saying Satan is a man or a woman, but that it's being played by a man and a woman as the best way to do it in this production.[31]

In the end Thomson had to pull out because she took a job outside York, and Parkinson had to shoulder the 'satanic duties' alone, although he did benefit from the assistance of Jenny Burrage-Smith, who 'smoulder[ed] like a sexy vamp' in the role of 'Satan's Snake.'[32]

Theatre of the People

The interest in the women of the 1996 mysteries virtually eclipsed the fact that this was 'Theatre of the People,' the first all-amateur, all-local performance since Edward Taylor's Museum Gardens production of 1969. Disappointingly, it even almost eclipsed Rory Mulvihill, the Leeds solicitor and member of the York Light Opera Company chosen to take on the starring role of Christ. Mulvihill's performance was no mean feat. Whereas in 1969 Taylor had been fearful that a single amateur would not have the stamina to play the central figure of the mysteries for the entire season and so cast a trio of actors to share the burden, Mulvihill proved, and perhaps with less credit than he deserved, that it was possible go it alone. He played Christ as a man of the people, and, because of his 'singing prowess as a musical actor,' doubled as the balladeer who told the Cain and Abel story through song.[33] The Theatre Royal was perfect for musical performance and, as Jansson had done in 1992, Catherine Jayes, the musical director and composer for 1996, used her actors as singers. Music was also used anachronistically and to great comic effect as was evident, for example, when the strains of 'Somewhere Over the Rainbow' rang out over the 'Flood' scene.

Unfortunately, however, Mulvihill's versatile Christ was largely ignored by the national press where attention remained fixed on the woman who was, as Lyn Gardner, the reviewer for the *Guardian*, flamboyantly put it, 'born to play God.'[34] He did rate a mention in the *Daily Telegraph*, however, where his performance was described as 'humane and commanding' although his 'immaculately groomed appearance ... just the thing in his solicitor's chambers, seem[ed] more than a little absurd here, especially when he ha[d] just emerged from the wilderness.'[35] The reviewer for the *Northern Echo*, perhaps unfairly and overly mindful of expectations of well-known professional stars in the role, rated Mulvihill as a 'capable rather than a charismatic choice.'[36]

Tony Morris, Poet in Residence (1996)

The 1996 production offered another variation on the notion of 'Theatre of the People'; it had not only a local director and an all-amateur cast but also a local 'poet in residence,' Tony Morris, who provided an artistic commentary on the lead-up to the production.[37] Morris took up 'residence' at the theatre to observe the progress of the plays as 'a fly-on-the-wall, at marketing meetings, front of house meetings, backstage, rehearsals, young people's workshops, movement sessions, music rehearsals, voice training and text study sessions.'[38] As he records the 'process' through verse in his collection *Poet in Residence*, he considers the 'people' of this community play such as Burrage-Smith, who was doubling as 'Satan's Snake' and Mary Magdalene, the role she had taken in two successive productions. The poet questions the notion of fixed traditions that can become frustrating even for the community that creates them when he asks if she was to be stuck in such roles forever – or would they let her play 'Mrs. Noah' one day (48)? Morris concludes his poems with an epilogue where he offers an insider's view of the motives for belonging to what he describes as the 'community/Of hewers for history' (60). Some participants have religious motives, he claims, while others are devoted to the past and to local tradition, a clear reflection of the mysteries of the Middle Ages as they are portrayed in the much less personal records among the documents in the city archives.

Millennium Fears

Rumours were running hot in the lead-up to the 1996 season at the theatre. Because of the somewhat exaggerated perception of the absence of council support for the mysteries in the 1990s, fears were raised for the millennium: would York celebrate this important moment in modern history 'without a festival,' and, by implication, would the mysteries, which had been the 'spiritual and cultural core' of the local Arts festival enter into another period of darkness?[39] John Shannon, chairman of the York Civic Trust, expressed disapproval of the handling of the festival since 1988, but offered great hopes for the future by suggesting that the 'successful annual York Early Music Festival could be expanded to embrace elements of York's best quadrennial festivals' and that the mysteries might be staged 'in York Minster itself or in the Minster Gardens (i.e., Dean's Park) in 2000.'[40] Shannon was correct on both counts: with Delma Tomlin at the helm, the Early Music Festival, which was formally established in 1978 and has since gained national and international recognition, became a key to the continuation of the mysteries into the twenty-first century, and, to general applause, the Minster took the plays under its vaulted roof as the flagship event of the city's millennium celebrations.[41]

The Greg Doran Production, 2000

The Minster was preparing for the year 2000 long before the second Theatre Royal mystery play run began in 1996. The dean, the Very Rev. Raymond Furnell, states in the program notes for the millennium production that discussions were already underway in 1994. And in a letter of August 1996 to Jane Oakshott, who was herself preparing for the wagon production of 1998, Paul Chesemore, director of Leisure Services for the York City Council, explained the position as it then stood: the dean and chapter would 'offer the City the Minster for the plays in 2000 provided that they were assured about the production company ... and that the Minster would not be worse off financially'; and the dean 'thought that this was a good moment to commission a new script,' although, understandably, it would need to be approved as being 'compatible with current theology.'[42]

In a magnificent show of faith in the local plays, the Minster embarked on a concerted effort on the project in 1997. The York Millennium Mystery Plays board was formed with the dean as its chairman and Tomlin of the York Early Music Foundation as chief executive. Fundraising efforts were set in motion and the Royal Shakespeare Company's charismatic Gregory Doran was secured as director. A new script was commissioned from professional dramatist Mike Poulton, who already had experience with Middle English texts, having successfully adapted the medieval saint's legend, *St Erkenwald*, for the RSC in 1997.[43] The scriptwriter assured traditionalists and potential new audiences that this was not to be 'an academic museum piece' but that his 'rule of thumb was ... to hear ... gutsy language resonating around the building,' and to retain as much of the 'original language' as possible while making it 'comprehensible and accessible' to modern ears.[44] His reverence for the fifteenth-century verse of the plays was similar to that espoused by Rev. J.S. Purvis as he embarked on the first revival script for 1951, but almost fifty years after the cautious approach to the text for the Festival of Britain year by a man who was a historian rather than a creative writer, this professional scriptwriter, like Lochhead, had the necessary artistic qualifications. Consequently, when Mulvihill, having switched to the diabolic role for this production, bounded onto the stage as a comically extroverted Satan, audiences were reduced to raucous laughter as his outlandish exclamations of 'Bollocks!' and 'Oh, Hell!' boomed beneath the soaring roof of this most sacred building signalling his defiant fall from grace. The script won the approval of audiences for the millennium production as it had previously won the approval of the dean and chapter, who clearly agreed with Poulton that 'humour lubricates these Plays.'[45]

The millennium, like the 1951 Festival of Britain, was a time for thanksgiving and renewal, and the Labour government of Tony Blair was, as Andrew Rosen puts it, 'in search of the monumental.'[46] Once again London had its 'Dome,' but the Millennium Dome was scarcely the popular success that its forerunner, the Dome of Discovery, had been in the dying days of the Clement Attlee Labour government. While the building itself was 'monumental' enough, there was a 'problem of what to put in it' because the millennium, unlike the 1951 Festival, was not 'an inherently British occasion' and the exhibits finally chosen for the Dome were 'designed to offend no one' and, consequently, failed to please anyone.[47] But although this new Dome was a disappointment as the centerpiece of the London celebrations in 2000, this was not true of the mystery plays in York, where once again they were the triumphant focus of the city's rejoicing. As in 1951, the mysteries had a freshly modernized script, a high-profile director, and a performance space that resonated with time-honoured spirituality, and as in 1951, the plays fitted the occasion in a special way. In the Festival of Britain the plays had declared themselves as monumentally and 'supremely York,' a perfect expression of faith in Britishness; at the millennium, and in the context of their performance in the largest Gothic cathedral in northern Europe, they were supremely appropriate in the year that marked two thousand years of Christian history.

By the end of the second millennium, Britain was a largely secular society; in terms of numbers world religions were predominantly non-Christian; and there was a strong trend towards using the non-Christian referencing 'BCE' and 'CE' in the universal calendar. But for all this, the dawning of the third millennium was accepted as a moment for reflection on Christian themes. Hollywood cashed in on the notion of 'doomsday' and Arnold Schwarzenegger, the epitome of the action hero in the late twentieth century, did his duty and saved the world by defeating the devil in *End of Days* (1999, dir. Peter Hyman), and in Rome, Pope John Paul II, celebrating 2000 as a Holy Year of Christian Jubilee, embraced popular interpretations of the Christian story by approving the rock musical *Jesus Christ Superstar* as part of his May Day festivities, thus negating decades of fundamentalist disapproval.[48]

In the Middle Ages the York mysteries were a secular event that celebrated the Real Presence of Christ on Corpus Christi Day; in 2000 they reached back to celebrate that Presence once again as a largely secular event but, as with *Superstar* in Rome, one that was taken to the ecclesiastical bosom when it was staged within the Minster walls. As had been the case in 1951, York was not the only local community preparing to perform their mysteries. Chester's offering, however, unlike their usual large-scale triennial fixed-place productions, was disappointingly low-key in the millennium year; their 'Mysteries in the Street' consisted of only a single fixed-'wagon' stage that presented the history of the world in thirty minutes.[49] Elsewhere however, larger projects came to fruition, projects that, as in York, built on existing modern traditions. In Coventry, where mysteries have been played since 1951, local groups joined with the Belgrade Theatre and Polish company, Teatr Biuro Podrozy, to perform their own version of the mysteries in the ruined cathedral.[50] In the majestic hill-top cathedral in Lincoln, Keith Ramsay, who inaugurated a mystery play performance tradition there in 1978, directed his final production, an adaptation of the N-Town mysteries that the local community has made its own.[51] Smaller communities also gave their all to medieval plays. Blockley village in the Cotswolds, for example, took the opportunity of the turn of the millennium to set down what may be the basis for an ongoing modern mystery play tradition with a production of a New Testament cycle built on the medieval Coventry plays.[52] Ancient mysteries were not alone in the millennium context; there were also newly devised community-based mysteries, such as the *Greenwich Passion Play* and the *Southwark Mysteries*,[53] and in the professional theatre there were productions of the Harrison *Mysteries* at the Cottesloe Theatre and Nativity plays by the Birmingham Rep and the Young Vic.

Mysteries and the Minster

In York the Minster and the mysteries came together in the millennium year in ways that would have been astonishing to the inhabitants of the Middle Ages. The dean and chapter certainly signalled their approval of the plays in the period of their first flowering and honoured the city and the guilds by watching the wagons as they stopped to perform at the Minster gates on Corpus Christi Day; but it was an enormous leap to take out a theatre licence and turn the cathedral church itself into a stage, disrupting the progress of visitors and the comfort of worshippers for over a month while preparations were made and the production completed its run. Much had changed since 1579 when the city council tentatively agreed to a performance of the mysteries in 1580 on the proviso that 'first the booke shalbe caried to my Lord Archebisshop and Mr Deane to correcte.'[54] Much had changed since Archbishop Cyril Garbett expressed his doubts about the appropriateness of these antique biblical dramas as part of the 1951 Festival of Britain.

In the excitement of the millennium year people could have been forgiven if they thought that the York mysteries had finally come home to their medieval roots. Just as the magic of a perfect summer's evening in the Museum Gardens worked on audiences to evoke an illusion of the plays rising out of the abbey ruins, so too the magnificence of this new production as it fitted into its new surroundings encouraged similar misconceptions. Although Paul Toy contributed a succinct overview of the medieval history of the plays to the program to explain the original performance conditions, there was a strong sense in which the 2000 production could not help but proclaim itself as belonging to the Minster. The huge stage stepped up into the nave, so perfectly coloured to match the Minster stone as to become part of the fabric of the building just as many of the Museum Gardens stages had found their niche in the abbey walls (see plate 7). Designer Robert Jones followed Doran's suggestion of using the colours of the famed Minster glass; as a consequence the costumes were fitted to the site and the production was studded with medieval-style tableaux. This was particularly impressive in the 'Flood' scene as Noah and his family looked out in wonder over the blue waters that billowed down the full length of the set – a tribute to modern theatrical ingenuity and to the medieval artists who had created the 'Flood' scene for the Minster's Great East Window.

The Minster was a superb indoor setting for the millennium production, but the idea of using the building for mystery play productions had been

Plate 7. Assembled cast and crew of the Minster production, 2000. The sheer number of participants with some of the props for the 'Creation' suggests the scale of the set that was fitted between the columns of the nave.

contemplated as long ago as 1910 in the wake of Louis Napolean Parker's *York Historic Pageant*. As mentioned in chapter 1, Rev. Charles Bell, vicar of St Olave's, was so enchanted with the ancient Corpus Christi plays that he had looked forward to their being played to an audience of thousands in the Minster within five years. It took ninety years, but at last the Minster opened its doors to the mystery players and an enthusiastic public.

Other Community Projects in York for the Millennium

For 2000 the mysteries were complemented by community projects promoted by the city council and by the activities of the York Early Music Foundation. More efforts than ever before were made to ensure that the plays were available to as many people as possible and special provisions were made for hearing- and visually impaired patrons. Local schools were offered free tickets for all weeknight performances and York Card holders could purchase their tickets at a discount. Children from two primary schools made props for the 'Creation' episode and a number of school-based educational projects took their inspiration from the Minster and the mysteries that were to be performed there.

While the children who made the props had to wait until the preview performance to see the impact of their labours, other student-created events were complete before the mysteries opened: the *Carnival of Time* in the Museum Gardens and *A Creative Mystery* in the Minster in 1999, and *Hourglass* in the Theatre Royal at Easter 2000. In addition to these ancillary projects, Graham Sanderson of Fulford School and Cathryn Dew, educational co-coordinator on the Minster production team, compiled a Teacher's Pack that offered another means of taking the mysteries to a broader community, infiltrating various areas across the national curriculum, from Business Studies and Religious Studies to Drama and English. This was a mystery play season that brought together the Minster, the city council, the Early Music Foundation, the amateur performers, and the wider local community in ways that had been successful in the past and also through innovations prompted by the sense of this year being special.

The Minster as Entertainment Space

The Minster had, of course, allowed theatrical productions within its walls before, although nothing of the magnitude of what was contemplated for the year 2000. In 1968, for example, there had been a single performance of

Philip Turner's *Christ in the Concrete City*, presented in the nave by boys from Eton College, making 'history' as the first 'modern Passion drama' to be played there.[55] This play both made history and repeated history as the actors alternated between the representation of biblical and contemporary characters, thus replicating the original mystery players' overlay of biblical past onto their own present time. Later, in 1972, there were performances of T.S. Eliot's well-known cathedral play *Murder in the Cathedral* in the north transept by the resident company of the Theatre Royal to mark the 500th anniversary of the completion and re-dedication of the Minster in 1472.

The Minster had also functioned on many occasions as a concert hall. This had been one of its traditional roles in the York Festivals of the Arts of the twentieth century, but even before this, the Theatre Royal, St Michael-le-Belfrey, the Assembly Rooms, and the Minster all played host to musical events in the eighteenth and nineteenth centuries,[56] although as was so often the case with the concerts in the twentieth-century festivals, the prices for admission were too high for most York residents. In the early part of the nineteenth century, the dean, the Very Rev. George Markham, would not allow music festivals in the Minster because of his 'fears of possible damage to the ... fabric,' but with the accession of a new dean, the Very Rev. William Cockburn in 1822, the Yorkshire Musical Festivals were set up in the nave of the cathedral church in the following year.[57] The conductor of the Minster performances at this time, Thomas Greatorex, complained that the building was unsuitable, 'so preposterously large that no band that can be procured in England can be found to fill it – there is only one worse place for music and that is out of doors.'[58]

Music in the Minster, 2000

The acoustics of the Minster still presented problems in 2000, especially for the actors, but attempts were made to overcome the difficulties by the use of a computerized audio system designed by the Dutch company, Duran Audio. Still, as E. Martin Browne had intimated in his objections to using microphones in the Museum Gardens, it was sometimes difficult for members of the audience to locate the natural source of the voice on the huge Minster stage and there were some complaints, with Jeremy Kingston, reviewing for *The Times*, claiming that the 'miking turn[ed] most of the lines into gabble.'[59] But while there was some difficulty with human voices, the music composed by Richard Shepherd, then headmaster of the Minster School and subchamberlain of the Minster, was triumphant.

As other mystery play revival composers had done before him, Shepherd responded to the musical cues of the original playbook, such as the singing of the *Magnificat* in the 'Annunciation' episode. He also wove into his score elements that would meet the expectations of a modern audience regarding musical themes and sound effects. He would have liked a huge orchestra, 'with a sumptuous string section, quadruple woodwind, a generous brass section ... [and] a devastating battery of percussion instruments,' but financial constraints allowed him only ten musicians: an oboe, a clarinet, two trumpets, two French horns, a cello, two percussionists, and the Minster organ. The trumpets were needed for angelic announcements on a number of occasions, the oboe and clarinet underscored Noah's raven and dove,[60] the horns made 'a suitable Roman sound for Pilate's court,' the organ provided 'a wonderful rumbling sound ... for some of God's more portentous statements' and a 'suitably churchy sound under Simeon's rather long speech when the infant Jesus [was] presented in the temple.'[61] The entry of the umbrella-animals for the 'Flood' scene was visually and aurally impressive, provoking a thrill in the audience that can be compared with the stunning impact of the parade of the animals in the acclaimed musical *The Lion King*.[62] Shepherd claims that his 'jaunty' music for this sequence 'was designed to emphasise the processional nature of the animals' entry into the ark,'[63] again responding to the needs of the script in ways that are similar to the responses of the medieval practitioners by providing music to enhance the 'movement of characters' and to mark a 'scene-division.'[64]

Shepherd's musical expertise and first-hand knowledge of the Minster helped to transform this sacred space into a theatre of thanksgiving in the millennium year, defying the acoustic problems inherent in a building that was designed for worship to the glory of God rather than as a concert hall. As the assembled cast joined in the hymn of praise at the end of the performance, 'a three verse adaptation of the Easter *Exultet*,'[65] members of the audience wept, overcome by the sheer magnitude of the sound and the palpable energy emanating from the stage. John Hall had been commanding as God the Father, and Ray Stevenson, the only professionally paid actor in the cast, had been a warm and almost larger-than-life Christ, but now both of them were just actors, part of the team beefing out the final chorus. This closing burst of music allowed for a breaking of the stage illusion as the actors stepped outside their stage characters and become worshippers. It also signalled the divine harmony associated with music in the Middle Ages and conformed with one of the 'dynamic functions' of music that Richard Rastall has identified in the medieval mysteries to mark the 'end of play.'[66]

8 Theatre of the Streets

The Single-Wagon Tradition Begins, 1954

Raising the curtain on a biblical stage show was a risky business in 1951 and E. Martin Browne was cautious not to allow any scholarly sympathy for medieval practice to seduce him towards the even greater hazards of wagon production. In his view the revival of the drama of the Middle Ages must err in the direction of conformity to current theatrical norms and the life of the modern city must take precedence over historical accuracy; so it was that the abridged mysteries went on in the Museum Gardens without any untoward disruption to traffic or commerce. All the same, Browne did not abandon the 'Theatre of the Streets' entirely in 1951; both he and the Rev. J.S. Purvis outlined the basics of this unfamiliar process through the newspapers and in public lectures, while the program notes offered those who saw the plays against the abbey ruins a brief account of the original staging conditions.

In 1954, when the mysteries were the acknowledged and widely advertised centrepiece of the York Festival and special events were devised to complement them, Browne went one step further in this regard and arranged a separate wagon performance of the 'Flood' as an adjunct to the central mystery play event. Noah's Ark floated majestically through the streets on a suitably disguised railroad baggage cart and audiences saw it free of charge at two playing stations.[1] One wagon play at two stations was light years away from forty-eight wagons and twelve stations envisaged by scholars in the 1950s as the norm in medieval times, but it was, nonetheless, a significant beginning.

This first modern 'Flood' was horse-drawn, a method that prevailed until 1966, when the medieval practice of using manpower was adopted and a team of sturdy youngsters from Archbishop Holgate's Grammar School manoeuvered another 'Flood' wagon between the stations. In 1954, the horse, like the other wagon play presenters, was attired in medieval costume, a mounted herald rode ahead to deliver the fifteenth-century proclamation, and the actors, escorted by a policeman, took up the rear.[2] With this curious equipage a second revival tradition of mystery playing in York made its debut, and from 1954 until 1988, a single wagon play, joined in 1969 and 1973 by a 'river play' and by a second wagon in 1980, was officially associated with the Museum Gardens mysteries (see appendix 3 B).

Browne's 'Flood,' 1954

Browne regarded the 1954 'Flood' as no more than a successful experiment, deficient because it did not allow the audience to 'enjoy the Mystery Plays as a whole' or 'the actors to display their full talents'; its only virtue was that it was 'a means of restoring to our knowledge the quality of the original popular show.'[3] He consistently played down the importance of the supporting act, claiming in 1963 that 'the effect of this isolated unit has been amusing and attractive but no more,'[4] and in 1981 that his wagons, although they gave 'an idea of what the pageants looked like ... and of the vivacity that can be engendered in their confined space,' could not rival 'the elaboration in which the Guilds competed with each other.'[5]

In 1954 the wagon complemented the Museum Gardens extravaganza as a pre-show entertainment but by no means upstaged it. As the single-wagon tradition continued it was customary that only an episode that was excluded from the main production would be seen in the streets, the sole exception being in 1988 when the 'Harrowing of Hell' was seen on the wagon as well as in the Gardens.

The wagon play was chosen on the basis of lively action and comic stage business: this was to be a showcase of the merry Middle Ages, a form of museum theatre, while the Museum Gardens production continued to provide the experience of real theatre for the modern audience. Keeping a tight rein on the wagon in 1954, Browne cast tried and trusted local actors from the 1951 revival in the starring roles, with Hubert Dryland as Noah, Lilian Pickering as Noah's Wife, and Nicholas Evans from the Northern Children's Theatre School as the First Son.

Because the 'Flood' was not included in the published 'shorter version' of the cycle, Purvis prepared a text that was printed locally as part of the wagon-play program, a convention that continued even after the 'complete version' of the cycle became available in 1957, thus taking modern-spelling texts of the York plays to an ever-widening public.[6] Purvis himself was happy with idea of the 'Theatre in the Streets,' recommending to the board that the 'Flood,' along with 'parts of the Mystery Plays [i.e., the Museum Gardens mysteries],' be filmed 'by an amateur photographer' and requesting permission to take this film on a lecture tour of the United States planned for later in the year.[7] The film, which now appears to be lost, was to be used to publicize future Museum Gardens productions as well as to provide a suitable visual aid for the scriptwriter's historically based lectures.

In 1954 the 'Flood' was held back until Thursday 17 June, five days into the festival. This delay had a purpose: it meant that the first modern re-enactment of medieval stage practice in York coincided with the date of Corpus Christi, thus honouring the ancient tradition. Echoing the sentiments of the 1951 Festival of Britain, this was also a wagon play for the present. Consequently, in a whimsically modern gesture, a special ceremony was devised to launch it. The Ark pulled up in St Helen's Square in front of the Mansion House, the Lord Mayor's official residence, the herald read the proclamation, and the local dignitaries responded to their cue:

The Lord Mayor and Lady Mayoress, the City Sheriff and his lady, and Dr. J.S. Purvis walked from the Mansion House and stepped onto the movable stage. The Sheriff then reminded the crowd of the historical significance of the mystery plays and, especially, of the pageant wagon. The performers ... waited beside the wagon as the Sheriff's lady christened the Ark by breaking a bottle of champagne over its bows, saying:

Good ship with fortune free
I set thee forth to fare,
And Noah's Ark shall be,
The name that you shall bear.[8]

The actors did not perform at the launch site, even though the Mansion House location corresponded roughly to the medieval playing station (at the gates of the Common Hall, i.e., the Guildhall) reserved for the Lord Mayor and aldermen in the Middle Ages. After the champagne ceremony, the wagon moved to the first playing station at the west front of the Minster (not far from where the dean and chapter saw the medieval plays at the Minster gates) and then on to King's Square (near the original playing station at the corner of Girdlergate and Petergate). Performances were given at the Minster and Thursday Market (St Sampson's

Square, which approximates to the station on the Pavement occupied by the Lady Mayoress and the aldermen's wives), except on the launch day and other Thursdays, when the second station was at King's Square to avoid disruption to the market.

Browne notes in his autobiography that the 'Flood' required 'two adults and half-a-dozen young people who could be drawn from secondary schools,'[9] and implies that local schoolmaster Stewart Lack, who played Peter in the Museum Gardens in 1954, was involved with him in his inaugural wagon production. There is no documentary evidence to support this and Browne is credited in the program as the director of this first wagon play. Nonetheless, Lack is widely regarded as the mainstay of the single-wagon play tradition, a perception that has a good deal to recommend it.

In the Wake of the 'Flood'

Reviewers reacted variously to the 'Theatre of the Streets' in 1954. John Buckingham found the 'Flood' merely 'interesting but not outstanding,' preferring the Museum Gardens production because it was not, like the wagon play, 'a diverting slice of medieval England' but, rather, 'full of dramatic power and truth.'[10] Celia Henderson, writing for *Time and Tide*, was kinder to the wagon play, although she recorded traffic chaos on the evening of the launch, thus vindicating Browne's concerns: the police had omitted to reroute traffic, with unfortunate results after closing time at the local factories, when workers on their bicycles and motor-bikes almost literally collided with the wagon and its entourage.[11]

The *Yorkshire Herald* reported that the 1954 wagon performances were 'altogether delightful ... and if anything were necessary to encourage people to see the longer cycle ... this would be just the thing.'[12] But at least one festival official was convinced that the wagon play could have quite the opposite effect. T.C. Benfield, the town clerk and secretary to the York Festival Society, was more than somewhat negative:

> I always feel that 'The Flood' gave a completely wrong impression to people witnessing it because I imagine they thought that that was the type of play which was performed in the Museum Gardens ... people seeing the waggon play would quite easily say that if that was one of the Mystery Plays, they had no desire to see more.[13]

But, clearly, there were other members of the York establishment who entertained more positive opinions of the 'Flood,' which has been immortalized in the Guildhall. Until 1956, when the city council decided to restore it, this building stood derelict, an unhappy monument to the Baedeker bombing raid of 29 April 1942. The restoration work included a new west window designed by H.W. Harvey, a prominent local glass painter; in its central panel, representing civic affairs, the 'Ark' as designed by Norah Lambourne takes pride of place, complete with the mounted herald, the police escort, and representatives of the cast and audience.

The 'Exodus,' 1957

After the 1954 'Flood,' the Festival Society board considered further street productions for 1957. Browne made several suggestions, including 'Christ before the Elders' (i.e., 'Christ and the Doctors') and the 'Presentation in the Temple' (i.e., 'The Purification') on the grounds of their 'human interest,' and the 'Shepherds,' which, in his view, might work if played by 'some good rustic actors,' although on the whole he preferred the 'Exodus' (i.e., 'Moses and Pharaoh') for its 'element of quaint humour.'[14] There was concern that the board might be accused of selecting the 'Exodus' in order to capitalize on the political upheavals in the Middle East that ended only a few months before the festival, when the Suez Canal was reopened to shipping, but this worry was set aside. Purvis made an effort to deflect criticism and increase interest in the production by deliberately drawing attention to the issue in the Festival Supplement in the local paper, where he claimed that the ancient play in which 'Israelites and Egyptians' clashed was 'chosen not because it was topical, but rather in spite of that.'[15]

The 'Edoxus' saw the arrival of Archbishop Holgate's Grammar School on the wagon-play scene. From that time onwards, the wagon play became a 'school play' and responsibility for it remained with Archbishops through to 1984, with teachers as directors, sometimes also acting alongside the boys and combining with the staff and students of local girls' schools. The teachers from Archbishops had formed an early alliance with the Museum Gardens productions: in 1951 and 1954 Kenneth Parsons appeared in the role of Adam, Michael Vonberg played Gabriel in 1954, and in the same year Stewart Lack played Peter, a part he was to retain for a number of years to come. These three men were also the backbone of the wagon play in 1957, with Parsons, the art master at Archbishops, as 'associate director' and also playing Pharaoh, Vonberg as Moses, Lack as God, and twelve boys from the school in the minor roles. Until

1973 the teachers were referred to as associate directors of the wagon plays while the current Museum Gardens director was given top billing. Although this convention lent kudos to the wagon play by linking it to the professional in charge in the Gardens, it almost certainly under-acknowledges the contribution made by the professionals at the school.

The 1957 'Exodus' wagon was popular and audiences were large: 'six to seven hundred if it were raining' and 'in the vicinity of a thousand' if it were fine.[16] The wagon set off from the school, then situated in Lord Mayor's Walk, and journeyed to the first station at the west front of the Minster; the herald and his attendant trumpeter and halberdiers headed the procession, and the players followed with their police escort. 'So far, so quaint,' wrote Robert Speaight, promising the readers of the *New Statesman* that they need not expect, nor, he implied, need they fear more 'pleasures of quaint-ness' in the Museum Gardens.[17] Undeterred by such slights, however, Archbishops held onto their association with the wagon tradition.

'Christ before the Elders,' 1960

Lack was the associate director for the 1960 'Christ before the Elders' wagon. Keith Mellor, the Museum Gardens designer, based the wagon on 'a fifteenth-century British Museum print of a Royal Entry pageant wagon,'[18] and Lack played it 'end-on,' that is with the shorter side of the stage rather than the longer one used as the 'front' (see plate 8). The 'end-on' configuration, one that was also favoured by a number of academic directors in later productions, theorizes the original staging conditions, with the wagons in procession along the streets approaching their audi-ences with the shorter 'end' in sight. Both the design and Lack's direction anticipated later scholarly arguments for 'end-on' staging by, among oth-ers, Meg Twycross and John McKinnell, whose work was similarly based on illustrations of antique processions and on modern Spanish Holy Week celebrations, from which Twycross extrapolates the wagon as a 'thrust stage surrounded on three sides by the audience.'[19]

Sister Bernarda Jaques notes that in 1960 Mary and Joseph used the street area around the wagon in their search for their lost son.[20] Clearly, Lack's school production in 1960 anticipated not only Twycross's aca-demic experiments with 'end-on' playing in York in 1988 and 1992 but also the 'off-wagon' playing by Jane Oakshott and Peter Meredith as Mary and Joseph in the version of the same episode performed in Toronto in 1998.[21] The question of using the streets as well as the wagon stage was

Plate 8. 'Christ before the Elders' wagon, 1960. The waggon plays 'end-on' at the West Front of the Minster. The mounted herald stands by (left) and the audience arranges itself on three sides of the stage.

one of the issues hotly debated by theatre scholars in the symposium associated with the York mysteries in Toronto in that year, but due credit should be given to Lack in his experiments with the possibilities of street playing almost forty years earlier.[22]

'Abraham and Isaac,' 1963

In 1963 'Abraham and Isaac' was chosen as the wagon play, again with Lack as associate director. The heart-rending subject matter enhanced the 'Theatre of Cruelty' in William Gaskill's Museum Gardens mysteries, and whereas previous wagon productions had used elaborate superstructures in their designs, John Bury, Gaskill's designer, opted for a bare stage, again in keeping with the minimalist style in the Gardens in that year. Jaques comments that there was 'a great flag pole with a lamb painted on its banner' to 'counteract this bareness' and that Abraham and Isaac rode on the wagon, something that concerns for health and safety issues would now prohibit, 'to add life and color.'[23] Potentially, Lack's handling of the Archbishops cast on the bare stage allowed for the 'all-round' playing option that Philip Butterworth chose for his 'Crucifixion' in 1992, with the audience able to see the actors from all four sides of the wagon.[24] Jaques records that by 1963 the wagon play tradition 'had grown so popular that this year the spectators far to the back were observed using periscopes and mirrors to see over the heads of the crowds.'[25]

Another 'Flood,' 1966

Browne returned to the Museum Gardens in 1966 and, perhaps recalling the success of his 1954 wagon play, decided on a new production of the 'Flood.' In 1964 Hans Hess, the artistic director of the festival, in pursuit of the imprimatur of the academy, had consulted Professor Neville Coghill of the University of Oxford for advice on the next wagon play. Coghill was an inspired teacher, famous for his modern English version of Chaucer's *Canterbury Tales* (1951), and noted also for his brilliantly eccentric productions of plays, particularly Shakespearean plays, for the Oxford University Dramatic Society.[26] He was known as the creator of stunning special effects in open-air productions, including a real 'flood' issuing on cue from the lock gates at Pinkhill Lock on the Thames where he directed a 'medieval *Noah's Flood* with a group of unemployed Welshmen at a camp organized by the University.'[27] His advice to Hess in 1964 offered no such excitement, however, and he suggested that the wagon play be transformed into a fixed-place event, 'performed on a raised and static platform high enough to be seen by everybody.'[28]

Happily Hess and Browne ignored this advice in 1966 and the wagon was on the move again as Archbishop Holgate's Grammar School combined with the York College for Girls, with associate director Lack playing Noah opposite Rosemary Whitaker, music mistress at the College, as his wife (see plate 9). For the first time, the Museum Gardens designer was not involved and Michael Rogers, a history teacher at Archbishops, provided the design, adapting his ship on wheels from a medieval sculpture in the Chapter House of Salisbury Cathedral. In another departure from previous tradition, the students from the two schools rather than the Museum Gardens team made the properties and painted the set, which was built by Ossie Heppell, a Museum Gardens stalwart. Costumes were, as usual, provided by the wardrobe mistress for the larger production, but the wagon play was becoming more independent of the Museum Gardens and more fully a school project than it had been in the past.

The 'Exodus' and the 'River Play' of the 'Flood,' 1969

The year 1969 saw an influx of foreign academics as mystery play volunteers. Meg Goin, an assistant professor of English at Keuka College, New York, was Taylor's assistant stage director in the Museum Gardens and also his associate director for the 'river play' of the 'Flood.' Reiner Sauer, then a graduate student supervised by John Leyerle at the University of Toronto, was particularly interested in the medieval mysteries and took on the position as Taylor's associate director for the main production and directed the 'Exodus' as the wagon play, providing his own script rather than accepting the Purvis version used by previous wagon-play directors.[29] Besides the usual street performances, the 'Exodus' was presented four times in the Guildhall, delivered in Middle English, a forerunner of the original pronunciation productions of the Lords of Misrule, the drama group of the Centre for Medieval Studies at the University of York. Archbishops provided an all-student cast for the 'Exodus,' with the set designed again by Rogers, built by Heppell Shopfitting, and painted by boys from the school.[30] Sauer experimented with a variation of Glynne Wickham's recently published theory that additional wheeled 'scaffold carts' were used in the Middle Ages to extend the acting area of the wagon stage.[31] In 1969, Rogers designed permanent scaffolds for the two performance sites and the wagon itself 'pulled up behind these ready built apron stages which were then used for most of the action of the play.'[32]

Plate 9. 'The Flood' wagon, 1966. Noah (Stewart Lack) struggles, with the help of his sons, to bring his reluctant wife (Rosemary Whitaker) on board the ark.

The river play directed by Museum Gardens director Edward Taylor was both colourful and popular in 1969. The Royal Navy provided the Ark and its crew and the cast arrived via the River Ouse, disembarking to perform at Marygate Landing and St George's Field. Adults took the lead roles of Noah and his wife, as in previous productions of the 'Flood.' John de Frates was Noah and Edna Shann played his wife, both Museum Gardens actors in previous years. Following Archbishops' lead, other local schools became involved; the minor roles were taken by students from St George's Secondary Modern School, while boys from St George's Roman Catholic School took the parts of the animals in masks made by the York School of Art.[33]

'Herod and the Three Kings' and the 'River Play' of the 'Flood,' 1973

The river play was repeated in 1973, when its companion piece was Lack's 'Herod and the Three Kings' (i.e., 'Coming of the Three Kings to Herod'). Like Sauer in 1969, Lack, who was finally billed in this year as the director rather than associate director, prepared the text himself. According to the custom established when the single-wagon play tradition began in 1954, the text was printed in the program, with generous acknowledgment to the 'debt to the late Canon Purvis, to whose work on the Plays anyone concerned with their production must be beholden.'

The 'Last Judgment,' 1976

The unusual shape of the Museum Gardens mysteries imposed by director Jane Howell was much to the advantage of the wagon players from Archbishops in 1976. As discussed in chapter 5, Howell closed her show with the general joy of the 'Ascension' rather than what she saw as the discriminatory triumph of the 'Last Judgment.' This was a happy and timely decision as far as the wagon players were concerned as the episode was now free to be taken up on the wagon. This gave the Archbishops team the opportunity to present the grand finale to the mysteries in something approaching the medieval format.

Wagon playing had received an unexpected boost in the early 1970s with the publication of the previously unknown York Merchant Adventurers' pageant masters' indenture of 1433, a document that contained some details about the 'Last Judgment' wagon-stage itself as well as an inventory of costumes and properties.[34] Lack responded with scholarly interest to this find. He had remained in contact with Browne and they continued to discuss the mystery play revivals and developments in medieval theatre studies long after the inaugural director had ceased to be involved with the Museum Gardens productions.[35] After his 1973 production of 'Herod and the Three Kings' Lack wrote to Browne about speculations by James Young on the dimensions of the original York wagons and pointed out that practical experience had taught him that Young's hypothetical wagon was too large.[36] Young had suggested a mighty 10' by 20' wagon, but as John Marshall commented, 7' by 12' wagons at Leeds in 1975 made excellent stages.[37] Clearly Lack, with his years of experience in York, was of a similar view.

Lack noted that when he presented 'Herod and the Three Kings' in 1973 the audience solemnly accepted the actors' insistence that the kings were approaching Jerusalem from a great distance even when that 'city' was only two feet away, thus confirming the dynamics of playing in confined spaces in the streets, and he was already pondering the practical implications of the 1433 document, questioning Young's placement of Hell for the 'Judgment' and speculating on how the separation of the good and bad souls might be achieved.

When Keith Daggett directed the 'Last Judgment' for Archbishops in 1976, Lack made a substantial contribution to a reconstruction of the wagon on the basis of the 1433 indenture.[38] Daggett himself prepared the script from the Lucy Toulmin Smith edition (1885), acknowledging, as Lack had done in the previous year, the contribution of the Purvis text and the Museum Gardens productions to the cause of making the 'work of our forefathers increasingly accessible.'

The 'Building of the Ark' and the 'Flood,' 1980

A conflation of the two episodes associated with Noah was derived from the Toulmin Smith edition for the 1980 festival and in this year the wagon-play cast for director John Osborn was all-male, thus taking a step away from the earlier 'Flood' productions by Archbishops in which the female roles had been filled by staff and students from the Queen Anne Grammar School or York College for Girls. On this occasion the masters played God and Noah, while senior boys played Noah's Wife and the elder son, junior boys the younger sons and the daughters, and the eleven-year-olds featured as the animals. This was an important statement on the medieval convention of cross-dressing that predates Meg Twycross's extensive academic experimentation with all-male casts in 1982–3.[39]

The casting also reflected the hierarchy of masters, journeymen, and apprentices of the medieval guilds. Lack himself pointed out the likeness of the school community to the ancient guilds in the 1973 program notes, claiming that the boys from the grammar school were 'renewing in a modern context the concept of the guild or closed fraternity responsible for the original productions.'

Archbishops had readily assumed the stewardship of the single-wagon tradition in 1957 and absorbed it into their own tradition. The stability of the school as an organization, the ongoing presence of interested staff, and the benefits to the school as a whole and for the individuals involved in the production were a firm foundation for continuity. Like all school drama, the wagon plays offered desirable outcomes such as building personal self-esteem for the young players, strengthening bords within the institution, fostering appreciation of literature and drama, and in this case, highlighting local history. The wagon play was also a much more public performance than most school plays could hope to be and, consequently, Archbishops could derive satisfaction from the contribution a successful production made to their public image.

The 'Harrowing of Hell,' 1984

The last of Archbishops' wagon plays was Daggett's 'Harrowing of Hell' in 1984. In 1985 the school was renamed as 'Archbishop Holgate's School' and reorganized as a coeducational comprehensive establishment. At this time the 'new' school began a new tradition of 'staging Broadway successes,'[40] a factor that, along with the departure of teaching staff, may have contributed to the severance of its association with the wagon plays after the 1984 Festival. The wagon itself subsequently passed into the hands of the Lords of Misrule, who continued to put it to good use.

The 'Exodus,' 1988

The last of the Museum Gardens' productions was in 1988 and in this year the single-wagon production, the last of its kind, was a performance of the 'Exodus' by the MAPA Drama Group from Bradford, presented at only one station, untraditionally located at the Marygate entrance to the Gardens, the back door to the St Mary's Abbey ruins. But even as the single-wagon tradition appeared to be fading in York, a bold venture originating even further afield than Bradford, brought medieval theatre to the streets of modern York with greater brilliance than ever before.

Meg Twycross: Multiple-Wagon Traditions Begin in York, 1988[41]

In 1988 Meg Twycross organized a production of four wagon plays from her base in the English Department at the University of Lancaster. Wagon teams from Copenhagen, Durham, and Lancaster converged on York to join the local drama group from the Centre for Medieval Studies at the University of York, the Lords of Misrule (see appendix 3 C). The challenge of the York streets had long been a dream for academic directors: Twycross was determined to seize upon it. She was given permission to use a section of the original pageant route, thereby at least partly fulfilling the heartfelt wish expressed by Jane Oakshott in her reflections on her own ground-breaking 1975 wagon production of the York cycle in Leeds:

> One would like to take over the city of York, ban modern traffic from it for a day, and use the medieval playing-places. That way, we should learn a great deal ... no modern setting will otherwise give an exact 'feel' of the space originally available.[42]

On the evening of Saturday 9 July and Sunday 10 July 1988, starting at 7 pm, four 'medieval' wagons performed in procession at four playing stations in Low Petergate, a major breakthrough for the modern traditions of York mysteries and for the academic study of medieval plays in performance. This enterprise yielded positive proof of the power of the medieval theatrical methods and a more precise 'feel' of the original spaces than had ever been possible before. The Lords of Misrule, directed by Paul Toy, who has been closely involved with later mystery play productions, made a further statement by presenting their wagon play in Middle English, using original pronunciation in original performance spaces and thus well ahead of developments in the professional Shakespearean theatre, where it was not until 2004 that there were experiments with 'original pronunciation' performance at the reconstructed Globe in London.[43] In 1988, following the trend evident in the single-wagon tradition, directors were turning away from the Purvis texts and either fashioning their own from the new scholarly edition by Richard Beadle or using the modern spelling edition by Beadle and Pamela King.

The emphasis in 1988 was on authenticity and experimentation; in the words of the program notes, the production set out to 'recreate the last four plays of the York Cycle as they might have been seen in the 1470s along a section of the original route.' This time frame was a deliberate choice. It coincided with the completion of the register of the play texts (1463–77) and with official statements made in 1476 regarding the examination of the players to ensure their fitness to perform and the restriction of those who passed scrutiny to play 'but twise' on Corpus Christi Day.[44] The program notes encouraged audiences to break their ingrained habit of watching 'all four plays in sequence' and take the option of 'follow[ing] one play through several performances.' There was clearly a desire to engage the audience as part of an on-site experiment as well as to present them with the fruits of the experimentation of the presenters with 'stage machinery and "devices" for which medieval craftsmen were famous.'

Authenticity featured in the investigative creative work of John Brown, then a postgraduate student at the University of Lancaster, who was put to work by Tywcross as the director of the devils for her production on the 'Last Judgment' wagon. For Brown this was to be a means of 'testing out ideas' for his thesis, '"The Function of Devils in the Mystery Plays,"' to see if he could 'create a reasonably authentic, yet popular, demonic crew.'[45] The devils, he observed, 'brought the action of the play to the audience' and recreated some part of the original 'spirit,' a 'feeling of fun tinged with fear' that made them particularly popular with children in his audience.[46]

There was no way of knowing in advance just how a procession of 'medieval' pageant wagons would be greeted even by those who met them purposefully as an 'audience' in 1988, let alone by others who came upon them by accident. John McKinnell from Durham University, director of the 'Assumption of the Virgin' wagon, commented on some hostility encountered on the streets:

> Some … may have been ordinary citizens of York who simply felt that we were intruders, getting in the way, or making an implicit criticism of 'their' mystery play in the Abbey gardens. But most, especially on the Saturday night following the York Races, were young people who had come into the city from elsewhere in order to get drunk. In Petergate, this group generally restricted themselves to a bit of jostling (except for a brawl during *The Last Judgement*, which I didn't see). But in the larger space of King's Square, some of them felt brave enough to shout abuse or mockery, and a few deliberately drove past blowing their car horns.[47]

McKinnell was also able to note, however, that even serious attempts at disruption in 1988 did not 'destroy the atmosphere of the play,' and he was heartened that the efforts of his team to perform the play 'with integrity according to our best historical understanding' was not met with 'indifference,' even when the reaction was sometimes unpleasant.[48]

Meg Twycross: 1988 Wagon Play Director

When she brought off her impressive coup in 1988 and led her wagon players into the streets, Twycross was already well known in scholarly circles for her medieval productions and for her work on the actor/audience dynamic of street performance. In her York 'Resurrection' pageant at the Nuffield Theatre Studio at the University of Lancaster in 1977, Twycross lacked an authentic streetscape and so was obliged to content herself with an artificial 'street-shaped space, with a standing and potentially mobile audience.'[49] Even with this artificiality, further increased by the fact that this was an indoor production, Twycross was able to observe an audience 'more actively implicated than we are used to' in the theatrical event by virtue of their proximity to the play as the actors moved between the wagon stage and the simulated street space.[50] Her work in York was a valuable extension of this 1977 experiment, by 1988 further informed by her interest in masking in medieval theatre, her analysis of the playing stations on the York route, and her speculation that the York wagons were designed to be played 'end-on,' as Lack had elected to do with his 'Christ before the Elders' wagon in 1960.[51]

The 1988 wagons offered audiences a sequence of plays chosen from the latter part of the medieval cycle and allowed them to see the Marian episodes that had been all but obliterated from the fixed-place mysteries. Their presentation by the Twycross team reinforced the origins of the plays and their association with Catholic belief, and as this Marian group is followed in the original playbook by the 'Last Judgment' episode, there was an authentic grand finale that allowed for yet another attempt to interpret the 1433 pageant inventory, justly described in the program notes as 'a thrilling but frustrating document.'

Responses from the Academy to the 1988 Wagons

Although there had been little scholarly comment on earlier wagon productions, academics responded to the Twycross enterprise in print. Peter Happé, for example, saw the experience as a means of making 'speculations about the nature of medieval acting, particularly in respect of communication between performers, the level of interchange with the audience and the types of characterization.'[52] Alexandra Johnston, the driving force behind a wagon production of the York cycle in Toronto in 1977, came from Canada in eager anticipation. She was delighted to see 'that the acoustics in street performance are very good indeed,' and when darkness came down on the Last Judgment wagon she was able to conjecture that, as may have been the case in Coventry in 1457, 'the final stations were not always used by the last plays.'[53] Unlike McKinnell, she did see the 'scuffle between drunken race goers and the crowds seeing the plays' and chastised the local authorities for not foreseeing that the performance would block off 'the short cut between the favorite pubs and the car parks and bus station.'[54] The academic dialogue was well underway as Johnston compared aspects of the 1988 York performance unfavourably with the Toronto wagons of 1977; she was not pleased with the size of the wagons in York, which she considered too big, nor with the 'end-on' playing that seemed to her to be inappropriate for the York streets; nevertheless, she conceded that this was a 'valuable experiment both for its strengths and its weaknesses.'[55]

The Twycross Wagons 1992

Twycross followed her first multiple-wagon production with a second, five-wagon program in 1992. Although her wagons were strictly independent of the mysteries in the Museum Gardens (1988) and the Theatre Royal (1992), they, like the single-wagon plays of earlier years, were presented during the performance run of the fixed-place productions. This fact, taken with the restricted number of the wagon performances compared with the much longer season of the more culturally familiar and better-publicized mysteries on the big stage, meant that they were somewhat overshadowed.

Twycross repeated her experiment with a similar team of academic players, this time with five wagons at four stations on a route that had been extended to include Stonegate. The starting time was brought forward to 3 pm on Saturday and Sunday, 20 and 21 June, a decision that proved an unhappy one when the congestion in the streets during trading hours on Saturday caused problems for retail establishments.

In the 1992 production Twycross initially grouped three of her playing stations in tight formation along Stonegate to test the effects of concurrent performances within hearing distance of one another. Browne had been concerned about the lack of spectacle in the single-wagon tradition – now there was the colour, bustle, and possible confusion of a processional performance as well as the potential for the liveliness of cooperative competition as different groups of players vied with each other to impress the onlookers. As it happened, audiences were not unduly distracted by adjacent wagons: the real competition was a battle for space between the wagons and their audiences as opposed to people who were intent on pleasures other than seeing the plays. When the crush of people and wagons in Stonegate became a problem on the first day and the shopkeepers started to complain, Twycross immediately relinquished one of the sites and relocated to the less problematic but also less authentic site at King's Square.[56]

In 1992 Twycross concentrated on the Passion of Christ, beginning with the 'Crucifixion' and ending with 'Christ's Appearance to Mary Magdalene,' thus presenting her audiences with a slice of the original cycle that showcased its major focus. She gave a 'free hand' to the performance groups as to how they dealt with their individual episodes,[57] replicating the autonomy of the episodes in the Middle Ages, when there does not appear to have been an overarching artistic policy that would attempt to smooth out unevenness in artistic approach and achievement. Only the local Lords of Misrule chose to play their wagon 'side-on';[58] the Durham and Lancaster university groups played 'end-on'; and the Groningen and Bretton Hall groups opted for 'all round' playing and hence included only minimal superstructure in their set design, in the case of the 'Appearance to Mary Magdalene,' a leafy garden archway placed at the back of the wagon, and in the case of the 'Crucifixion,' only the cross, which was raised on one end of the wagon (see plate 10).

In his discussion of the production, Philip Butterworth, who directed the Bretton Hall production of the 'Crucifixion,' includes some of his notes to the company referring to recent scholarly speculations about 'medieval acting style.'[59] The express purpose of his contribution to the 1992 experiment was to identify 'an appropriate form of direct communication with a mobile audience'; Butterworth was particularly interested in developing the suggestions made by David Mills about direct address.[60] His soldiers spoke directly to (and hence 'through') members of the audience and the effect was magnificent. The words of the text, always chilling, became even more so when they were directed not only between the soldiers on the wagon stage, but also, and very pointedly, to the onlookers as if they were part of the action:

2 SOLDIER: He must be dead needlings by noon.
3 SOLDIER: Then is good time that we begin.
4 SOLDIER: Let ding him down, then is he done –
    He shall not dere us with his din.

Plate 10. 'The Crucifixion' wagon, 1992. The soldiers raise the cross while the 'audience' on the street (and in the windows above) look on intently or, alternatively, pass by intent on pleasures other than those of the theatre.

1 SOLDIER: He shall be set and learned soon,
    With care to him and all his kin.
2 SOLDIER: The foulest death of all
    Shall he die for his deeds.
3 SOLDIER: That means cross him we shall.
4 SOLDIER: Behold, so right he redes.[61]

Members of the audience who were addressed felt uncomfortable while those who were spared were conscious of their own relief not to have been chosen. This was 'Theatre of Cruelty' at its most powerful.

In her own commentary on the 1992 event, Twycross concentrated on the orientation of the wagons, the use of space, and the importance of the wagon itself as a constant visual element in street production, 'a trailer, an anticipation stirrer' that would entice audiences to congregate.[62] One of her major concerns was to prove to herself and others the power of playing in the streets in the traditional processional mode.

Even as Twycross demonstrated the theatricality of processional performance, she also showed only too well the truth of Browne's fears of the disruptions inherent in wagon playing in the modern city. Along with health and safety issues, the opposition of some local traders following the 1992 event worked against subsequent use of the original route for wagon productions, with further complications evident when Sunday trading was introduced in July 1994, just in time for the first of Jane Oakshott's wagon productions in York.

Jane Oakshott's Mystery Play Campaign Begins: Leeds 1975

Oakshott was awarded a well-deserved MBE for services to community drama in the New Year Honours list announced on 29 December 2007, but the story of her involvment with the community of the York mysteries begins almost thirty years earlier and in Leeds rather than in York itself. Then a recent graduate with an MA in Medieval Studies from the University of Leeds, Oakshott organized an (almost) full cycle of thirty-six of the forty-eight episodes in the York manuscript, enlisting performers from both university and community groups, who performed together in what was a splendid finale to her university's centenary celebrations in 1975. Her main agenda, one that she shared with Twycross, was to provide proof of the vitality and viability of medieval processional performance by replicating, as far as possible, the circumstances of such a performance. The fixed-place revival productions in York, Oakshott believed, were based on the assumption that 'a wagon is unsuitable as a stage ... in short, that the audience will be bored.'[63] As mentioned in chapter 1, there had been alarming attacks on 'Theatre of the Streets' in the early 1970s by scholars, notably Alan Nelson, who dismissed processional production as unworkable in medieval York and therefore insisted that the guilds did not perform in peripatetic mode on the Corpus Christi festival in those long-gone days. Even before Twycross began her experiments in Lancaster in 1977, Oakshott had shown the way as she set out to defend wagons by playing on them.

In her account of the 1975 Leeds production Oakshott remarks that universities have a duty to lead the community through research.[64] She convinced her own institution to take the lead by staging a large-scale re-enactment of medieval theatre. She created a street-shaped space in the university precinct by arranging fair-stalls so as to mark out 'a rather narrow corridor as the processional route in which everything happened.'[65] The successful 1975 York mysteries in Leeds, presented at three playing stations and over two days, under sunny skies and in the festive atmosphere of a medieval-style fairground, were the inspiration for another York production at the University of Toronto in October 1977. At that time, David Parry, the Robert Gill Fellow for 1977–8 in the Graduate Centre for Study of Drama, directed an ambitious full-cycle wagon production organized by a committee chaired by Johnston.[66] This, too, was an attempt to prove that processional wagon performance was both viable and theatrically engaging. In addition the organizers hoped that it would also show, in defiance of Nelson, that the entire cycle could be performed in processional format on a single day. This was not to be since heavy rain drove much of the production indoors. In her assessment of the event, Johnston emphasized that it was 'not a re-creation but an experiment' and that it would take 'many more experiments' before 'a re-creation' would be possible.[67]

Oakshott was already conducting further experiments. Earlier in the same year as the Toronto production, 1977, she set up a production of twelve of the Towneley mysteries in the pedestrianized shopping precinct in Wakefield, at that time still widely regarded as the medieval home of this cycle of plays. The repatriation of early theatre to its places of origin was high on her list of priorities, and she was delighted in 1980 when the drive towards a second production in Wakefield, this time a much larger one with twenty-nine of the thirty-two Towneley plays performed in Middle English, came from within the local community. The community still needed the academy, however, and was heavily reliant on Oakshott and on Peter Meredith of the University of Leeds, who prepared the performance text.

In the 1980s Oakshott's campaign was well underway, and in 1983 she turned her attention to the Chester mysteries, presenting the whole cycle at three playing stations at the University of Leeds for the Renaissance Festival organized by the Centre for Medieval Studies, with Meredith as artistic director and Twycross as costume designer. Subsequently, a minicycle of eight plays from this production travelled to Chester itself to perform at two playing stations, one of them an original location at the Cross in Watergate, and the other a non-authentic site in Eastgate.[68] Six of the plays were presented by Leeds groups, while Twycross brought the Joculatores Lancastrienses to perform 'The Purification and Doctors,' and John McKinnell, the scholarly director who came with Twycross to York in 1988 and 1992, led the Durham Players with 'Moses, Balaam and Balaak.'

Jane Oakshott in York, 1994 and 1998

When the Friends of the York Mystery Plays invited Oakshott to their city to direct her first multiple-wagon production there in 1994, the original medieval pageant route enjoyed by the Twycross team was off-limits. Disappointing as this undoubtedly was for Oakshott, it paved the way for creative decisions on a new route and a new set of playing stations to suit the current conditions. These new performance sites were located in open, virtually off-street spaces, where sizeable audiences could gather without the possibility of their conflicting unduly with the needs of others. While this compromised authenticity, there was a possible advantage in that there was now space for positioning stands where audiences could pre-book a seat from which to see the plays in relative comfort. It was a compromise that took audiences a small step closer to their counterparts who witnessed the fixed-place revival performances and to those members of the medieval audience who watched from the comfort of the buildings along the route.

Oakshott had one advantage over Twycross in that her 1994 production was taken in under the umbrella of the York Early Music Festival and was not attached to or in competition with the fixed-place mysteries. She set the base for a new quadrennial performance pattern: her wagon productions (1994 and 1998) fell midway between the fixed-place productions, coinciding with the annual Early Music event, a factor that afforded the wagons greater visibility and also increased their credibility by virtue of their being 'the' mystery plays for those years rather than an adjunct or an alternative to what was and is still widely perceived as the main production.

Under Oakshott's direction, the multiple-wagon tradition became community-driven. She was of the view that the fixed-place productions in York failed as 'Theatre of the People' and therefore as a true revival of the medieval originals because of the importation of an outsider as director.[69] An outsider herself, Oakshott advocated her own departure to allow the repatriation of the York mysteries to their traditional owners. In 2002 her vision was fulfilled and the York guilds assumed full responsibility, appointing York born-and-bred Mike Tyler as director and inviting him back for a second production in 2006.

Oakshott's 1994 production had nine episodes and she increased the number to eleven in 1998 (see appendix 3 D). Each episode was presented by a different group under its own director, while Oakshott, as she says in the program notes, gave 'momentum' without 'interfering with individual patterns' beyond insisting on a set-up time of no more than 30 seconds before each group of wagon-players began to perform. Given the difficulty of obtaining a wagon that could be converted into a stage, two of these groups, St Luke's Church Players ('Entry into Jerusalem'), and the Poppleton Players ('Way to Calvary'), performed without a wagon, an innovation forced upon them by necessity, but one that set a precedent for future 'wagon' plays.

The achievement in 1994 was considerable, but Oakshott managed to outdo it in 1998, for not only did she enlist the participation of the guilds, the closest fit possible with the original performance groups of the Middle Ages, but she also presented audiences with an abridged version of the Creation to Last Judgment story (see appendix 3 E). Whereas Browne's mysteries had achieved the panorama of biblical history by reducing the number of episodes and cutting heavily, Oakshott's mysteries in 1998 reduced the number of episodes much more drastically but did not cut the texts of the individual episodes. Although the whole production, which started at midday, took around six hours, an audience member who stayed at one station could see all eleven plays in 1998 in a maximum of three to four hours. In terms of physical endurance this was not much more demanding on the audience than the Browne abridgement for the Museum Gardens in 1951.

The Mike Tyler Productions, 2002 and 2006

After two productions Oakshott was anxious to move on and for the next multiple-wagon project in 2002 the guilds, which were now combined as a unit by virtue of their shared involvement with the plays, took control, appointing local amateur director Mike Tyler to oversee the event. Oakshott was delighted that she had achieved her objective of guiding the local community to the point where they were prepared to take over the mysteries themselves; she had turned the concept of these plays as community theatre into a reality in which the community firmly took the helm.

Tyler, an enthusiastic member of the Lords of Misrule and a member of St Luke's Church Players, had contributed to Oakshott's wagons, playing the Porter in the 'Entry into Jerusalem' in 1994, and Satan in the 'Harrowing of Hell' in 1998 (which he also codirected). His links with the amateur theatre groups in the city, particularly those interested in the mysteries, are further evident in his association with the Friends of the York Mystery Plays and Festival, for whom he played Christ in Ray Alexander's 'Harrowing of Hell' in 1996 and Elijah (as a recorded voice-over) in the same director's 'Life of Christ' in 1998. Tyler combines academic scholarship with his experience in amateur theatre and a lifetime's understanding of the city where he was born and grew up. He is, strictly speaking, a historian, but his graduate research has been strongly focused towards the York mystery plays.[70] With a local director who had both a scholar's and an amateur theatre practitioner's interest in the mysteries leading the project, and with other local directors, many of whom were already experienced with wagon playing, and likewise fascinated with the historical tradition in which they were working, the guilds presented their own Creation to Last Judgment play, with ten episodes performed at five playing stations, on two successive Sundays in July 2002, starting at midday and concluding right on schedule at 7 pm (see appendix 3 F).[71] For 2006, the guilds, with Tyler again in charge, went for a slightly grander production in terms of size, offering a twelve-episode set of mysteries played at four stations (see appendix 3 F).[72]

After three productions in which the guilds have been involved some observations can be made regarding continuity of sponsorship of particular episodes. While there were some changes in the responsibility for individual wagon episodes in the medieval performance life of the mysteries, there was overall a remarkable stability in pageant sponsorship. A number of the modern guilds have chosen to emulate this tradition, but the experience so far indicates that stability of pageant responsibility does not necessarily entail stagnation. When he made his final report on the 2002 production, Tyler suggested to the guilds that they consider varying their contribution from time to time. He offered them a scheme whereby the plays recorded in the original fifteenth-century manuscript could be divided fairly evenly among the seven modern guilds while still retaining an appropriate fit between each modern guild and a medieval equivalent.[73] This meant that there could be variation in the episodes played. 'The Creation to the Fifth Day' could be replaced by, say, 'The Creation of Adam and Eve,' to represent the Creation sequence; the 'Death of Christ' could be replaced by the 'Crucifixion' to mark the central moment of the Passion; and the 'Incredulity of Thomas' could be replaced by another post-Resurrection episode, say 'Christ's Appearance to Mary Magdalene.' The guilds might not take up these options in the short term, but they remain as possibilities for the future.

The Builders' 'Creation,' 1998–2006

As stated in the 1998 program notes, the Guild of Building was formed in 1954 'to encourage communication between the many different sections of the building industry.' This guild has no specific medieval underpinning but can claim links with the diverse skills of the building trade represented in the Middle Ages by a number of separate guilds. Consequently the Builders have a large range of plays to choose from, including the 'Building of the Ark' (Shipwrights), the 'Nativity' (Tilethatchers), 'Herod and the Three Kings' (Masons and Goldsmiths), the 'Second Trial before Pilate' (Tilemakers), the 'Crucifixion' (Pinners), the 'Resurrection' (Carpenters), and the episode they chose in 1998 and have maintained ever since, the 'Creation to the Fifth Day' (Plasterers). As Oakshott has explained, the 'Creation' appealed to this group in 1998 'because it offered the scope for construction skills as much as dramatic ones.'[74] The set displaying the wonders of Creation was carefully designed to respect the expertise, the materials, and the technology available to the original presenters. The inventive wagon was, in fact, the star attraction of the Builders' show in 1998. God was only a voice-over, delivering his lines through a speaking tube, another example of medieval technology, but one that was abandoned because it created rather than solved audibility problems and kept the audience at too great a remove from the action on the wagon. The Builders learnt from their experiences, but while they dispensed with the speaking tube, they were not about to scrap their ingenious wagon, although they modified it for its second outing and for its third in 2006 – much to the delight of returning audiences as they waited to discover what new special effects the group had devised.

In 2002 and 2006 the Builders' God had a separate pulpit stage from which he directed the work of his colleagues behind the scenes (see plate 11). In 2006, he delivered some of his lines in plainchant, adding a nice medievalizing

Plate 11. 'The Creation to the Fifth Day' wagon, 2006. God (Brian Wilson) speaks from his pulpit stage beside the Creation wagon.

touch to his monologue, again to the surprise of returning audiences.[75] The initial investment in the wagon and its machinery is a factor that will ensure that the Builders will retain their association with this particular play for some considerable time, a factor that may also have contributed to the stability of pageant ownership in the medieval production run. A costly and effective set is a strong incentive for stasis.

In 2002 the Butchers, the Scriveners, and the Merchant Adventurers, like the Builders, retained their play from 1998, but their commitment to their particular episode can be understood as a desire to accept responsibility for the play belonging to their more direct medieval counterparts.[76] Their interest in continuity rests in their sense of the ancient tradition and pride in their current ownership of what was once 'theirs,' although Tyler convinced the Scriveners to take on a wagon-less 'Christ and the Doctors' and the Butchers to perform the 'Crucifixion' in 2006.

The Merchant Adventurers' 'Last Judgment'

As was the case with the Builders, the retention of the same episode by the Merchant Adventurers, performed over three productions by the York Settlement Players, did not result in sameness. In 1998 Mike Rogers, formerly designer for the Archbishops wagons, and his set-production team constructed a medieval-style wagon that matched well with the indenture of 1433, but in 2002 Rogers worked from director Richard Digby Day's drawings to develop a very different set with three towers representing heaven, offering a setting that could still be appreciated as a reflection, although less of a 're-creation,' of the fifteenth-century document (see plate 12). The care taken by Digby Day and the Settlement Players to respect the medieval tradition was clearly evident in 2002; modern costume was chosen for the souls coming to judgment, a daring departure from the traditional modern use of medieval costume to signal the plays' antiquity. This choice underlined the medieval practice of costuming the actors in contemporary dress and also made a clear statement that the plays were not a form of museum theatre with only an oblique reference to the present. The costuming blended a number of historical periods and was a visual reminder that the mysteries present the whole of human history. The inhabitants of heaven were in recognizably 'medieval' garb; the devils came from the nineteenth century; the apostles represented the twentieth century; and the souls appeared to have chosen something from their own wardrobes at home and emerged seamlessly from the audience, one of them carrying a Mystery Play program. The

Plate 12. 'The Last Judgment' wagon, 2002. The angelic singers (Thomas Meredith, left, and Paul Toy, right) disappear behind the wagon. God (Jack O'Brien and Ruth Ford) and Christ (John Gray) take centre stage, while the good souls (Charles Hunt and Helen Wilson) look up in adoration below (left) and the bad souls (Robin Sanger and Julie Craggs) cringe in terror (right). The devils (from left, Emma Jane Wheelan, Tim Holman and Neil Ward) play up to the 'on-stage audience' of youngsters in medieval dress.

respect for the original text was detailed even down to the processing of the choristers, Paul Toy and Thomas Meredith, from opposite sides of the wagon, a form of homage to the Latin stage direction in the original text that requires the melody of angels 'crossing from place to place.'

Going one better in 2006, Digby Day and Mike Rogers set the 'Judgment' in a post-apocalyptic modern world (see plate 13). Gone were the splendid towers and the shining trumpets of the angels, replaced by instruments made from what looked like 'found' objects. Christ wore torn jeans and a grubby T-shirt, modern dress that took the audience back to the Middle Ages and the conventions of anachronistic transposition of the biblical story onto the present of the audience. The Merchant Adventurers and the Settlement Players, the oldest surviving amateur theatre group in the city, whose members had been prominent in the casts of the revival mysteries since 1951, were also concerned with the modern traditions; this was reflected in the choice of Ruth Ford as God (the Father) in 2002 and 2006, a comment on her controversial casting in this role for the 1996 Theatre Royal production.

The Medieval and the Modern: Continuity and Change

Tyler's two productions made reference to the involvement of the people of York in the modern revivals by means of the choice of playing stations. Returning mystery play devotees might have been reminded of the millennium production or earlier wagon productions by the selection of the playing stations around the Minster, and the last station in the Museum Gardens was both an excellent off-road choice with plenty of space for the performance and for the wagons to reassemble, and, as Tyler has put it, 'marked something of a symbolic return to the home of the York Mystery Plays' chosen for the Browne production in 1951.[77] The guilds were celebrating the modern history of their plays in 2002 as well as re-enacting the medieval past.

Not all the guilds chose to present their 1998 offering a second time. The Merchant Taylors, whose medieval antecedents were assigned the 'Ascension,' observed this tradition in 1998 but in 2002 chose to present the 'Exodus' and in 2006 'Herod and the Magi.' The drama group performing on their behalf in 2002 and 2006 was from All Saints' Roman Catholic School and, knowingly or not, the students were involved in another form of stewardship, taking up these wagon episodes from the former Archbishops students and staff and presenting them as a 'school play.' The Cordwainers, likewise the inheritors of a traditional play that they

Plate 13. 'The Last Judgment' wagon, 2006. God (Jack O'Brien and Ruth Ford) and Christ (Paul Stonehouse) take centre stage, with apostles (from left, Roberto Machado and Julie Craggs), while the good souls (from left, Robin Sanger and Barbara Miller) assume an attitude of prayer.

duly presented in 1998, made changes in 2002 and 2006, and the Freemen, without any guild underpinning in the medieval context, also took on a different play in 2002 but returned to their original choice in 2006. The mixture of continuity and change that has been evident in the guild productions to date provides a balance between the allure of heritage and the fear that interest in the wagons for both the presenters and their audiences might wane if too fixed a format were to be instituted.

Further variation in the multiple-wagon format lies in the recruiting of the additional community groups, particularly evident in the expanded cycle of 2006. The Young York Civic Trust, renewing the link between the Trust and the mysteries forged in 1951, launched the production with their stately Creation play of the 'Fall of the Angels'; St John's College, whose staff and students, led by lecturer David Henshaw as Satan, starred in the diabolic sequences of the 1966 Museum Gardens production, provided an interpretation of the temptation of Adam and Eve in which Satan's angelic alter ego seduced Eve on the wagon while his gross demonic manifestation roamed the audience space. Pocklington School joined for the first time, delighting everyone with their enthusiasm and particularly with their pot-throwing dance (repeated as an encore at a number of stations) that paid homage to the Potters, the original presenters of the 'Pentecost' episode that the school had chosen.

There were, of course, faithful groups returning yet again, like the St Luke's Church Players, whose policy is to present an episode that lends itself to a large cast of extras so as to accommodate all parishioners who wish to participate. They reverted to the 'Entry into Jerusalem,' their chosen episode in 1994. This time, instead of being content with a free-standing 'Jerusalem' as they had to be in their previously wagon-less presentation, they had the luxury of a wagon. Although they did not perform in modern dress, this group made a strong statement about the continuity of the biblical past, the Middle Ages, and the present as the burghers escorted Christ through a replica of Bootham Bar, an essential destination for every modern tourist to York (see plate 14).

Following a second guild production in 2006 and with a successful one-day guild conference on the mysteries at Bedern Hall in 2007, the York community can be said to have taken over the leadership role from the academy, a reversal of what Oakshott saw operating in the Leeds experiment in 1975 and what was envisaged decades earlier in the Bristol symposium that Browne attended in 1951. The guilds have, metaphorically at least, assumed the scholar's mantle as they search for workable solutions to the problems of reactivating the medieval texts. Differences of opinion will

Plate 14. 'The Entry into Jerusalem' wagon, 2006. Peter (Martin Sheppard, centre left) and Philip (Martin Davies) speak with the Porter (Dion Smith) about the donkey that Christ is to ride as he enters Jerusalem. The set on the wagon presents Bootham Bar, York, as the gates of Jerusalem.

always remain about matters such as those that were discussed at the Toronto symposium of 1998: the orientation of the wagon stages and the use of additional playing space, whether it be by providing extensions to the wagon itself or appropriating the available area on the street level. There is now, however, considerable consensus about wagon playing as a familiar format that modern audiences can enjoy as theatre rather than endure as momentarily pleasurable only through its 'quaintness' as observed by Robert Speaight in 1957. Further, with the multiple-wagon productions of Twycross and Oakshott, followed by those under Tyler's direction, there has now been sufficient experimentation for the 're-creation' that Johnston foreshadowed after the Toronto production of 1977, although perhaps not in the form that she might have envisaged. The guild wagons could not claim to be a perfect facsimile of the medieval performance tradition, but their re-enactment of the community effort, with groups committed over the longer term, comes closer to the past than any strictly academic under- taking, whether it be on foreign soil or in York itself. As the guilds continue to orchestrate the wagon plays in the twenty-first century, their steward- ship of the tradition offers material for scholarly consideration. Long-term commitment can have both strengths and weaknesses. On the one hand, it can lead to the reluctance to change and fixity of presentation style that Hans Hess warned against amid the euphoria of reactions to the Browne productions in the early 1950s; on the other hand, continuities safeguard against inefficiencies that can accompany inexperience.

While the infrastructure and the function of the modern guilds are not the same as those of their medieval antecedents, there are possibilities for broad observations of the mysteries as a community project. When he com- mented on the various merits of the 'full-length scholarly' production of the York mysteries in Toronto in 1998 and Oakshott's shorter community- focused wagon production in York in the same year, Peter Meredith con- cluded that academic experimentation has probably gone as far as it could and that scholars should look to 'the community and ... smaller-scale experimentation' for inspiration.[78] In 1998, shortly before the second Oakshott production in York, the international academic community had been drawn to the University of Toronto for the one-day extravaganza in which the complete cycle of the York mysteries was performed at four play- ing stations on the campus of Victoria College. Many of those who attended the plays and the symposium associated with them then proceeded across the Atlantic to attend the International Medieval Congress at the University of Leeds and to see the wagon production in York.[79] Although most of the published commentary on the 1998 'York' productions has focused on the Toronto venture, some of those who were present for both events recognized that the community production was instructive.[80]

Observation of local referencing and of the continuities and changes in the modern wagon plays over time can offer scholars windows into the past. What can be seen in these productions is, and will be in the future, the ways in which a community holds onto its heritage and maintains its affection for the past by renewing it and adapting it to current constraints and possibilities and to the responses of their audiences. In 1994 the St Luke's Church Players and the Poppleton Players proved that they could perform a 'wagon play' without a wagon, and in 2006 the Scriveners did the same. This may be an affront to authenticity, but it is also a challenge to scholars to speculate on diversions from assumed norms that may have operated in the Middle Ages.

Since the Oakshott mysteries of 1994, the multiple-wagon productions have reinvented themselves as a major theatrical event, taking on many of the trappings of recent fixed-place productions, including the glossy program, the list of patrons, and the ancillary publication of a Teachers' Pack based on mystery play material.[81] Just as the Museum Gardens-style mysteries became entrenched in York, so too the local guild wagon plays, increasingly more confident, are gaining status locally and globally as a viable mystery play format for modern audiences.

Epilogue: Ongoing Mysteries

Academics like myself with an interest in the theatre of the Middle Ages customarily ask themselves what they have learned as audience members at modern productions of mystery plays. In the years spent on this study I have learned a great deal, even from the many mysteries that I have seen only through the eyes of others. In some ways what I have learned seems almost too obvious: that a community like York, modern or medieval, must adapt its theatrical traditions to suit changing times and changing enthusiasms; that continuity depends on infrastructure, money, and active participants with a real interest in maintaining continuity; and that none of this comes without struggle and disagreement. Anthony Minghella wrote his 1983 play, *Two Planks and a Passion*, he tells us, as 'an attempt to understand why the medieval Corpus Christi cycle, a collection of apparently innocuous religious plays, aroused so much political intrigue and civic rivalry.'[1] His guildsmen, anachronistically at times, battle out their differences over finances, casting, and new words and new moves to commit to memory; they display their jealousy of other guilds and grumble about their own lot; but in the end their performance for a visit by Richard II and Queen Anne is recommended to the king by the earl of Oxford as 'Humble, sir. Very special' (II.13). His players are not 'rude mechanicals' like those who reduce Duke Theseus and his Hippolyta to laughter in Shakespeare's *Midsummer Night's Dream*; these men of York move the queen to sincere tears. Minghella may not have answered his own question as to 'why' there was 'intrigue' and 'rivalry' associated with the plays, but at least he showed that it was worth it. Interpersonal difficulties and disappointments can, indeed, be read through the lines of the theatrical documentation in the medieval records of York as they can in those of the modern era; such divisions are part of what continues to sustain the mysteries.

There are two types of 'ongoing mysteries' in York. For the theatre historian seeking to re-imagine the medieval mystery plays in performance there will always be unknowns to be pondered and long-standing debates to be continued. Despite exhaustive efforts in private study and extensive collaborative endeavours in the open forums of practical stage experiment and conference discussion, the York mysteries stubbornly withhold some of their secrets. Their origins, in particular, and the reasons for their association with the feast of Corpus Christi, remain a focus of interest. Pamela King's monograph, *The York Mystery Cycle and the Worship of the City* (2006), makes the most recent contribution to this area of enquiry by tying the plays back to the liturgy and to ecclesiastical politicking of the period; press releases in February 2007 on the discovery of a 'lost' Pater Noster roll suggested the still lost York Pater Noster Play was the 'ancestor' of the mysteries.[2] This claim proved to be without basis in the document itself, and the announcement opened old wounds in the academy inflicted by the long-discredited evolutionary approach to medieval biblical drama, but at the same time it proved that the mysteries maintain their ability to provide good copy.

The second sense in which the mysteries will continue to go on in the heritage-conscious city of York is through future performance, on wagons and in fixed-place settings. In 1951 mystery plays were virtually unknown in Britain, but by the twenty-first century they were so well known that they could be performed in the village of 'Ambridge' in 'south Borsetshire.' The on-air community of the long-running BBC Radio 4 soap, *The Archers*, had its own 'Nativity Play' for Christmas 2003; the project began in late September and eventually, after considerable squabbling and several disasters averted, a stunning production was staged in the village hall on 24 December. The play consisted of episodes from the Chester cycle: the 'Nativity,' the 'Shepherds,' the 'Magi,' and the 'Slaughter of the Innocents,' with a cheerful epilogue written by the director, Lynda Snell, to counterbalance the unsettling impact of the Slaughter. The Chester mysteries also received vicarious acclaim through the moving reinterpretation offered in the South African Broomhill Opera's *Yiimimangaliso: The Mysteries*. This production opened in London's East End at the Wilton Music Hall in 2001 with such success that it transferred to Shaftesbury Avenue (Queen's Theatre) in 2002 and by 2003 was being broadcast on BBC Four.[3]

Meanwhile in twenty-first century York, the local community has a firm grip on its homegrown mysteries. The Minster authorities are considering their next extravaganza possibly in 2010 or 2012, and at the same

time the guilds are so confident of the wagon plays that the idea of coinciding with a second Minster production holds no fears for them and they
are pushing ahead for 2010 with Paul Toy and Lesley Wilkinson as directors. As the local mystery play community ages, of course, there must be
some succession plans if the plays are to continue. The city council is taking steps towards making this happen and have announced a four-month
youth festival that focuses on the mystery plays. Colin Jackson, a drama
consultant for the council, is working with the University of York St
John, the University of York, York Theatre Royal's Youth Theatre, Riding Lights Youth Theatre, and York College on this project, which will
come together in June 2008.[4] On with the modern mysteries!

For me, the greatest of the York mysteries left over from the Middle
Ages has always been the logistics of processional performance of forty-
eight wagon episodes at twelve playing stations. In chapter 1 I mentioned
Alan Nelson's claim at the 1968 Modern Languages Association conference that this mode of production was unworkable and that the medieval
mysteries could only have been performed at a single fixed-place site.[5]
Encouraged by Professor A.C. Cawley, who was supervising my doctoral
dissertation at that time, I responded with evidence from medieval records
in the York archives to argue that the wagon plays were 'seen and heard'
at the various playing stations.[6] I championed the idea of a twenty-hour
all-day production of all the wagons at all the stations; and in his 'Postscript' on my work, Martin Stevens, who supported Nelson, commented,
quite rightly, that 'good sense dictates against the likelihood that such a
performance ever took place.'[7] I later tempered my enthusiasm, suggesting that the productions may have been shorter because not all the episodes were necessarily presented in any one year and that a wagon
performance of around thirty episodes suggested in documentation from
1535 could reduce the time to tolerable levels.[8] Thirty-odd years on and
with the benefit of considering the practical experimentation in York,
Leeds, and Toronto discussed in this study, I have now come to agree
with the notion first put forward by Stanley Kahrl, based on a York
record of 1476, when the register of the plays was in the final stages of
completion, that, at least at that time, the preferred option was for each
wagon to perform only twice rather than twelve times over on Corpus
Christi Day.[9]

Observation of the recent wagon productions by the guilds has convinced me that modern audiences can appreciate the Creation to Last
Judgment story through a selection of episodes and that a time frame of
four to five hours is satisfactory for an outdoor event of this kind. I am

not about to claim that modern audiences are in any way 'medieval' audiences who just happen to be living four hundred years on. The system that I am advocating is, however, one that may have suited the elite audiences at the official playing stations in the Middle Ages, audiences that were dividing their attention on the festival day between watching the play and observing their own social rituals as they ate and drank in the rooms overlooking the pageant route. As Alexandra Johnston suggested in her comments following the Toronto production of the York cycle in 1998, it could well be that the 'primary audience' for the medieval mysteries may not have been on the streets themselves but, rather, above the mud and the filth in the 'raised viewing spaces in the houses that lined the route.'[10] Such a scenario can easily accommodate my interpretation of the notion of 'playing twice,' that is, at only two of the appointed playing stations, and help to explain how the processional performance worked in medieval York, not for all time perhaps, but at least for a period in the late fifteenth century.

If the evidence of the seventeenth-century antiquarian accounts of the Chester mysteries in the Rogers *Breviary* can be believed, processional production in medieval Chester was a well-organized and efficient process. The *Breviary* explains that there was an 'excedinge orderlye' system in place there, with word being taken to each wagon in the procession when its predecessor was about to complete its performance at one of the playing stations, thus giving the following group warning to move into place in good time to begin their own play.[11] It is possible, given that the *Breviary* is an antiquarian volume rather than one that was contemporary with the Chester plays, that the orderly system is one that has been invented by Robert or David Rogers in an effort to make sense of the processional mode and bring glory to the ancient Cestrians. Furthermore, the differences between the Chester and York situations are considerable and comparatively speaking, the logistical difficulties in medieval Chester were minimal. Chester had a much smaller number of playing stations (five), the number of episodes was half that of York (twenty-four),[12] and by the sixteenth century the Chester mysteries had been transferred from the one-day festival of Corpus Christi to Whitsun, and the twenty-four episodes were spread over the three days of celebration, thus reducing the timing problems inherent in processional staging.[13] But if Chester went to such lengths to ensure efficient management of its civic theatre, how, then, did York cope with the complexities of the performance of its mysteries?

When she assessed what had been 'learned' from the Toronto production of 1998, Johnston claimed, among other things, that 'contrary to much sceptical speculation,' the academic community could now rest easy with the proof that it is possible, and by implication was possible under the original playing conditions, to present all forty-eight episodes of the York cycle in one day.[14] But the Toronto production actually lent weight to Nelson's argument against this method, for although all the episodes were performed over a very long day they were seen not at twelve playing stations but only at four. The York records, however, consistently refer to twelve stations from the late fourteenth through to the sixteenth century, the only exceptions being when the number was reduced to ten in 1551 to avoid 'long taryeng' because there was a threat of plague, and when it was increased to seventeen for what was to be the last medieval production in 1569.[15] Could the medieval presenters, who supposedly performed at at least three times the number of stations used in Toronto, have outpaced the modern wagon teams so substantially?

The wagon productions directed by Mike Tyler in York in 2002 and 2006 have only served to increase my concern in this regard. Even with careful planning and a strict schedule, the ten and twelve wagons, respectively, took almost seven hours to complete their run through the five, and in 2006, four, stations.

The Chester solution of a three-day production has had a considerable appeal for York enthusiasts, but only in fiction could it happen in medieval York. Netta Syrett takes this option in an early twentieth-century educational novel for children, *The Old Mirade Plays of England*, in which she presents an imaginative recreation of a day at the York mysteries. Two youngsters, Colin and Margery, travel with their parents from the outlying countryside to see the first day of the plays from the 'Creation' through to 'Christ and the Doctors,' a suitable episode with which to end for a young audience because it features Christ as an exemplary twelve-year-old hero. Syrett's medieval Master Gyseburn explains to the children how processional production works:

> The plays will go on all day to-morrow, and the next day too, I expect ... It very seldom happens that any town gets through all its pageants on one day. Certainly not here in York, where we generally act forty of them.[16]

Syrett suggests that there is no advance planning for a division of the plays over the three days. In real life the results of a haphazard division decided on the spot on the grounds of failing light or falling rain would not have been positive ones. Certainly it would have been inconvenient, to say the least, for those players who had waited all day only to find that they had to come back the following morning or even the day after that as well. Whatever the real life situation in medieval York, it is unlikely that the plays extended beyond a single day or that the conduct of the production was as haphazard as Syrett suggests.

Jane Oakshott used a variation of the Chester solution in her production of the York mysteries in Leeds in 1975. Her cut-down version of thirty-six episodes divided into three five-to-six-hour 'sessions' was performed comfortably at three stations over two days.[17] Like the Toronto production of 1998, Leeds 1975 proved the vitality and appeal of wagon performance, but also supported the notion of the impracticality of a one-day forty-eight times twelve version of the York plays. Yet the medieval records stubbornly imply this kind of performance for the original mysteries. The challenge for the theatre historian is to reconcile the compelling evidence of the documentation from medieval York that it could be done with the equally compelling physical evidence of modern production practice that it could not.

The late fifteenth century was a significant time for the York mysteries, with the civic authorities organizing the compilation of their official playbook and the plays displacing the civic procession from the Corpus Christi festival itself to the following day. In 1476 the city council legislated that during Lent they would send out four experienced actors to examine the players and pronounce on their worthiness to play their part in the mysteries.[18] The ordinance also states that players should perform 'but twise' on the day of the play, and that 'he or they' who played more than twice would incur a fine of forty shillings. Johnston assumes, along with numerous other scholars, that the injunction is against taking a role in more than two episodes, that is, it allows doubling between wagons suitably spaced in the procession, with an actor completing his twelve performances on one wagon and then returning to join another wagon at the first station to start in the performance run of another episode.[19] As Nelson remarked in 1970, however, this is a practice fraught with danger,[20] for delays in performing a player's first episode could result in even worse delays in the second episode still waiting for him to return to join his fellow players at the gates of the church of Holy Trinity Priory in Micklegate.

Could there be another way of looking at it? What if the wording of the 1476 ordinance was intended to ensure that each player, and therefore each episode, actually performed for only two audiences? Does this necessarily make nonsense of the twelve stations? Would the occupants of the houses along the route and their guests for the festival day have welcomed the

sight of the wagons progressing slowly past the windows, sometimes halting to play and sometimes not playing, and have been content with seeing
only a selection of the wagon performances? Could this be something that
might actually suit the processional format and the festival atmosphere of
the day?

Imagine what might happen if each group of players performed their
episode only twice, carefully avoiding the temptation to present their
show a third time to people they wanted to impress or to importunate
friends. The procession of the pageants sets off from Toft Green, where
they have been checked off by the common clerk, who has the register
there. Scholars have usually assumed that this register was the playbook
and that the clerk observed the performance and noted discrepancies. But
as the city council was in the habit of calling a large number of its official
books 'registers,' this one could have simply contained a list of plays that
the clerk, acting as an event manager, used for checking off the wagons as
they drew up in proper order and ensuring that they moved off from the
starting point in a timely manner. Perhaps the first wagon does not perform at the first station, but the play simply begins its progress as a procession of decorated floats through the city, rather like the Abraham and
Isaac wagon with its players on board in 1963. The actors and their wagon
stages are on display, the wagons follow each other swiftly as they are
enjoined to do in the official proclamation, and the actors perform at only
two of the authorized stations marked by the official city banners. The
leading wagon does not perform until it arrives at a station where the pageant master, or possibly a council officer, has decided in advance that the
first performance should be given.

Perhaps in an imagined performance of this civic play, we can assume
that the first episode is seen first at the gates of the Common Hall, the
eighth of the twelve stations, where the lords of the city, the mayor and
aldermen, who are also the authorizing body for the mysteries and
therefore their ultimate overseers, are assembled in their feasting chamber. By this time we can assume that there are eight wagons on the route
and that one of them occupies each of the first eight stations. After performing, the first wagon moves off and performs at its second performance site, perhaps at the twelfth and final station on the Pavement for
the Lady Mayoress and the aldermen's wives, who are traditionally
assembled there. There are now twelve wagons on the streets and some
of them have performed twice and must therefore progress through the
system to make room for the players that follow. If one wagon team

ignores the 'but twise' instruction and performs a third time, their additional performance will produce a flow-on effect and result in a lengthy traffic delay for those episodes yet to come. This would certainly warrant the large fine of 40 shillings with which those who performed more than twice were threatened in 1476.

Using this method – with the forty-eight episodes in the registered text in mind and privileging the Lord Mayor and his associates at the eighth station and the Lady Mayoress and the wives of the aldermen at the twelfth – produces some interesting results. Viable mystery cycles, although not all ending with the 'Last Judgment,' are on display at the major stations for the local dignitaries and at the other stations along the route as the following examples show:

Station 1 (Holy Trinity Priory church gates)
1. The Building of the Ark
2. Moses and Pharaoh
3. The Slaughter of the Innocents
4. The Temptation
5. Christ before Herod
6. The Resurrection
7. Pentecost
8. The Last Judgment

Station 5 (End of Coney Street, opposite Castlegate)
1. Adam and Eve in Eden
2. The Building of the Ark
3. Coming of the Three Kings to Herod
4. The Slaughter of the Innocents
5. The Last Supper
6. Christ before Herod
7. Christ's Appearance to Mary Magdalene
8. Pentecost

Station 8 (Lord Mayor and aldermen at the gates of the Common Hall, i.e., the Guildhall)
1. The Fall of the Angels
2. The Fall of Man
3. Joseph's Trouble about Mary
4. Coming of the Three Kings, the Adoration
5. Woman Taken in Adultery/Raising of Lazarus
6. The Agony in the Garden and the Betrayal
7. The Death of Christ

8. The Supper at Emmaus
9. The Last Judgment

Station 10 (Dean and Chapter at the Minster gates)
1. The Creation of Adam and Eve
2. Moses and Pharaoh
3. The Shepherds
4. The Temptation
5. The Conspiracy
6. The Road to Calvary
7. The Resurrection
8. The Coronation of the Virgin

Station 12 (Lady Mayoress and aldermen's wives on the Pavement)
1. The Fall of the Angels
2. The Flood
3. Joseph's Trouble about Mary
4. Christ and the Doctors
5. Woman Taken in Adultery/Raising of Lazarus
6. Christ before Pilate 2: The Judgment
7. The Death of Christ
8. The Death of the Virgin

This is a radical redefinition of the notion of 'playing' the Corpus Christi Play in medieval York in the 1470s although it should not be assumed to have operated throughout its entire medieval history; other methods may have been tried and may also have been successful. This form of 'playing,' however, has its attractions; it is a leisurely progress combining performance and processional display. Each station sees all the forty-eight wagons go by and interspersed with this procession there is a performance of seven, eight, or nine episodes. The experience of the actual 'performance' is one that is comparable to those on offer in the modern multiple-wagon productions in York. Better still, the whole 'processional play' from the crossing of the first wagon at the starting point at the gates of the church at Holy Trinity Priory through to the parading of the 'Last Judgment' wagon past the final station on the Pavement, all going well, takes under five hours, thus allowing for delays along the way without courting logistical disaster.

This is not conventional theatre for post-1951 audiences where a play is to be seen from beginning to end if you are to get your money's worth. It is a play that is a hybrid form, a procession as much as a play and, hence, we need to build into our understanding of it our own reception of street processions as well as our reception of theatre. With a production of the kind I have suggested, the traditionally understood 4:30 am start that Meg Twycross has brought into question is no longer necessary for the mysteries to be performed efficiently in a single day.[21]

Could modern York open its gates and close off the pageant route to allow for an experiment with such a production? Perhaps it could, but perhaps only at the expense of modernizing its wagons as the Merchant Adventurers did in 2006, taking the adventurous decision of using motor vehicles rather than 'authentic' pageant wagons. In 1951, the organizers of the Chester revival passed over a bold plan for a processional performance using 'side-tipping lorries' suggested by Graham Webster, curator of the Grosvenor Museum.[22] Webster was ahead of his time and the Chester organizers opted for an indoor production, but now that the 'Last Judgment' of 2006 has taken the York wagons forward into the motorized age, this may be a possibility that would allow relatively easy access to a large number of 'wagons' and relatively swift movement through the streets.

With twenty-one major productions in York since 1951 there is already ample material for theatre historians to grapple with and to use as a basis for debate. What is abundantly clear and indisputable, though, is that a community that takes up a performance tradition as vehemently as the people of York did in the Middle Ages – and as their modern counterparts did again in 1951 – will hold onto that tradition through good times and bad, through economic downturn and through factional conflicts of various kinds. The strength of such traditions lies in continuity and change, in the determination of the current stewards of the ancient custom of mystery playing to make the performance distinctly their own. John Elliott listed religion, nostalgia, aesthetics, novelty, and local pride as forces behind the longevity of the revivals through to 1980;[23] these forces remained in place in 2006; the purpose in this study has been to show them at work and to examine them more fully and in the light of the ongoing tradition. Some of those who continue to play their part in the history of the York plays look back to the medieval past for their inspiration, others look back to 1951 and the glories of the Museum Gardens, but we can conjecture that many look to the future of the tradition and hope that their particular contribution to it will not be the last.

Appendix 1: Music in the Outdoor Mysteries

As mentioned in chapter 7, the nineteenth-century conductor Thomas Greatorex complained that the only place that was more challenging for musicians than York Minster was the great outdoors. This is an observation that past directors of the Museum Gardens mysteries would undoubtedly confirm, but according to Richard Rastall, the more confined open-air spaces of the medieval street performances were not necessarily inhospitable to the musicians who accompanied the plays. Rastall argues that these medieval singers and instrumentalists would have been both audible and visible on the wagon stages, and that some of the wagons may have had a solid backing, that, along with the 'roofing ... would focus the sound forward.'[1]

Music in the Modern Wagon Plays

In the modern wagon productions in York, portable sound shells of the sort envisaged by Rastall have not been used, nor, except on some rare occasions, have the revival wagon players had the acoustic benefits of the backing of the narrow medieval streetscape to assist them. Nevertheless the performance of early music has been an important feature of the recent wagon productions, both as part of the plays being presented and as entertainment between the acts. Richard Rastall and Paul Toy have been appointed as musical directors in recent years to oversee the musical element and to give expert advice to the performance groups, and a number of church choirs and individual singers have been enlisted to swell the onstage sound. The York Waits have done sterling service accompanying the wagons and their players through the streets and have delighted audiences in the intervals between the performances themselves; and in 2006 the musical strength and joyousness of the wagon event was increased by the generous contribution of a number of visiting troupes of specialist early music practitioners.[2] The ongoing presence of the wagon plays as a feature within the York Early Music Festival and the prestige of that festival and the National Centre for Early Music that stands behind it will surely encourage further experimentation with the musical aspect of the performances.

Music in the Museum Gardens

E. Martin Browne was very conscious of the difficulties for music-makers when he embarked on his first York production in 1951. He was aware that the huge number of performers necessary to create sufficient volume out of doors was impossible in terms of the expense involved and impractical given the lack of space for accommodating such a group on the site he had chosen. In 1951 he had only a choir of sixty-four voices and eight instrumentalists to accompany them and still he struggled to find an appropriate position for them in his improvised outdoor theatre. He did not place them on the stage where they would have had the advantage of the sounding-board of the abbey walls behind them because he did not see them as part of the action as Rastall has argued musicians were on the medieval wagons;[3] nor did he have the equivalent of a modern orchestra pit in which they could have been neatly tucked out of the way. He originally placed the musical performers facing the stage so that the sound was directed away from the audience, and when this proved unsatisfactory, he located them at 'the back of the side stand' with the result that 'the music sounded very unbalanced.'[4] After this failed attempt with live music in 1951, Browne had to conclude that the only solution for his next production in 1954 was to prerecord the music,[5] a practice that he followed for all his subsequent productions in the Gardens.

As director Greg Doran was to do for the millennium production, Browne looked for local musical talent, using Alan Wicks, who had been assistant organist at the Minster but was now at Canterbury Cathedral, as his musical director, and James Brown, a specialist in sacred music then a lecturer in the Music Department at the University of Leeds, as his composer. His experience as the director of adaptations of medieval religious plays had convinced Browne that the music 'should be contemporary with the plays' and he suggested to aspiring directors of this kind of theatre that the raw material could be drawn from the 'carols of the period' and from 'plainsong.'[6] Accordingly, the music for the 1951 mysteries included some liturgical pieces that dated back to the Middle Ages, such as the *Vexilla Regis*, a processional hymn associated with Good Friday, to accompany Christ as he carried the cross to Calvary, and the *Dies Irae*, usually sung at Requiem Mass, for the 'Last Judgment' sequence. When he moved to recorded music, Browne commissioned scholarly musicologist, Denis Stevens, who, as his obituary in *The Times* describes him, became the 'popular face of early music' in the 1960s and 70s,[7] as his musical director. Browne retained the London recordings made for this production, with some minor changes and additions, through to his last Museum Gardens mysteries in 1966.[8]

Following Browne for the 1960 mysteries, David Giles eventually had to agree that 'pre-recorded music' was 'much more secure because it could be cued from the control booth with proper timing, volume, and placement,'[9] and his composer, Frederick Marshall, recorded the music, sung by the choir of the York Musical Society, in Manchester. Originally, however, Giles had hoped to allow some of the music to 'arise naturally' out of the onstage action.[10] He had arranged for four ceremonial trumpeters from the 4th/7th Royal Dragoon Guards to 'take the part of angels and play the trumpets at the required places,' but these military men were not natural actors and although they attended the 'last few rehearsals' and dutifully donned their angelic robes, 'they found it impossible to master their cues, and this idea ... had to be abandoned.'[11]

William Gaskill's Brechtian mysteries of 1963 also used recordings, but the music composed by Marc Wilkinson, in tune with the departures from tradition that marked the 1963 production, moved away from the medieval models and was based on 'a Byzantine, middle-Eastern mode' with some Stravinsky thrown in for good measure; overall the music was 'somewhat medieval in tone, but sounded a more contemporary note by the use of the Stravinsky counterpoint and harmony.'[12] Wilkinson also varied the Museum Gardens tradition by introducing a number of musical themes for 'God, Angel, Devil, Jesus, Prayer, Pomp, and a pastoral theme which the composer called "Wales" music,'[13] inspired perhaps by his previous work with Gaskill on a production of *Cymbeline* in 1962.

Edward Taylor's all-amateur production of 1969 favoured traditional sounds, mostly from 'fourteenth and fifteenth century carols and liturgical music' with the score composed by 'Christopher Butchers, an Oxford graduate who manage[d] the record and music library in York.'[14] According to Sister Bernarda Jaques the music was declared 'exciting' by Wilfrid Mellers, Professor of Music at the University of York, 'but it was too difficult for the musicians at the disposal of Mr. Taylor,' and had to be recorded by the King's Singers in London and the Brian Parker Brass Ensemble in

York.[15] For Taylor's second production in 1973, Edward Jones was both the musical director and one of the three musicians who, according to the program, performed the medieval music using 'authentic instruments.'[16]

Jane Howell's production of 1976 made further changes to the mystery play music. Well-known composer, Edward Gregson, was commissioned to write the score for the production using funds allocated specially for that purpose by the Arts Council of Great Britain. The York Celebrations Choir provided the singers while three local brass bands, the Rowntree Mackintosh Works Band, the York Citadel Salvation Army Band, and the York Railway Institute Band were assigned a number of performances each at which they supplied live music. The voluble success of the bands meant that they were used again in 1980 by Patrick Garland, who invited the audience to join in community singing to further swell the sound in the outdoor setting and to mark the end of the two parts of the play: *Jerusalem* before the interval, and *Psalm 100* after the 'Judgment.' Toby Robertson (with musical director Robert Walker) reverted to recorded music in 1984, while Stephen Pimlott (with composer Chris Monks) in 1988, seeking the immediacy of live performance, took a chance with a choir provided by the Mount School and the local Scout Association and a small group of instrumentalists that included the players of the City of York Pipe Band. In all the different approaches used in the Museum Gardens, the music for the open-air performances struggled against the venue, and it was not until the mysteries moved indoors, as discussed in chapter 7, that the potential of any musical style could be realized fully.

Appendix 2: Biographies

This material is by no means comprehensive and many contributors to the modern mysteries in York remain unsung. This appendix supplements information in the text and notes; only persons and local groups not given sufficient coverage elsewhere are included. Abbreviations are used to refer to the various York productions: (MG) Museum Gardens; (TR) Theatre Royal; (M) Minster; (WP) Wagon Plays; (F) mystery plays presented by the Friends of the York Mystery Plays and Festival

Harry Bridge local mystery play actor: Joseph/Disciple (MG) 1976; Joseph/3rd Knight (MG) 1980; Joseph/Longeus/Jew 1/Duke 2/Master/ Pilgrim 2/ Burgess 2 (MG) 1984.

Jenny Burrage-Smith local mystery play actor: Woman Taken in Adultery/crowd (MG) 1988; Mary Magdalene (TR) 1992; Mary Magdalene and 'Satan's Snake' (TR) 1996.

Percy Corry lighting designer (MG) 1951, 1954, 1957, 1966; author of a number of books on theatre, for example, *Stage Planning and Equipment for Multi-Purpose Halls* (London: Strand Electric and Engineering Company, 1949); *Lighting the Stage* (London: Pitman, 1954); *Planning the Stage* (London: Pitman, 1961); *Amateur Theatrecraft* (London: Museum Press, 1961); and *Community Theatres* (London: Pitman, 1974).

Father Hugh Curristan local mystery play actor: Pilate's Beadle (MG) 1976; Chorus (Doctor)/Duke/Priest in Temple/Master (MG) 1984; Priest/Pharisee (MG) 1988; Balthasar/Butler (TR) 1992; King Caspar/ Joseph of Arimathea (TR) 1996; First Good Soul ('Last Judgment' WP) 1998; Lawyer (M) 2000; Caiaphas ('Death of Christ' WP) 2002; religious advisor to the Museum Gardens production 1988.

Howard Davies local mystery play actor: King/Roman Soldier (MG) 1969; translator of medieval plays for the London Festival in 1971 and 1972 (Towneley and Coventry Mysteries); scriptwriter (MG) 1973.

John de Frates local mystery play actor: Devil/5th Burgher (MG) 1963; Herod/Burgher (MG) 1966; Noah ('Flood' WP) 1969; Beelzebub ('Harrowing of Hell' F 1996).

Alec de Little local mystery play actor: Pilate (MG) 1951 and 1954; Caiaphas (MG) 1957; First King/Nichodemus (MG) 1960; King (MG) 1969.

Kathleen (Kay) de Little property mistress (MG) 1951, 1954; property mistress and wardrobe mistress (MG) 1957, 1960.

Judi Dench local mystery play actor and later professional star of stage and screen: Angel (MG) 1951; Angel of the Resurrection (MG) 1954; Virgin Mary (MG) 1957.

Olave Dench local mystery play actor: crowd (MG) 1954; citizen (MG) 1957; crowd (MG) 1960; Wife to Zacchaeus (MG) 1966 and 1969; wardrobe mistress (MG) 1951, 1954, 1957, 1960; member of the wardrobe group (MG) 1966.

Reginald Dench local mystery play actor: Annas (MG) 1951 and 1954; Abraham (MG) 1957; Joseph (MG) 1960.

Richard Digby Day freelance professional director trained at RADA: director at the York Theatre Royal (1971–6); director for York Settlement Players ('Last Judgment' WP) 1998, 2002, and 2006.

Betty Doig local mystery play actor: Mary the Mother (MG) 1976; Martha (MG) 1980; Anna/Wailing Woman (MG) 1984; Noah's Wife (MG) 1988. Friends of the York Mystery Plays: a custodian of the mystery play wardrobe; wardrobe mistress for the wagon plays (1994).

John Doyle professional director: director (TR) 1996; Coventry Mysteries in the ruins of Coventry Cathedral 1997; *Greenwich Passion Play* in Greenwich Park 2000.

Ruth Ford local mystery play actor professionally trained for the stage: Percula (MG) 1973; Mary Magdalene (MG) 1976; God (TR) 1996; First Bad Soul ('Last Judgment' WP) 1998; Noah's Wife (M) 2000; God ('Last Judgment' WP) 2002 and 2006.

Friends of the York Mystery Plays and Festival established as independent registered charity in 1975 to assist with the York Festivals. In recent years the Friends' activities have included a number of small-scale mystery play productions directed by Ray Alexander (with codirector Paul Toy in 2001). In 1996 they presented a single-wagon play ('Harrowing of Hell') in association with the Theatre Royal mysteries and the Early Music Festival. In 1998, alongside Oakshott's wagon plays, they staged the 'Life of Christ' in All Saints' Church, Pavement, a composite text with extracts from episodes between the 'Baptism of Christ' and the 'Entry into Jerusalem.' In 2000 they braved the competition of the mysteries in the Minster with 'Herod and the Magi' in the Barley Hall. In 2001, their play was 'Divine Intervention,' showing the work of God the Father through the Old Testament sequence of eleven original texts, again in All Saints' Church, Pavement. In 2004, the Friends presented the 'Last Supper' in the Stagecoach Youth Theatre in Monkgate, an abridged sequence of plays leading up to the Betrayal of Christ. Their chairman of many years, Robert Ward, announced that the group had been formally wound up in 2007. The mystery play costumes and props, of which they had been custodians, were disbursed to the National Centre for Early Music archive and to a local costume hire company.

David Giles professional actor and director, studied with Esmé Church and Geraldine Stephenson, at the Northern Children's Theatre School in Bradford: Angel Gabriel (MG) 1951; director (MG) 1960.

Ursula Groom Friends of the York Mystery Plays: treasurer and wardrobe mistress for many years; wardrobe mistress ('Resurrection' WP) 1994; ('Life of Christ' F) 1998; ('Divine Intervention' F) 2001; ('Death of Christ' WP) 2002.

John Hall local mystery play actor: Pilate (MG) 1988; Herod (TR) 1992; Herod/Musician (TR) 1996; God (M) 2000.

Ossie Heppell local mystery play actor: Roman Soldier (MG) 1951; Roman Soldier/First Shepherd (MG) 1954; Isaac (MG) 1957. His family firm, Arthur Heppell & Co., made sets for the Museum Gardens' productions 1954, 1957, 1960, and 1963, and built the wagon play sets from 1954 to 1966. Heppell designed the set and codirected the 'Temptation of Christ' wagon play in 1998.

Hans Hess (OBE 1958) curator of the York City Art Gallery, artistic director York Festival 1954, 1957, 1960, 1963, 1966; left York to take up an academic post at the University of Sussex in 1967 after his public altercation with Councillor Jack Wood over the program for the 1966 festival; highly regarded as a curator. According to Mark Fisher, *Britain's Best Museums and Galleries* (London: Allen Lane, 2001), 413, Hess was 'determined that this modest provincial gallery [in York] should become of national importance' and worked this transformation during his tenure there.

Barbara Hughes local mystery play actor: Portress (MG) 1951 and 1954; Mary Cleophas (MG) 1957.

Peter Jackson local mystery play actor: Peter (MG) 1976; Lucifer/Annas (MG) 1980; Caiaphas/Third Master/Isaiah/ Burgess/Bad Soul (MG) 1984.

John Jacob assistant curator of the York City Art Gallery, played God in the 1954 Museum Gardens mysteries, arranged the exhibition of medieval alabaster carvings that coincided with the 1954 York Festival.

Rev. David Johnson local mystery play actor: God (MG) 1973; God/ Disciple/Burgher (MG) 1976; vicar of Thornton, Allerthorpe, and Melbourne, and drama advisor to the archbishop of York.

John Kay local mystery play actor: Caiaphas (MG) 1951; Caiaphas (MG) 1954; Burgher/Joseph of Arimathea (MG) 1960.

Stewart Lack local mystery play actor and director: member of the York Settlement Players; Peter (MG) 1954, 1957, 1960 and 1969; Nichodemus (MG) 1966; God ('Exodus' WP) 1957; Noah ('Flood' WP) 1966; came to York in 1952 and taught French at Archbishop Holgate's Grammar School, later becoming head of Art at the York College for Girls; member of the Yorkshire Architectural and York Archaeological Society from 1952 until his death in 1993; elected president in 1992 after holding other offices in the society with great distinction.

Sue Morris local mystery play actor: Innkeeper/Mother/Crowd (MG) 1988; Percula (TR) 1992; Caiaphas (TR) 1996.

Tony Morris local mystery play actor: Annas (MG) 1984; Caiaphas (MG) 1988; poet in residence (TR) 1996.

Rory Mulvihill local mystery play actor: Christ (TR) 1996; Satan (M) 2000.

Dave Parkinson local mystery play actor: James ('Assumption of Mary' WP) 1994; Satan (TR) 1996; First King ('Herod and the Magi' F) 2000; God ('Divine Intervention' F) 2001; Pilate ('The Death of Christ' WP) 2002; director for York Settlement Players' production of Anthony Minghella's

Two Planks and a Passion in 1995. He described this play in the program notes as 'a sort of follow up to the Mystery Plays … with people of York again playing their predecessors from six centuries ago.'

Leonard Pickering local mystery play actor: Joseph/Beadle (MG) 1951; Joseph (MG) 1954.

Lilian Pickering local mystery play actor: Poor Woman (MG) 1951; Noah's Wife ('Flood' WP) 1954; Wife to Zacchaeus (MG) 1954: Portress (MG) 1957 and 1960; Woman by the Fire/Bad Soul (MG) 1963; Blind Woman (MG) 1966.

Mike Poulton professional scriptwriter (M) 2000. Other 'medieval' scripts: *St Erkenwald* and a two-part adaptation of Chaucer's *Canterbury Tales*. Poulton currently has an adaptation of Sir Thomas Malory's medieval prose masterpiece, *Le Morte Darthur*, under commission from the RSC.

Ben Pugh event manager (M) 2000 and the 2002 and 2006 wagon productions; compiled feasibility report for the return of the mysteries to the Museum Gardens for the York Mystery Plays Association (2003/4).

Edna Shann local mystery play actor: Martha (MG) 1960; Mary the Mother (MG) 1963 and 1980; Mary Cleophas (MG) 1966; Noah's Wife ('Flood' WP) 1969; Mary Salome (MG) 1973 and 1976; Elizabeth/Veronica/Mary Cleophas/Angel (MG) 1984; Elizabeth (MG) 1988.

Margaret Sheehy professional director, writer, and producer; in the 1990s she established the Community Plays Archive and Database; dismissed from post of artistic director of the 1992 York Festival in 1991.

J.L. Styan academic: staff tutor/senior staff tutor in Literature and Drama, Department of Adult Education, University of Hull 1950–65; later appointed as Professor of English at a number of American universities: University of Michigan, Ann Arbor, 1965–74; University of Pittsburgh 1974–7; Northwestern University 1984–7.

Keith Thomson (CBE 1952) artistic director of York Festival (1951) and secretary to the Academic Development Committee of the York Civic Trust, which was working to establish the University of York; grandson of William Thomson, archbishop of York (1863–91); played the flute in the Max Reinhardt's *Midsummer Night's Dream* for OUDS in 1933; invited to become secretary to the Religious Drama Society by E. Martin Browne after the 1951 York Festival but declined.

Delma Tomlin (MBE 2008) administrator for the 1984 York Festival; director of the National Centre for Early Music and York Early Music Festival.

Paul Toy local mystery play actor professionally trained for the stage, director, and musical director: director (WP) 1988; Jesus/assistant director/musical director ('The Life of Christ' F) 1998; Malchus/assistant director (M) 2000; codirector ('Divine Intervention' F) 2001; singer/musical director (WP) 2002; director/musical director (WP) 2006. MA in Medieval Studies, Centre for Medieval Studies, University of York, thesis: 'Medieval Acting Techniques.'

John White local mystery play actor, turned professional under the name Richard Conway: Adam (MG) 1957, Gabriel (MG) 1960, God the Father/Jesus/Judas (MG) 1969, Pilate/Archangel Michael (MG) 1980; after retirement became involved with the amateur players in York again, directing *Richard III* for the York Shakespeare Project (2002) and performing with the York Settlement Players.

David Wilde local mystery play director; Lord Mayor and patron of the wagon plays (1994); presented a puppet play of the 'Flood' based on the York, Chester, and Towneley cycles as part of 'The Citizens Play' associated with the 1996 Theatre Royal mysteries; see also appendix 3 for his work as a wagon play director.

Keith Wood mystery play enthusiast: member of the lighting team (MG) 1969; 1980 vice-chairman and 1984 chairman of the board of the York Mystery Plays and Festival Ltd; 1980 and 1984, chairman of the Mystery Plays Working Group, a subcommittee of the board; chairman York Mystery Plays Association dedicated to a return to the Museum Gardens (2003/4).

York Civic Trust founded by J.B. Morrell, Oliver Sheldon, and the dean, the Very Rev. Eric Milner-White in 1946; a body committed to raising public interest in local architecture and history. The Trust was concerned with preserving the existing fabric of York's heritage, with new buildings, and with the provision of educational facilities, its most ambitious project being the establishment of the University of York, a project that came to fruition in 1963.

York Early Music Festival a York Early Music Week was held in 1977 and the York Early Music Festival was established in the following year with the York Early Music Foundation set up to support it. In 2000 the

Festival had strong links with the Millennium Mysteries in the Minster; and the National Centre for Early Music, funded by a National Lottery Grant to the York Early Music Foundation, was formally opened in the city. Umbrella organization for recent wagon play productions.

York Festival Committee (1951) appointed to oversee the organization of the Festival of Britain celebrations in York. A.S. Rymer, the sheriff (1950), was the chairman of the committee, and J.B. Morrell, the Lord Mayor (1949–50), was vice-chairman. The committee was made up mostly of elected members of the council, with the addition of co-opted members; these included the dean, the Very Rev. Eric Milner-White, Oliver Sheldon, joint-secretary of the York Civic Trust (with Milner White), and Geoffrey Staines, director of Productions at the Theatre Royal. The Town Clerk, T.C. Benfield was secretary.

Yorkshire Evening Press local newspaper and mystery play supporter (1905–96); renamed *York Evening Press* (1996–2006); then *The Press* (2006–).

Yorkshire Philosophical Society founded in 1822 and acquired three acres of land on which to set up a 'scientific garden.' In the 1840s Sir John Nasmyth designed the Museum Gardens to complement the Yorkshire Museum (opened 1830) and the surviving ruins in the area. The Society retained control of the site until 1961 when it passed to the York City Council.

Appendix 3: Digest of Plays, Directors, and Performers

A. Abridged Cycles: Directors and Actors (Christ and Satan)

Year	Director	Actor playing Christ	Actor playing Satan
1951 ☼	E. Martin Browne	Joseph O'Connor	John van Eyssen
1954 ☼	E. Martin Browne	Joseph O'Connor	John van Eyssen
1957 ☼	E. Martin Browne	Brian Spink	Robert Rietty
1960 ☼	David Giles	Tom Criddle	Harold Lang
1963 ☼	William Gaskill	Alan Dobie	Ian McShane
1966 ☼	E. Martin Browne	John Westbrook	David Henshaw
1969 ☼	* Edward Taylor	* Peter Blanshard * Gerald Lomas * John White	* Christopher Butchers
1973 ☼	* Edward Taylor	John Stuart Anderson	Joseph Copley
1976 ☼	Jane Howell	David Bradley	Raymond Platt
1980 ☼	Patrick Garland	Christopher Timothy	* Peter Jackson
1984 ☼	Toby Robertson	Simon Ward	Philip Tait
1988 ☼	Steven Pimlott	Victor Banerjee	Dave McDade
1992 ◠	Ian Forrest	Robson Green	Jonathan Mellor
1996 ◠	John Doyle	* Rory Mulvihill	* Dave Parkinson
2000 †	Greg Doran	Ray Stevenson	* Rory Mulvihill

Notes: The names of the directors and actors who were local amateurs are marked with an (*).
☼ designates Museum Gardens productions
◠ designates Theatre Royal productions
† designates Minster production

B. Wagon Plays Associated with the Museum Gardens' Productions

Performed at two playing stations
(usually the west front of the Minster and King's Square)

Year	Wagon Play	Director	Associate Director	Performers
1954	Flood	E. Martin Browne	–	Museum Gardens cast
1957	Exodus	E. Martin Browne	Kenneth Parsons	Archbishop Holgate's GS
1960	Christ before the Elders	David Giles	Stewart Lack	Archbishop Holgate's GS/ Queen Anne GS
1963	Abraham and Isaac	William Gaskill	Stewart Lack	Archbishop Holgate's GS
1966	Flood	E. Martin Browne	Stewart Lack	Archbishop Holgate's GS
1969	Exodus	Reiner Sauer	–	Archbishop Holgate's GS/ York College for Girls
1969	Flood (river play)	Edward Taylor	–	see Notes below
1973	Herod and the Three Kings	Stewart Lack	–	Archbishop Holgate's GS/ York College for Girls
1973	Flood (river play)	Edward Taylor	–	see Notes below
1976	The Judgement Day	Keith Daggett	–	Archbishop Holgate's GS
1980	Building of the Ark and the Flood	John Osborn	Keith Daggett	Archbishop Holgate's GS
1980	Exodus	unknown	–	Lords of Misrule
1984	Harrowing of Hell	Keith Daggett	–	Archbishop Holgate's GS
1988	Exodus	unknown	–	MAPA Drama Group, Bradford

Notes: The titles of the wagon plays are as given in the programs. The river plays were performed at Marygate Landing and St George's Field by local amateur players with assistance from schools. In 1973 the Mill Mount Grammar School provided musicians for the river play, while the animals and angels were from the Junior Schools of St Peter's School and York College for Girls. In 1980 the Lords of Misrule, the drama group of the Centre for Medieval Studies at the University of York, presented John Heywood's *Johan Johan* along with the 'Exodus.' Their performances began at 12:30 pm on Monday, Wednesday, and Friday. Archbishop's 'Noah' was presented twice at 5 pm and 5:30 pm daily except on Saturdays. In 1984 the Lords of Misrule's wagon presentation was 'The Confessions of the Seven Deadly Sins.' Their performances began at 1 pm on Monday, Wednesday and Friday. Archbishop's 'Harrowing of Hell' was presented twice at 4:30 pm and 5 pm Monday to Saturday with performances at 2:30 pm and 3:15 pm on Sundays.

C. Wagon Plays Organized from the University of Lancaster

1988: 9 and 10 July (during the York Festival)
Director: Meg Twycross
Four plays performed at four playing stations in Low Petergate (1. Minster Gates; 2. Junction of Low Petergate and Grape Lane; 3. Goodramgate Head; 4. King's Square).

Wagon Play	Director	Drama Group
Death of the Virgin	Lene Christensen, Dennis Omø, Birgitte Lomborg	Unicorns of Copenhagen
Assumption of the Virgin	John McKinnell	Durham Medieval Drama Group
Coronation of the Virgin	Paul Toy	York Lords of Misrule
Doomsday	Meg Twycross, John Brown	Joculatores Lancastrienses

1992: 20 and 21 June (during the York Festival)
Director: Meg Twycross
Five plays performed at five playing stations in Stonegate and Low Petergate
(1. Stonegate, opposite Little Stonegate; 2. Stonegate just beyond the Star Inn arch;
3. corner of Stonegate and Low Petergate; 4. corner of Low Petergate and Grape Lane,
modified on the following day to omit the Star Inn site and replace it with King's Square
as the fourth station).

Wagon Play	Director	Drama Group
Crucifixion	Philip Butterworth	Bretton Hall College
Death and Burial of Christ	David Crouch	York Lords of Misrule
Harrowing of Hell	John McKinnell	Durham Medieval Drama Group
Resurrection	Meg Twycross	Joculatores Lancastrienses
Christ's Appearance to Mary Magdalene	Femke Kramer	University of Groningen

Note: The titles of the wagon plays are as given in the programs.

D. Wagon Plays Presented by the Friends of the York Festival and Centre for Medieval Studies, University of York

1994: 10 July (during the Early Music Festival)
Director: Jane Oakshott
Nine plays (seven on wagons) performed at five playing stations (1. Dean's Park; 2. King's Square; 3. York Market; 4. St Sampson's Square; 5. Parliament Street).

Wagon Play	Director	Drama Group
Building of the Ark	John-Paul Cherrington	Centre for Medieval Studies University of York
Noah and the Flood	David Crouch	York Lords of Misrule
Annunciation and Visitation	Helen Taylor	Early Music Singers
Nativity	Sharon Scott	Foxwood Community Centre Players
Shepherds	Mike Carter	Howdenshire Live Arts
Entry into Jerusalem	Philip Cunningham Mark Reilly	St Luke's Church Players
Way to Calvary	Sally Roberts	Poppleton Players
Resurrection	Ray Alexander	Arts York
Assumption of Mary	Ray Alexander	York Settlement Players

Notes: The titles of the wagon plays are as given in the program. The 'Entry into Jerusalem' and the 'Way to Calvary' were played without wagons.

E. Wagon Plays Presented by the Guilds of York and City Drama Groups

1998: 12 July (during the Early Music Festival)
Director: Jane Oakshott
Eleven plays performed at five playing stations (1. Dean's Park; 2. King's Square;
3. York Market; 4. St Sampson's Square; 5. Parliament Street).

Wagon play	Director	Drama Group
Creation to the Fifth Day	Anthony Ravenhall	York Guild of Building and York College of Further and Higher Education
Creation of Adam and Eve	Roy Francis	Parish of Wheldrake
Fall of Adam and Eve	Sue Foster	Poppleton Players
Flight into Egypt	Sharon Scott	Foxwood Community Centre Players
Temptation of Christ	Ossie Heppell David Wilde	Guild of Freemen
Agony and Betrayal of Christ	Kathleen Foster	Company of Cordwainers
Death of Christ	Mike Carter	Howdenshire Live Arts for the Company of Butchers of the City of York
Harrowing of Hell	Mark Reilly Mike Tyler	St Luke's Church Players
Incredulity of Thomas	Philip Bowman	Guild of Scriveners
Ascension of Jesus Christ	David Crouch	York Lords of Misrule for the Company of Merchant Taylors
Last Judgement	Richard Digby Day	York Settlement Players for the Company of Merchant Adventurers

Note: The titles of the wagon plays are as given in the program.

F. Wagon Plays Presented by the Guilds of York

2002: 7 and 14 July (during the Early Music Festival)
Director: Mike Tyler
Ten plays performed at five playing stations (1. Dean's Park; 2. Minster South Door;
3. St William's College Green; 4. King's Square; 5. Museum Gardens).

Wagon Play	Director	Drama Group
Creation of the World to the Fifth Day	Anthony Ravenhall	York Guild of Building
Building of the Ark and Noah and the Flood	Mark Reilly	St Luke's Church Players
Moses and Pharaoh	Ged Cooper	All Saints' RC School for the Company of Merchant Taylors
Angels and Shepherds	Carolin Esser	York Lords of Misrule
Baptism of Christ	Lee Maloney	St Paul's Church, Heslington
Woman Taken in Adultery and the Raising of Lazarus	Kathleen Foster	Company of Cordwainers
Conspiracy against Jesus	David Wilde	Guild of Freemen
Death of Christ	Ray Alexander	Company of Butchers
Incredulity of Thomas	Philip Bowman	Guild of Scriveners
Last Judgement	Richard Digby Day	York Settlement Players for the Company of Merchant Adventurers

Note: The titles of the wagon plays are as given in the program.

2006: 9 and 16 July (during the Early Music Festival)
Director: Mike Tyler (pageant master)
Twelve plays performed at four playing stations (1. Dean's Park; 2. St William's College Green; 3. St Sampson's Square; 4. Museum Gardens).

Wagon Play	Director	Drama Group
The Fall of the Angels	Paul Toy	Young York Civic Trust
Creation of the World to the Fifth Day	Anthony Ravenhall	Guild of Building
The Creation and Fall of Man	David Richmond	York St John University College
Herod and the Magi	Ged Cooper	All Saints' RC School for the Company of Merchant Taylors
Christ and the Doctors in the Temple	Philip Bowman	Guild of Scriveners
Temptation of Christ	David Wilde	Guild of Freemen
Entry into Jerusalem	Mark Reilly	St Luke's Church Players
Crucifixion	Simon Tompsett	Company of Butchers and St Chad's Parish Church
Harrowing of Hell	Kathleen Foster	Company of Cordwainers and the choir of St Olave's Parish Church
Christ and Mary Magdalene and The Resurrection	Lee Maloney	Heslington Church
The Descent of the Holy Spirit at Pentecost	Alan Heaven Emma Cunningham	Pocklington School
Last Judgement	Richard Digby Day	York Settlement Players for the Company of Merchant Adventurers

Notes: The titles of the wagon plays are as given in the program. 'Christ and the Doctors' was played without a wagon.

Notes

Preface

1 For transcriptions of medieval archival material relating to the plays see Johnston and Rogerson, *York*.
2 Mills, *Recycling the Cycle*, 6–11, deals succinctly with the wide range of terminology used in medieval theatre scholarship; see also Twycross 'Medieval English Theatre: Codes and Genres.'
3 Cawley, *Everyman and Medieval Miracle Plays*, vii, n. 1.
4 Dodsley, *A Select Collection of Old Plays*, x, xii.

Prologue

1 For lists of productions in England before 1951, see Child, 'Revivals of English Dramatic Works, 1919–1925'; and Elliott, *Playing God*, 145–6.
2 Wickham, 'Introduction: Trends in International Drama Research,' 5.
3 For an overview of the 1951 festival in York, see Harrison, 'The York Festival of 1951.'
4 Mills, 'The 1951 and 1952 Revivals of the Chester Plays,' 116.
5 Shepherd and Womack, *English Drama*, 47.
6 Mills, 'The 1951 and 1952 Revivals,' 122.
7 'Rio,' 'The Mystery Plays.'
8 See, for example, Beckwith, *Signifying God*, 18; Elliott, *Playing God*, 142; and Normington, *Modern Mysteries*, 85–6.
9 For discussion of the Chester revivals, see Elliott, *Playing God*, 101–7; Mills, 'The 1951 and 1952 Revivals,' 'Replaying the Medieval Past,' and *Recycling the Cycle*, 206–19; and Normington, *Modern Mysteries*, 64–71. For an account of the Coventry revivals from 1951 to 1993, see King and Davidson, *The Coventry*

Corpus Christi Plays, 59–60. For an account of the 2000 production, see Normington, *Modern Mysteries*, 106–18; and Rogerson, '"Everybody Got Their Brown Dress."'

10 For discussion of this play see Walker, *The Politics of Performance in Early Renaissance Drama*, 138–62.

11 For discussion of this play, see Shapiro, *Oberammergau*.

12 Walker, *Medieval Drama*, 536.

13 For discussion of the 1948 Edinburgh production, see Bruce, *Festival in the North*, 25–9.

14 Williams, 'Lyndsay and Europe,' 342, explains that Lindsay himself had 'strong ties' with Edinburgh.

15 'Festival Centre Choice is Seen as – York's Superb Opportunity,' *Yorkshire Evening Press*, 11 September 1948: 2.

16 'York Festival,' *Manchester Guardian Weekly*, 7 June 1951: 6.

17 Elliott, *Playing God*, 29.

18 Sponsler, *Ritual Imports*, 126.

19 For discussion of interest in Oberammergau in Victorian England, see Elliott, *Playing God*, 25–41; and for its impact in America, see Sponsler, *Ritual Imports*, 126–34.

20 'The Passion Play: Renewal of Oberammergau after Sixteen Years,' *The Times*, 18 May 1950: 7.

21 'Powerful Appeal of the Mystery Plays: Outstanding Feature Free from Sophistication,' *Yorkshire Gazette*, 8 June 1951: 5.

22 Browne, *The Production of Religious Plays*, 37.

23 Palliser, *Tudor York*, 1. Goldberg, *Medieval England*, 44–5, asserts that York's 'frequently cited claim during the later Middle Ages to be second only to London in importance ... appears to have been cultivated' but 'had little substance by the later fourteenth century.'

24 Quoted in H.P. Dixon, 'Mystery Plays Again: Dr. Purvis Explains Some of the Festival Pleasures in Store at York,' *Yorkshire Post and Leeds Mercury*, 8 February 1951: 2.

25 York City Archives, YDV, Festival 1963. Hans Hess, 'The First Ten Years 1951–1961,' 2. Elliott, *Playing God*, 97, referring to Edward Taylor's Museum Gardens production of 1973, complained that the plays were becoming increasingly like Oberammergau in terms of script, style, casting, and references to the starring role as 'The Christus.'

26 Elliott, *Playing God*, 71–100.

27 Normington, *Modern Mysteries*, 50–63.

28 York City Archives, YDV, Festival 1954. York Festival Society, 'Summary of Informal Meeting Held at the Art Gallery on Friday, 12th September, 1952,' 7.

29 York City Archives, Acc. 159, 'York Festival 1976,' 5.

30 Dobson, 'Craft Guilds and City,' 92.

31 'Must Go on as Counter to Gloom,' *Yorkshire Evening Press*, 26 October 1976: 8.

32 York City Archives, YDV, Festival 1988. Jude Kelly, 19 April 1988, 'History of 1988 York Festival,' n.p.

33 For an account of the seven guilds now constituted in York, see Oakshott, 'York Guilds' Mystery Plays 1998,' 274–7.

34 Twycross, 'Civic Consciousness in the York Mystery Plays,' 72.

35 Raymond Furnell, in an interview with Delma Tomlin for the National Centre for Early Music, 26 June 2002, *York Mystery Plays: Illumination – From Darkness into Light.* http://www.yorkmysteryplays.org/achive16.shtml.

36 Pugh, 'York Mystery Plays Feasibility Report.' I am grateful to the author for providing me with a copy of this report.

37 Ibid., 29.

38 Dave Parkinson, 'Why All the Fuss?' *York Evening Press*, 5 July 2003: 11.

39 Eliot, 'The Responsibility of the Man of Letters in the Cultural Restoration of Europe,' 245.

40 For discussion of this painting, see Rogerson, 'Rediscovering Richard Eurich's "York Festival Triptych."'

41 For discussion of these texts, see Rogerson, 'Records of Early English Drama: York, volume 3, the "Revivals."'

42 McNeir, 'The Corpus Christi Passion Plays as Dramatic Art,' 601.

43 Yates, 'The Critical Heritage of the York Cycle,' 214.

44 Wickham, 'Conclusion: Retrospect and Prospect,' 115; see also Wickham, 'A Revolution in Attitudes to the Dramatic Arts in British Universities, 1880–1980.'

45 Browne, 'The Amateur Theatre and the Universities,' 82.

46 For the papers and discussion, see *Proceedings of the Colloquium Held at the University of Leeds 10–13 September 1974 on The Drama of Medieval Europe.*

47 Dobson, 'Craft Guilds and City,' 91.

48 See also the discussion of change in Rogerson, 'Living History.'

49 See entries in the *A/Y Memorandum Book* for 1399 and 1417 in Johnston and Rogerson, 11, 28.

50 Legg, 'Religious Life in York since 1800,' 149.

51 Kirk, 'York and Social Boredom,' 665.

52 E. Martin Browne Archive, University of Lancaster. Telegram dated 14 June 1951; and letter dated 15 June 1951.

53 Oakshott, 'York Guilds' Mystery Plays 1998,' 273. The chaplain to the Guilds of York sat on the Board of Management for the wagon plays in 2002 (Rev. David Porter) and 2006 (Rev. Canon Simon Stanley).

54 Beckwith, *Signifying God*, 12–13, 190.

55 David Mills has argued for the Chester mysteries as heritage events in the late medieval period in 'The "Now" of "Then."'

56 Lowenthal, *Possessed by the Past*, xiii.

57 Samuel, *Theatres of Memory*, 176–7.

58 Cusick, 'Religion and Heritage,' 289.

59 Ibid., 306. Billington, *State of the Nation*, 302, lists 'religious nostalgia … the aesthetic persuasiveness of theatre' and 'a political' appreciation of 'an alternative creed to the culture of greed and the social Darwinism' of the 1980s as positive elements contributing to the success of Tony Harrison's *Mysteries*.

60 Smith, *Uses of Heritage*, 83.

1. From Medieval Religious Festival to the Festival of Britain

1   Keown, 'Festival Time,' 195.

2   The exhibition highlighted W.L. Hildburgh's theory of the influence of medieval theatre on alabaster carving published in *Archaeologia* in 1949. Hildburgh gave a lecture on the topic in York on Monday 14 June to mark the exhibition opening. More recent scholarship downplays this theory. See, for example, Cheetham, *English Medieval Alabasters*, 18.

3   These Latin music dramas were directed by E. Martin Browne, who also directed the Museum Gardens mysteries in 1966.

4   The re-enactment was devised by David Clarke, who was assistant director of the Museum Gardens mysteries in 1980.

5   *Noyes Fludde* is based on the Chester mysteries.

6   Maynard Keynes, quoted in William Rees-Mogg, preface to *The Glory of the Garden*, iii.

7   For discussion of the Corpus Christi festival, see Rubin, *Corpus Christi*. For discussion of the relationship of the York mysteries to the festival, see, for example, Beckwith, *Signifying God*, and King, *York Mystery Cycle*, 7–29.

8   R.N. Swanson, *Church and Society in Late Medieval England*, 259.

9   Homan, 'Ritual Aspects of the York Cycle,' 306–7. Anachronism continues to fascinate medieval theatre scholars; see, for example, Alakas, 'Seniority and Mastery.'

10 Styan, *The English Stage*, 16. For further discussion of the relationship between the York mysteries and the devotional lives of their players and audiences see Hill-Vásquez, *Sacred Players*, 102–21.

11 Rubin, *Corpus Christi*, 200.

12 Johnston and Rogerson, *York*, 3. The date given by Johnston and Rogerson is 1376, but Peter Meredith corrects this to 1 January 1377. See his 'The City of York and Its "Play of Pageants,"' 40–1, n. 3.

13 Johnston and Rogerson, *York*, 8.
14 There were three independent liturgical processions of Corpus Christi in medieval York, each confined to the jurisdiction of those who regulated it: one in St Mary's Abbey, another in the Minster, and the third, the civic procession in the streets. See Cowling, 'The Liturgical Celebration of Corpus Christi in Medieval York'; and Weissengruber, 'The Corpus Christi Procession in Medieval York.'
15 Beadle, *The York Plays*, 29, argues that despite efforts by William Melton in 1426 to displace the mysteries, the procession was transferred to the day after the festival, possibly by 1468, certainly by 1476.
16 King, *York Mystery Cycle*, 2.
17 Martin Stevens believes Beadle made the 'wrong editorial decision.' See his *Four English Mystery Cycles*, 40, n. 28.
18 Dobson, 'Craft Guilds and City,' 103. Goldberg, 'Craft Guilds,' 152, disagrees, concluding that 'it was as much the pageants that created the gilds as the gilds that created the pageants.'
19 Schofield and Vince, *Medieval Towns*, 133. For an exhaustive study of the guilds of medieval York and Chester and their connectedness to the plays see Fitzgerald, *The Drama of Masculinity*.
20 Heather Swanson, 'The Illusion of Economic Structure,' 30–1.
21 Palliser, *Tudor York*, 150.
22 Rosser, 'Crafts, Guilds and the Negotiation of Work in the Medieval Town,' 6.
23 Normington, *Gender and Medieval Drama*, 41, takes the traditional view that only men performed in the mysteries. For the contrary view that women did perform, see Goldberg, 'Craft Guilds,' 146–8.
24 Johnston and Rogerson, *York*, xii–xiii.
25 Mills, 'Who Are Our Customers?'
26 According to Reginald Pecock, the controversial bishop of Chichester, in his *Repressor of Over Much Blaming of the Clergy* (c. 1450), the live actor was superior to the static image. See discussion by Lerud, 'Quick Images,' 222–4.
27 Johnston and Rogerson, *York*, 37, 43.
28 Ibid., 47–8. Butterworth, 'Substitution,' 212–15, discusses the disjunction between the comic and the didactic in this episode.
29 Swanson, 'The Illusion of Economic Structure,' 44, 48.
30 Davidson, 'York Guilds and the Corpus Christi Plays,' and Goldberg, 'Craft Guilds,' 152–4.
31 Goldberg, 'Craft Guilds,' 154.
32 Richardson, 'Craft Guilds and Christianity in Late-Medieval England,' 163.
33 For discussion of the performance route, see, for example, Higgins, 'Streets and Markets'; Twycross, '"Places to Hear the Play"'; and White, 'Places to Hear the Play.'

34 Wiles, *A Short History of Western Performance Space*, 76.

35 Johnston and Rogerson, *York*, 8, 10–12.

36 A revised version of the paper was published subsequently; see Nelson, 'Principles of Processional Staging: York Cycle,' reprinted with slight variations and additions in Nelson's extended work, *The Medieval English Stage*, 15–37.

37 Nelson, *The Medieval English Stage*, 65, suggests that all three of York's religious plays were performed in the Common Hall (i.e., the Guildhall). This notion has been countered effectively by Eileen White, 'The Tenements at the Common Hall Gates: The Mayor's Station for the Corpus Christi Play in York'; see also White, 'The Tenements at the Common Hall Gates 1550–1725.'

38 Stevens, 'The York Cycle: From Procession to Play,' 52–7.

39 Kahrl, *Traditions of Medieval English Drama*, 46.

40 Tydeman, *English Medieval Theatre*, 107.

41 For discussion of the station holders, see, for example, White, 'Places for Hearing the Corpus Christi Play in York'; and Crouch, 'Paying to See the Play.' In the 1417 the city council agreed to a scheme whereby station holders could erect scaffolds in the street to accommodate paying customers. Peter Meredith argues that this may have been a one-off arrangement that was not repeated; see 'The Fifteenth Century Audience,' 103–6.

42 In 1548, the year of the abolition of the Corpus Christi festival, in the reign on Edward VI, the episodes of the 'Death,' 'Assumption,' and 'Coronation' of the Virgin Mary were excluded from the York production. These episodes were reinstated in 1554 (reign of the Catholic queen, Mary) only to be excluded again in 1561 (reign of Elizabeth I); see Johnston and Rogerson, *York*, 291–2, 310, 331–2. See also discussion by Cross, 'Excising the Virgin Mary from the Civic Life of Tudor York.' The same process is evident in Chester and Coventry; see Mills, *Recycling the Cycle*, 125–7; and King and Davidson, *The Coventry Corpus Christi Plays*, 5.

43 Palliser, *Tudor York*, 55.

44 The last recorded performance of the Creed Play was in 1554/5 and of the Pater Noster Play in 1572. The playbooks were called in by the Minster authorities for examination and were not returned. For speculation on the content of these two lost plays, see Johnston, 'The Plays of the Religious Guilds of York,' and 'William Revetour'; and Wyatt, 'The English Pater Noster Play.' The Creed Play was sponsored by the Corpus Christi Guild, and the Pater Noster Play by the Pater Noster Guild (St Anthony's Guild after 1446). For details of the membership and functions of these religious guilds, see Crouch, *Piety, Fraternity and Power*.

45 Harding, 'Reformation and Culture 1540–1700,' 265.

46 Johnston and Rogerson, *York*, 405–8, 414–15, 417–23.

47 Ibid., 390.

48 Ibid., 392–3.

49 Horsler, *Elizabeth and Philip*, 4.

50 Olga Horner has discussed the censorship issue extensively in 'The Law that Never Was,' and '"The Law that Never Was" – A Codicil.'

51 Parker, *Several of My Lives*, 279.

52 Parker, *The Book of the York Pageant 1909:* foreword, n.p.

53 Trussler, *The Cambridge Illustrated History of British Theatre*, 310.

54 There were various productions of *Everyman*, for example, in London at St Thomas's Church, Regent Street, and St John's Church, Waterloo, and in Dawlish at the Dawlish Modern Secondary School.

55 *The British Drama League 1919–1959*, 19.

56 Murdoch, *Cornish Literature*, 44, points out that the *Ordinalia* has sometimes been 'referred to as "the Cornish Corpus Christi plays."'

57 County Borough of Derby, 1951, 'Festival of Britain Derby 1951 Programme of Events,' 34.

58 Browne, 'A Look around Britain,' 40.

59 Ibid., 38.

60 Browne, *Two in One*, 183.

61 Hennessey, *Never Again Britain*, 425.

62 Foulkes, 'Charles Kean and the Great Exhibition,' 133.

63 Coldewey, 'From Roman to Renaissance in Drama and Theatre,' 52.

64 Elliott, 'The York Mystery Plays, 8 June–2 July 1984,' 187.

65 Cyril Garbett, quoted in Browne, *Two in One*, 194.

66 Tania Long, 'Difficulties Beset Britain's Festival,' *New York Times*, 4 March 1951: 27.

67 Hennessey, *Never Again Britain*, 425.

68 Coward, *The Lyrics*, 344.

69 Frayn, 'Festival,' 351.

70 Martin S. Ochs, 'Gaiety Returns to London as the King Opens Festival,' *New York Times*, 4 May 1951: 1.

71 Frayn, 'Festival,' 347.

72 Powers, 'The Expression of Levity,' 49.

73 Forty, 'Festival Politics,' 36.

74 J.B. Priestley, 'The Renewed Dream of Merrie England,' *New York Times Magazine*, 15 July 1951: 10.

75 'Overwhelming Council Support for Festival.' *Yorkshire Evening Press*, 3 January 1950: 3.

76 'Mystery Plays Cast a Spell,' *Yorkshire Evening Post*, 4 June 1951: 4.

77 'The York Mysteries: Notable Revival after Four Centuries,' *The Times*, 5 June 1951: 6.

78 Herbert Read, 'The York Mystery Plays,' *New Statesman and Nation*, 9 June 1951: 650.

79 Eric Keown, 'At the Play: The York Cycle of Mystery Plays,' *Punch*, 27 June 1951: 778.

80 J.C. Trewin, 'Among the Mysteries,' *Illustrated London News*, 23 June 1951: 1036.

81 Browne, *Fifty Years of Religious Drama*, 7.

82 E. Martin Browne Archive, University of Lancaster. Letter dated 6 June 1951.

83 Cyril Garbett, quoted in Browne, *Two in One*, 194.

84 Browne, 'The Medieval Play Revival,' 132–3.

85 Elliott, *Playing God*, 75.

86 Pascoe, *York Historic Pageant Souvenir*, n.p.

87 Purey-Cust, *Last Words on the York Pageant of 1909*, 10.

88 C.C. Bell, 'The York Mystery Plays,' *St Olave's with St Giles's Parish Magazine* (January 1910), iv.

89 According to the program the text was 'arranged by Professor G.K. Chambers' from the York and Coventry mysteries. 'G.K. Chambers' is an error for E.K. Chambers, famous for his influential work, *The Medieval Stage* (1903). A copy of the York program for the 1925 production is among the Purvis Papers at the York City Archives, Acc. 87:649. Edith Craig had directed the same play for the Everyman Theatre, Hampstead, in 1920, with her mother, Ellen Terry, playing the Prologue. Chambers's initials are given correctly in the program for this production, *An Old English Nativity Play, Arranged by E.K. Chambers from the York and Coventry Cycles*, Theatre Museum Collection, London.

90 Browne, *Two in One*, 183.

91 York City Archives, BC 88, *Festival Minute Books*, 16 December 1948: 3–4.

92 York City Archives, YDV, Festival 1951. 'First Thoughts on the York Festival of 1951,' 6. The typescript bears the date '28 January, 1948,' but the year must be an error for 1949.

93 Ibid., YDV. 'An Outline Plan for the York Festival of 1951,' January 1949: 16.

94 Ibid., 10. By early 1950 the Priestley idea had been dropped; York City Archives, BC 88, *Festival Minute Books*, 8 March 1950: 68.

95 Ibid., YDV. 'Second Thoughts on the Festival,' undated 3–4.

96 Ibid., 'An Outline Plan,' 10.

97 Ibid., 10–11.

98 York City Archives, BC 88, *Festival Minute Books*, 29 September 1949: 27.

99 Mandler, 'Nationalising the Country House.'

100 Lowenthal, *Possessed by the Past*, 1.

2. Dramatic Transformations: Performance Spaces and Scripts

1 The much altered *ordo paginarum* of 1415 lists fifty-two episodes, while its accompanying 'second list' has fifty-seven, Johnston and Rogerson. *York*, 16–26. For discussion of later alterations to the registered plays, see Meredith, 'John Clerke's Hand in the York Register.' Only one prompt copy remains, a six-teenth-century version of the Scriveners' 'Incredulity of Thomas'; this confirms the ongoing process of textual revision. For discussion and an edition of the Scriveners' episode, see Cawley, 'The Sykes MS of the York Scriveners' Play.' The Scriveners' manuscript is held in the York City Archives, Acc. 104 G1.

2 Langhans, 'The Theatre,' 12, 14.

3 Twycross, 'Forget the 4.30 a.m. Start.'

4 Beadle and King, *The York Mystery Plays*, xii. Some scholars have disputed the assumption of clerical authorship; see, for example, Clopper, 'Lay and Clerical Impact on Civic Religious Drama and Ceremony,' 112–18, and *Drama, Play, and Game*, 207–14; and Taylor, *Four Levels of Meaning in the York Cycle of Mystery Plays*.

5 See also Johnston, 'The York Corpus Christi Play.'

6 J.S Purvis, quoted in H.P. Dixon, 'Mystery Plays Again: Dr. Purvis Explains Some of the Festival Pleasures in Store at York,' *Yorkshire Post and Leeds Mercury*, 8 February 1951: 2. The name 'J. de Taystek' may be a manuscript misreading of 'John de Gaytryg.' For discussion of 'Gaytryg' and his identification as a monk of St Mary's Abbey and author/translator of the archbishop's *Lay Folks' Catechism*, see Cawley, 'Middle English Metrical Versions of the Decalogue,' 129–32; and R.N. Swanson, 'The Origins of the *Lay Folks' Catechism*.' Johnston suggests a possible connection between the mystery play scripts and the Augustinian Friary at York; see 'The York Cycle and the Libraries of York.'

7 Purvis, *The York Cycle of Mystery Plays*, 6.

8 For discussion of Chester's mythology of authorship, see Mills, *Recycling the Cycle*, 142–3.

9 For discussion of the tensions between the city and the abbey, see King, 'The York Plays in Performance.'

10 For a facsimile of the manuscript, see Beadle and Meredith, *The York Play: A Facsimile of British Library MS Additional 35290*.

11 Shellard and Nicholson, *The Lord Chamberlain Regrets*, 153.

12 Ibid., 171.

13 Browne, *Fifty Years of Religious Drama*, 8.

14 Eliot, *On Poetry and Poets*, 79. For a history of the Canterbury Cathedral Festivals, see Pickering, *Drama in the Cathedral*.

15 Kelly, *How to Make a Pageant*, 5–6.

16 Browne, 'The English Mystery Plays,' 36.
17 Browne, 'A Note on the Production at York,' 13.
18 Jaques, 'Ancient Magic Distilled,' 121.
19 Lambourne, 'Designing for the York Cycle,' 17.
20 Browne, 'Acting out of Doors,' 26.
21 Parker, *Several of My Lives*, 280.
22 Mills, 'The 1951 and 1952 Revivals of the Chester Plays,' 114.
23 Lambourne, 'Designing for the York Cycle,' 16.
24 Davies, 'The York Mystery Cycle,' 315.
25 Browne, *Two in One*, 58.
26 Ibid., 59.
27 Browne, 'Producing the Mystery Plays for Modern Audiences,' 12.
28 Purvis admitted to the addition in his 1957 edition of the plays, *The York Cycle of Mystery Plays: A Complete Version*, 270, n.1, and in the program notes for the 1963 production.
29 Browne, *Two in One*, 191.
30 Sayers, *The Just Vengeance*, 65.
31 Elliott, 'The York Mystery Plays, 8 June–2 July 1984,' 187.
32 Brown, *'Ane Satyre of the Thrie Estaits* at the Edinburgh Festival,' 30.
33 Guthrie, introduction to Robert Kemp, *The Satire of the Three Estates*, viii.
34 Ibid., ix.
35 Miller, *The Edinburgh International Festival 1947–1996*, 14.
36 Craig, *English Religious Drama of the Middle Ages*, 126.
37 Browne, 'The English Mystery Plays,' 36.
38 Browne, *Two in One*, 184.
39 Browne advised amateur directors of religious plays to obtain the 'permission of the Diocesan Bishop or analogous authority.' See *The Production of Religious Plays*, 27.
40 Mills, *Recycling the Cycle*, 215.
41 Davies, 'The York Mystery Cycle,' 319.
42 Browne, 'Producing the Mystery Plays for Modern Audiences,' 7.
43 Browne, *Two in One*, 189–90.
44 Actors in more recent years are more likely to have tried to tune their speech to local 'Yorkshire' in recognition of the origins of the mysteries and in response to the acceptance of regional accents on the professional stage.
45 Holford, 'Language and Regional Identity in the York Corpus Christi Cycle,' 179, 186.
46 Goldberg, *Medieval England*, 44–5. Goldberg notes that this policy also encouraged the use of 'southern forms of building construction.'
47 Beadle and King, *The York Mystery Plays*, xxix.

48 York City Archives, Purvis Papers, Acc. 87:577. Lecture notes on the York Mysteries for an Extension Course in Leeds, 23 February 1951, 52.

49 Browne, 'The English Mystery Plays,' 34.

50 Elliott, 'The York Mystery Plays, 8 June–2 July 1984,' 187.

51 Trewin, 'The Drama of Daybreak,' 26–7.

52 O'Donoghue, introduction, in *Plays One*, 7.

53 York City Archives, BC 89/2, *Festival Minute Books*, 15 November 1961: 217.

54 York City Archives, YDV, Festival 1966. Letter dated 23 July 1964.

55 Ibid. Letter dated 27 July 1964.

56 This nervousness is recalled by Browne's designer, Norah Lambourne, quoted in Horner, '"The Law that Never Was" – A Codicil,' 104.

57 Purvis, *The York Cycle of Mystery Plays: A Complete Version*, 10.

58 Ibid., 11.

59 Nuttgens and Nuttgens, 'A Future for the Past,' 322.

60 York City Archives, BC 89/1, *Festival Minute Books*, 16 November 1955: 147.

61 Jaques, 'Ancient Magic Distilled,' 42.

62 Browne, 'The Medieval Play Revival,' 134.

63 Elliott, *Playing God*, 78.

64 Browne, *Two in One*, 191. The archbishop wrote to the board of the York Festival expressing his concerns about the Passion. His letter is referred to in the Festival Minutes, but has not been kept; York City Archives, BC 88, *Festival Minute Books*, 5 April 1950: 82.

65 Browne, 'The English Mystery Plays,' 36.

66 Ibid.

67 E. Martin Browne Archive, University of Lancaster. Letter dated 12 March 1951.

68 Ibid., 1951 script.

69 York seems to have escaped bad press on this issue. There was a very faint murmur from Glenn Loney in 1966 following the pronouncements of Vatican II and the denunciations of Oberammergau aroused by its last production in 1960; see Loney, 'Summer Production at York, England,' 284.

70 Shapiro, *Oberammergau*, 70.

71 York City Archives, BC 89/2, *Festival Minute Books*, 12 March 1958: 20; and 10 December 1958: 31.

72 Ibid., 14 January 1959: 39–40.

73 Richard Digby Day and Wilfrid Mellers, quoted in 'Where Does York Festival Go from here?' *Yorkshire Evening Press*, 16 October 1973: 6.

74 'New Translation of York Mystery Plays Under Way,' *Yorkshire Evening Press*, 5 July 1972, 11. A copy of the text is held in the E. Martin Browne Archive, University of Lancaster, with a letter from Davies dated 16 October 1973, which indicates that Browne had advised Davies on the script.

75 For extensive discussion of these medieval borrowings, see Happé, *The Towneley Cycle*.

76 Elliott, 'Playing the Godspell,' 127.

77 York City Archives, YDV, Festival 1966. 'The Future of the York Mystery Plays: Some Suggestions by E. Martin Browne, 1966.'

78 E. Martin Browne, quoted in 'Where Does York Festival Go from here?'

3. A Leap of Faith

1 Browne, *Fifty Years of Religious Drama*, 8.

2 For his account of his collaboration with Eliot, see Browne, *The Making of T.S. Eliot's Plays*.

3 *The British Drama League 1919–1959*, 1.

4 Browne, 'The Medieval Play Revival,' 136.

5 Browne's editions of mystery play scripts for amateur players were published in 1932 by Philip Allan in the Religious Plays Series, *The Play of the Maid Mary* and *The Play of Mary the Mother* (from the N-Town cycle), *The Brome Sacrifice of Isaac*, *The Towneley Second Shepherd's Play*, and *The York Nativity Play* (an abridgement of the eight episodes between the 'Annunciation and the Visitation' and the 'Flight into Egypt,' severely cut and reordered).

6 Coffman, 'A Plea for the Study of the Corpus Christi Plays as Drama,' 417.

7 Withington, 'The Corpus Christi Plays as Drama,' 582.

8 Jaques, 'Ancient Magic Distilled,' 397.

9 Browne, *Two in One*, 10.

10 Ibid., 115.

11 Browne, 'How Pilgrims Worked,' 57.

12 Ibid., 58.

13 Ibid., 57, 59.

14 Further honours fell to those associated with the York mysteries in the honours lists for 2008 when Jane Oakshott (wagon play director 1994 and 1998) and Delma Tomlin (director, National Centre for Early Music, York) received MBEs.

15 Rosenfeld, *The York Theatre*, 327.

16 Rowntree, *Poverty and Progress*, 373.

17 Browne, *Two in One*, 187.

18 E. Martin Browne, 'Business Man Who Helped Revive Mystery Plays Dies,' *Yorkshire Evening Press*, 2 June 1976: 7.

19 Browne, *Two in One*, 87.

20 Ibid., 89.

21 For an account of this experience, see Browne, *Two in One*, 87–90; for discussion of the York Civic Theatre project to 1947, see Rosenfeld, *The York Theatre*, 329–37.

22 Browne, 'Drama's Return to Religion,' 93.

23 Browne, *Two in One*, 188.

24 H.J.K., 'Did Local Actors Get Chance?' *Yorkshire Evening Press*, 23 May 1951: 2.

25 'Honesty in Mystery Plays Vital – Producer,' *Yorkshire Evening Press*, 10 November 1965: 8.

26 Browne, 'Drama's Return to Religion,' 19.

27 'Search for Anonymous Actor,' *The Times*, 17 October 1950: 8.

28 For all their nervousness about possible complaints the only formal objection received by the York Festival Society came from the Lord's Day Observance Society protesting against Sunday performances. A letter from this society was presented to the board meeting on 9 May 1951; York City Archives, BC 88, *Festival Minute Books*, 203. The board agreed to take no action on this or on a second letter of protest presented at a later meeting, 20 June 1951; BC 88, 212–13. The board had already considered the possible legal problems relating to Sunday performance on 6 December 1950, but had 'agreed to take the risk'; BC 88, 149. Similar protests were ignored in 1954 and 1957.

29 Browne, *Two in One*, 188. The entire cast of John Masefield's *The Coming of Christ*, the first of the Canterbury Cathedral Festival plays (1928), for example, was anonymous.

30 Herbert Read, 'The York Mystery Plays,' *New Statesman and Nation*, 9 June 1951: 650.

31 Jaques, 'Ancient Magic Distilled,' 173, 238, n. 51.

32 Peter Iveson, 'Mystery Plays Are Absorbing,' *Yorkshire Herald*, 8 June 1951: 15.

33 John Barber, 'In the Shadow of a Ruined Abbey … Nothing Like It for 400 Years,' *Daily Express*, 4 June 1951: 3.

34 Eric Keown, 'At the Play: The York Cycle of Mystery Plays,' *Punch*, 27 June 1951: 778.

35 York City Archives, BC 89/2, *Festival Minute Books*, 15 July 1959, 80.

36 'Star Turns Down Role of Christ,' *Yorkshire Evening Press*, 18 March 1980: 1. Garland also toyed with the idea of God the Father as a voice-over, using the talents of 'one of our distinguished actor-knights,' quoted in 'Famous Voice for Mystery Plays?,' *Yorkshire Evening Press*, 7 November 1979: 1. Ultimately, Timothy was the only actor employed professionally in 1980.

37 Actual cast numbers are uncertain. The program lists 170 names, with an additional eight musicians and a choir of forty-nine. Janet Leeper put the

number at 'nearly 200.' 'The York Cycle of Mystery Plays,' *Spectator* 186,
8 June 1951: 748.

38 McCaw, 'Lifelong Listening,' 20. The 'students' were from the Northern Children's Theatre School, Bradford, where Stephenson taught with Laban one
day a week, spending the rest of her time at the Art of Movement Studio in
Manchester.

39 A.L. Laishley, 'York: The Mystery Plays: Looking Back.' *Yorkshire Ridings
Magazine* 17.2 (1980): 54.

40 Browne, 'Drama Full of Real People,' *Yorkshire Evening Press*. York Festival
Supplement, 1966: 1.

41 H.P. Dixon, 'Mystery Plays Again: Dr. Purvis Explains Some of the Festival
Pleasures in Store at York,' *Yorkshire Post and Leeds Mercury*, 8 February
1951: 2. Strictly speaking there were only three 'existing York guilds' at the
time, the Butchers, the Merchant Adventurers, and the Merchant Taylors, but
in much of the 1951 publicity the Staple (Merchants of the Staple of England)
were classed as a fourth York guild.

42 I am grateful to Christopher Webb, Keeper of the Archives at the Borthwick
Institute for Archives, and Ivison Wheatley of the Merchant Adventurers
Guild for assisting me with this information.

43 E. Martin Browne Archive, University of Lancaster. Letter dated 28 June 1957.

44 Savidge, 'E. Martin Browne, 146.

45 Ibid., 56.

46 Ibid., 60. Browne sets out his views on production and acting in *The Production of Religious Plays*, 28–40. He gave instruction about the delivery of lines
to the Royal School of Church Music in 1954 that further elucidates his
approach in the theatre; see Browne, 'The Words of My Mouth.'

47 Savidge, 'E. Martin Browne,' 61.

48 Browne, 'Medieval Plays in Modern Production,' 312.

49 Browne, 'Producing the Mystery Plays for Modern Audiences,' 10.

50 Savidge, 'E. Martin Browne,' 84.

51 Judi Dench, quoted in Ann McFerran, 'Judi Dench and Her Brother Jeffery,'
The Sunday Times, 26 November 2006 http://www.timesonline.co.uk/tol/
life_and_style/article641440.ece. Both Judi and Jeffrey Dench (who was away
at drama school in 1957) state that their father played Joseph opposite Judi's
Mary, whereas he actually played Abraham in 1957 (Norman Tyrrell played
Joseph) and only took the role of Joseph in 1960. Judi Dench offers further
recollections of the 1951–7 mysteries in a 1993 interview with Keith
Ramsay, in *The Lincoln Plays*, xiv–xxii.

52 Judi Dench, quoted in John Miller, *Judi Dench with a Crack in Her Voice*, 18.

53 Norah Lambourne, quoted in Savidge, 'E. Martin Browne,' 245.

54 Browne, 'The Medieval Play Revival,' 136–7.
55 York City Archives, YDV, Festival 1954. 'Second Report: York Season of Mystery Plays, Music and the Arts 1954,' 26 September 1952, Appendix I, 7.
56 Ibid. Letter dated 19 January 1953.
57 Ibid. Letter dated 23 February 1953.
58 E. Martin Browne Archive, University of Lancaster. Letter dated 12 June 1951. Purvis quotes (with slight variation) the words of God the Father in Play III, The Cardmakers' Play, in Purvis, *The York Cycle of Mystery Plays: A Shorter Version*, 20.
59 'Revival of York Mysteries,' *Church Times*, 8 June 1951: 4.
60 John Buckingham, 'Returning One Day from the Middle Ages,' *British Weekly: A Christian Journal of News and Comment*, 22 July 1954: 5.
61 Trewin, 'The Drama of Daybreak,' 27.
62 Kirk, 'York and Social Boredom,' 665.
63 Lambourne details this friendship and her work with Sayers in 'Recollections of Designing for the Religious Plays of Dorothy L. Sayers.' In 1951 she was designing for Sayers's *The Emperor Constantine*, which had been written for Colchester's contribution to the Festival of Britain, as well as for Browne's York mysteries.
64 Sayers, Preface, in *Dressing the Play*, 6.
65 Reynolds, *The Letters of Dorothy L. Sayers*, 12.
66 Sayers, 'Types of Christian Drama,' 91.
67 Bernard Miles did not make this mistake in his 1961 production of the Towneley mysteries in the Mermaid Theatre. According to Jaques, 'Ancient Magic Distilled,' 340, n. 13, 'while the actor was being nailed to the cross, another actor was substituted for him. When it came time for the Harrowing of Hell, Christ was still hanging on the cross, yet he appeared on the other side of the stage.'
68 Lambourne, 'Recollections,' 6.
69 Leeper, 'The York Cycle of Mystery Plays,' 748.
70 Williams, *The Drama of Medieval England*, 176, 184–5.
71 Wickham, *Shakespeare's Dramatic Heritage*, 4.
72 Ibid., 4–5.
73 Wickham, *Early English Stages 1300 to 1660*, xxvi.
74 Craig, Review of Arnold Williams, *The Drama of Medieval England*, 696.
75 Lowenthal, *Possessed by the Past*, 170.
76 Bretton Hall (near Wakefield) was founded as a Teacher Training College in 1949. It is now amalgamated with the University of Leeds.
77 Quoted in Butterworth, 'Discipline, Dignity and Beauty, 52.
78 For discussion of these vexed issues, see, for example, Happé, *The Towneley Cycle*, 15–17, 103; and Palmer, '"Townelye Plays" or "Wakefield Cycle" Revisited.'

79 For further discussion of the Bretton Hall production, see Butterworth, 'Discipline, Dignity and Beauty.'

80 Letter to Miles from Eric Penn of the Lord Chamberlain's Office, quoted in Butterworth, 'Discipline, Dignity and Beauty,' 78.

81 For further discussion of Harrison's *Mysteries*, see Normington, *Modern Mysteries*, 81–91.

82 For discussion of this production, see Mitchell and Kemp, 'How Do We Live?' (an interview with David Jays); and Normington, 'Little Acts of Faith.'

83 Sahlins and Rudall, *The Mysteries: Creation*, 3.

84 Browne, 'The English Mystery Plays,' 36.

85 Quoted in McCaw, 'Old Theatre for New,' 280.

86 York City Archives, Purvis Papers 87:605. 'Lessons of the Festival,' Hans Hess, Artistic Director's Report, August 1954: 4.

87 Ibid., 5.

88 York City Archives, BC 89/1, *Festival Minute Books*. Hans Hess, 'Outline Plan for the 1957 Festival,' May 1955: between 133 and 134.

89 Ibid., 1 June 1955: 134; and 5 October 1955: 141. Browne made the suggestion to offer the role of God the Father to O'Connor; York City Archives, YDV, Festival 1957, undated letter.

90 Ibid., 11 January 1956: 155. O'Connor had to wait to play a biblical 'baddie' until 1969 when he played Pontius Pilate in Dennis Potter's controversial *Son of Man*.

91 Leeper, 'The York Cycle of Mystery Plays,' 748.

92 Geraldine Stephenson, quoted in McCaw, 'Lifelong Listening,' 20.

93 Robert Speaight, 'The York Festival,' *New Statesman and Nation*, 29 June 1957: 838.

94 York City Archives, BC 89/1, *Festival Minute Books*, 1 June 1955: 134.

95 The board resolved that Henzie 'would not take any part in the Plays but might assist with rehearsals,' ibid., 5 October 1955: 141.

96 Judi Dench, quoted in John Miller, *Judi Dench with a Crack in Her Voice*, 19.

97 Their partnership is acknowledged extensively in Browne, *Two in One*, and by Euphemia van Rensselaer Wyatt 'What Religious Drama Owes to E. Martin Browne.'

98 *Beginning of the Way* was originally written for the Pilgrim Players and was teamed with the 'York Nativity Play' at the Union Theological Seminary in New York in 1956, when Browne was visiting professor of Religious Drama; see Browne, 'Drama's Return to Religion,' 93. Browne describes *The Green Wood* as 'a dramatisation of the Presentation of Christ in the Temple,' *Two in One*, 220. *Who Is There to Ask* was written as a 'Porch Play' for Coventry Cathedral when Browne was drama advisor there, Browne, *Two in One*, 235.

 99 Browne, *Two in One*, 35.

100 Ibid., 181.

101 Jaques, 'Ancient Magic Distilled,' 176–7.

102 Browne was offered £250 plus an additional £200 for travel and accommodation while in York; York City Archives, BC 88, *Festival Minute Books*, 14 January 1953: 254. Henzie Raeburn was paid separately for her services as an actor.

103 York City Archives, YDV, Festival 1954. Letter dated 27 February 1954.

104 Hess, 'Lessons of the Festival,' 4.

105 York City Archives, YDV, Festival 1957. Letter dated 13 March 1957.

106 Browne, *Two in One*, 195.

107 Hans Hess, Editorial, 170.

108 York City Archives, YDV, Festival 1957. Undated letter.

109 York City Archives, BC 89/1, *Festival Minute Books*, 5 October 1955: 142. At the same meeting the board approved the engagement of students from the Royal Academy of Dramatic Art or the Northern Children's Theatre School, Bradford, if insufficient voluntary male actors were available for the minor roles; ibid., 141.

110 York City Archives, BC 89/2, *Festival Minute Books*, 'Report 27 September 1957': between 9 and 10 (1–2).

111 York City Archives, BC 89/3, *Festival Minute Books*, 12 January 1966: 183. In this year, as in 1957, no associate director appears alongside Browne's name in the mystery plays program, although Ted Slavin is named as 'Assistant to the Director': 8.

112 Jaques, 'Ancient Magic Distilled,' 212.

113 Lowenthal, *Possessed by the Past*, 1.

4. Theatre of Cruelty

 1 Artaud, *The Theatre and Its Double*, 84.

 2 Ibid., 85.

 3 Ibid., 93.

 4 Ibid., 99.

 5 For discussion of the influence of the 'Theatre of the Absurd,' see, for example, Bull, 'The Establishment of Mainstream Theatre.' 337–40.

 6 Eddershaw, *Performing Brecht*, 51.

 7 Germanou, 'Brecht and the English Theatre,' 215.

 8 Gaskill, *A Sense of Direction*, 13.

 9 York City Archives, BC 89/1, *Festival Minute Books*, 5 October 1955: 144. Brecht's play is referred to here as the *Beggar's Opera*, the title of the eighteenth-century work by John Gay on which it is based.

10 York City Archives, BC 89/1, *Festival Minute Books*, 16 November 1955: 150.
11 Ibid., 14 March 1956: 162.
12 Ibid., 11 April 1956: 169.
13 Ibid., 13 June 1956: 178.
14 The board also agreed to a Brecht exhibition proposed for the Hunt Room at the City Library and later the Merchant Adventurers' Hall in the fortnight
  · before the festival; ibid., 10 April 1957: 252.
15 Bill Lang, 'What's Wrong with York and the Festival?' *Yorkshire Life Illustrated* 11.6 (June 1957), 23.
16 Robert Speaight, 'The York Festival,' *New Statesman and Nation*, 29 June 1957: 837.
17 Hans Hess, 'Why This Festival of Ours is Unique,' *Yorkshire Evening Press*, York Festival Supplement, 8 June 1960: 4. The festival program also included 'rarely-seen traditional' shadow plays from Setzuan in St Anthony's Hall to complement the Brecht play.
18 Douglas and Greenfield, *Cumberland, Westmorland, Gloucestershire*, 219.
19 Fuegi, *Bertolt Brecht*, 137.
20 Ibid., 83.
21 Speaight, 'The York Festival,' 837.
22 Stevens, 'Illusion and Reality in the Medieval Drama,' 464.
23 Jeremy Noble, 'The York Festival.' *Observer*, 30 June 1957: 10.
24 Browne, 'Medieval Plays in Modern Production,' 306.
25 York City Archives, BC 89/2, *Festival Minute Books*: between 19 and 20. Hans Hess, 'Festival Outline 1960,' March 1958, 3. Anthony Yates had been stage director for the 1957 Museum Gardens mysteries, a task he accepted again in 1960.
26 Ibid.
27 Gaskill, *A Sense of Direction*, 2.
28 Southern's publications to that date include *Stage-Setting for Amateurs and Professionals* (1937); *Proscenium and Sight-Lines* (1939); *Changeable Scenery* (1952); and *The Open Stage* (1953).
29 Southern claimed that the medieval 'in-the-round' system accommodated very large audiences, whereas the current popular experiments with the form were 'limited to small theatres seating comparatively small audiences,' and for that reason his work on medieval stagecraft should be of interest to 'inquiring producers today.' See Southern, *The Medieval Theatre in the Round*, 139–42.
30 York City Archives, BC 89/2, *Festival Minute Books*, 13 November 1957: 9.
31 Ibid., 16 July 1958: 26–7.
32 Ibid., 16 July 1958: 26. Giles was offered £500 plus expenses for a three-month period; ibid., 10 June 1959: 71.

33 Ibid., 14 January 1959: 39–40. Jaques, 'Ancient Magic Distilled,' 251, comments that Guthrie had suggested wagon production. I have been unable to confirm this claim.

34 York City Archives, BC 89/2, *Festival Minute Books*, 11 February 1959: 45.

35 Ibid., 11 February 1959: 46.

36 Kenneth Mellor, 'No Designer Could Ask for More!' *Yorkshire Evening Press*, York Festival Supplement, 1960: 10.

37 Browne, *Two in One*, 198.

38 'York Mystery Plays in Abbey Ruins,' *The Times*, 24 June 1957: 14.

39 'Future of York Festival of the Arts: It's Bright,' *Yorkshire Evening Press*, 6 July 1960: 4.

40 'Will the Plays Survive?' *Yorkshire Evening Press*, 8 July 1960: 6.

41 'What a Member of the Cast Thinks,' *Yorkshire Evening Press*, 8 July 1960, 6.

42 'Amateurs Should Do It All,' *Yorkshire Evening Press*, 8 July 1960, 6.

43 'Professionals are Essential,' *Yorkshire Evening Press*, 8 July 1960: 6.

44 A. Alvarez, 'The York Cycle,' *New Statesman and Nation*, 18 June 1960: 890.

45 York City Archives, YDV, Festival 1960. Letter dated 25 October 1960.

46 Jaques, 'Ancient Magic Distilled,' 247.

47 Ibid., 248–9.

48 Ibid., 252.

49 Ibid., 251.

50 Ibid., 253.

51 Ibid., 265.

52 For Brecht's interest in Brueghel, see Brecht, *Brecht on Theatre*, 157–61.

53 Jaques, 'Ancient Magic Distilled,' 278.

54 Ibid., 266–7.

55 Ibid., 269.

56 Ibid., 269–70.

57 Ibid., 270. In 1961 the first production of a mystery play cycle in the professional theatre, the Bernard Miles rendition of Martial Rose's version of the Towneley (Wakefield) plays, replicated Giles's back-view of the Crucifixion.

58 Ibid., 271.

59 Ibid., 279.

60 Hans Hess, 'Shape and Style of the York Festival,' *Yorkshire Evening Press*, York Festival Supplement, 11 June 1963: 5.

61 J.S. Purvis, 'Origins and Development of the Mystery Plays,' *Yorkshire Evening Press*, York Festival Supplement, 11 June 1963: 4.

62 Jaques, 'Ancient Magic Distilled,' 295.

63 Ibid., 298.

64 Ibid., 294.

65 Purvis, 'Origins and Development of the Mystery Plays,' 4.
66 Vivian C. Brooks, 'Effective New Approach for the York Mystery Plays,' *Yorkshire Evening Press*, 15 June 1963: 3.
67 Knight, 'The Kitchen Sink,' 54.
68 Bamber Gascoigne, 'Noble York,' *Spectator*, 21 June 1963: 810.
69 Jaques, 'Ancient Magic Distilled,' 299.
70 Ibid., 313.
71 Ibid., 314.
72 'Mystery Plays in One Night: Lack of Wonder,' *Daily Telegraph*, 15 June 1963: 13.
73 Twycross and Carpenter, *Masks and Masking in Medieval and Early Tudor England*.
74 Jaques, 'Ancient Magic Distilled,' 311.
75 For further discussion of this text, see Rogerson, 'Records of Early English Drama: York, volume 3, the "Revivals,"' 150–3.
76 Jaques, 'Ancient Magic Distilled,' 309, 318.
77 Ibid., 318.
78 Brooks, 'Effective New Approach for the York Mystery Plays,' 3.
79 William Gaskill, quoted in '"Yorkshire Voices" Sought for Mystery Plays,' *Yorkshire Evening Press*, 1 April 1963: 6.
80 Jaques, 'Ancient Magic Distilled,' 315.
81 Browne, *Two in One*, 190.
82 William Gaskill, quoted in Jaques, 'Ancient Magic Distilled,' 315.
83 Jaques, 'Ancient Magic Distilled,' 315.
84 Ibid., 316.
85 Ibid., 299.
86 Ibid., 299–300, notes that Christ was the only character who wore scarlet and that after the 'Resurrection,' his tunic and cloak were white; before his fall, Satan wore a 'gold and red cloak' that was 'snatched from him' by the angels.
87 Brooks, 'Effective New Approach for the York Mystery Plays,' 3.
88 William Gaskill, quoted in Jaques, 'Ancient Magic Distilled,' 294.
89 Desmond Pratt, 'Faith with a Rough Dialect,' *Yorkshire Post*, 15 June 1963: 19.
90 York City Archives, YDV, Festival 1963. Letter dated 9 November 1963.
91 Elliott, *Playing God*, 92.
92 Dorothy Bacon, 'God and Man at York,' *Life International*, 27 June 1966: 79.
93 Johnston, 'Medieval Drama in England – 1966.' 84.
94 Ibid., 85–6.
95 'Theatre of Cruelty' is now acceptable in the York mysteries and Mel Gibson's extreme cinematic risk-taking in his controversial *The Passion of the Christ* (2004) has proven beyond doubt that audiences can and will tolerate the

contemplation of the agony of Christ in its most visible and violent form, at least at the distance of the movie screen. For discussion of Gibson's *Passion* see, for example, Beal and Linafelt, *Mel Gibson's Bible*. Jill Stevenson aligns this film with medieval affective piety; see 'The Material Bodies of Medieval Religious Performance in England.'

5. Theatre of the People

1 Jaques, 'Ancient Magic Distilled, 293.
2 Meg Twycross stresses in her study of medieval acting that 'there were no professional actors as such' in the fifteenth century; see Twycross, 'The Theatricality of Medieval English Plays,' 44. John Elliott regards paid actors as 'experienced … part-time professionals'; see Elliott, 'Medieval Acting,' 245.
3 Twycross, 'Theatricality in Medieval English Plays,' 44.
4 Mills, *Recycling the Cycle*, 215.
5 Ede, *Drama Festivals and Adjudications*, 11.
6 Wickham, 'Conclusion: Retrospect and Prospect,' 113.
7 Browne, 'The Amateur Theatre,' 75.
8 Jellicoe, *Community Plays*, 147–66.
9 Browne, 'The Amateur Theatre,' 81.
10 Ibid., 82.
11 Homan, 'Ritual Aspects of the York Cycle,' 314. See also Beckwith, *Signifying God*, 49. Beckwith notes that the Forty-eight ran the risk of fines if they did not attend meetings on matters relating to the plays.
12 York City Archives, BC 89/2, *Festival Minute Books*, 16 July 1958: 25.
13 Ibid., 14 January 1959: 42.
14 Ibid., 15 July 1959: 82.
15 York City Archives, BC 89/2, *Festival Minute Books*, between 19 and 20. Hans Hess, 'Festival Outline 1960,' March 1958, 3.
16 York City Archives, YDV, 1960 Festival. Letter dated 18 September 1959.
17 Ibid. Letter dated 23 October 1959.
18 Ibid. Letter dated 23 January 1959.
19 Ibid. Letter dated 27 January 1959.
20 York City Archives, BC 89/3, *Festival Minute Books*, 21 October 1964: 116.
21 Ibid., 21 October 1964: 118.
22 Eliot's play ran for thirteen performances at Sadler's Wells with up to 1,500 in the audience each night; it was a spectacular production with twenty-two scene changes, a mostly amateur cast of over three hundred actors, a choir, and a forty-strong orchestra.
23 Savidge, 'E. Martin Browne and the Revival of Verse Drama in England,' 173.

The pageant was presented by a cast assembled from branches of the Girls' Friendly Society all over the country.

24 Jaques, 'Ancient Magic Distilled,' 348.

25 This revision of Parker's *York Historic Pageant* of 1909 by George Reed extends to the 'Baedekker' bombing of the Guildhall in 1942, whereas the original pageant ended with the surrender of York to the Parliamentarians in 1644. In the 1971 version Richard II and his entourage for the 1483 visit to York exit to see the guilds perform their 'mystery play' offstage, but the audience does not witness the performance of a wagon play as they had done in 1909.

26 Elliott, *Playing God*, 94.

27 Teresa Forbes Adam (Mary) and Cyril Livingstone (Pilate) were professionally trained actors.

28 'Not So Amateur Mystery Plays,' *The Times*, 6 February 1969: 8.

29 Jaques, 'Ancient Magic Distilled,' 377.

30 Ibid., 377–8.

31 Elliott, 'Playing the Godspell, 125.

32 Roddy, 'Revival of the Cornish Mystery Plays,' 16. John Marshall expressed surprise almost thirty years later that, 'given the pride with which York promotes its heritage ... the authorities have not yet given permission to close the appropriate streets to traffic for twenty-four hours in order to present a fully processional performance on wagons along the original route'; see Marshall 'Modern Productions of Medieval English Plays,' 297.

33 Trussler, *The Cambridge Illustrated History of British Theatre*, 341.

34 Elliott, *Playing God*, 95.

35 Ned Chaillet, 'Mystery Plays: York,' *The Times*, 12 June 1980: 11. Chaillet predicted that 'some of the chaff' would be 'blown away from the overly extended scenes near the Crucifixion.'

36 'The York Mysteries,' *Solicitors' Journal* 124, 18 July 1980: 493.

37 'Nude Eve Shocks Cast,' *Yorkshire Post*, 13 June 1980: 2.

38 Jaques, 'Ancient Magic Distilled,' 361.

39 Ibid., 363.

40 York City Archives, YDV, Festival 1969. Letter dated 5 April 1968.

41 Elliott, *Playing God*, 96.

42 'This Christ "Flashes Like a Blade in the Sun,"' *Yorkshire Life* 27.6 (1973): 38.

43 Albert Hunt, 'Hie Thee Hence,' *New Society*, 12 July 1973: 92.

44 Kahrl, 'Medieval Drama in England, 1973,' 117.

45 York City Archives, YDV, Festival 1973. Gavin Henderson, 'Director's Report on the 1973 Mystery Plays and Festival of the Arts,' n.p.

46 Gavin Henderson, quoted in '"Drastic Revision" of Mystery Plays "Is a Must,"' *Yorkshire Gazette and Herald*, 12 October 1973: 10.

47 Wilfrid Mellers and Richard Digby Day, quoted in 'Where Does York Festival Go From Here?' *Yorkshire Evening Press*, 16 October 1973: 6.

48 E. Martin Browne, quoted in 'Where Does York Festival Go From Here?' 6. The twelve-year scheme was based on the assumption of quadrennial festivals.

49 Eliot's *Confidential Clerk* (dir. E. Martin Browne) was performed at the Edinburgh Festival in 1951; Christopher Fry's *A Sleep of Prisoners* was commissioned by the British Drama League and played in London at St Thomas Church, Regent Street; and Dorothy L. Sayers's *The Emperor Constantine* had been written for Colchester's contribution to the Festival of Britain.

50 Elliott, 'Playing the Godspell,' 125–6.

51 Beckwith, *Signifying God*, 182. Tony Harrison's *Passion* was first performed in 1977 on the terraces of the National Theatre, London. The *Nativity* (*Passion* Part 1: Creation to Nativity) and *Passion*, were performed at the Edinburgh Festival of 1980; and these were combined with *Doomsday* and performed at the Cottesloe and the Lyceum Theatres in London as *The Mysteries* in 1985.

52 'Woman to Direct Mystery Plays,' *Yorkshire Evening Press*, 10 July 1975: 11.

53 Ibid.

54 'Animals – and Fun – in Her Plays' Recipe,' *Yorkshire Evening Press*, 26 September 1975: 10.

55 'Carnival Mood is Revived for Plays,' *Yorkshire Evening Press Festival Guide*, 3 June 1976: 3.

56 The Rowntree Mackintosh Works Band was set up in 1903, while the York Railway Institute Band is even more antique, with origins in the Chaucer Street Mission Band founded in 1883; see Griffiths, *A Musical Place of the First Quality*, 179–80.

57 Music historians link the brass bands with the city waits of the Middle Ages. The medieval tradition of waits continued in York until 1835, at which time the remaining waits were 'disbanded under the Municipal Corporation Act,' but one of their number had already cofounded one of the two brass bands that were active in the city in the 1830s; Jones, *Brass Bands in York*, 5. The York waits were reformed in 1977.

58 Elliott, 'Playing the Godspell,' 129.

59 Rachel Semlyen, 'Festive Occasions with a Point,' *Yorkshire Ridings Magazine: York Festival & Mystery Plays Supplement*, 1976: xviii.

60 Michael Chaddock, 'Spectacle Supreme in York Plays,' *Yorkshire Evening Press*, 12 June 1976: 6.

61 'Woman to Direct Mystery Plays,' 11.

62 'Mystery Plays Set Unveiled,' *Yorkshire Evening Press*, 29 January 1976: 1.

63 'Mystery Plays Have Genuine Flavour of Middle Ages,' *Yorkshire Gazette and Herald*, 17 June 1976: 7.

64 David Johnson, 'Understanding the Plays,' *Yorkshire Evening Press*, 24 June 1976: 3.

65 John Barber, 'York Mystery Plays: Jollification Changes the Religious Cycle,' *Daily Telegraph*, 14 June 1976: 8.

66 Ian Stewart, 'Pageant for the People,' *Country Life*, 22 July 1976: 210.

67 Robin Thornber, 'York Festival: Mystery Plays,' *Guardian*, 14 June 1976: 8.

68 'Carnival Mood is Revived for Plays,' *Yorkshire Evening Press Festival Guide*, 3 June 1976: 3.

69 Jane Howell, quoted in '1340 and All That,' *Ideal Home*, June 1976: 163.

70 Elliott, 'Playing the Godspell,' 129.

71 John Peter, 'York,' *The Sunday Times*, 20 June 1976: 35.

72 Richard Oxtoby, 'A Festival for All the People,' *Yorkshire Evening Press Festival Guide*, 3 June 1980: 2.

73 Richard Gregson-Williams, quoted in 'Festival Chief Wants to Hear from Local Groups,' *Yorkshire Evening Press*, 12 October 1978: 4.

74 'Say for Working Men in Festival,' *Yorkshire Evening Press*, 13 October 1978: 11.

75 The Chester Mystery Cycle was filmed by the BBC in six episodes in 1976 (dir. Piers Haggard). Glover had been a 'guest star' in one of the episodes. Christ was played by Tom Courtenay.

76 'Brian Puts Back Calendar 500 Years,' *Yorkshire Evening Press*, 17 May 1980: 1.

77 Peter Purslow, 'Visitor's Praise for Festival Events,' *Yorkshire Evening Press*, 19 June 1980: 3.

78 John Barber, 'Showbiz and Solemnity in Mystery Plays,' *Daily Telegraph*, 9 June 1980: 15.

79 Lucy Hughes-Hallett, 'When the Little Devils Raised Hell,' *Now!* 20 June 1980: 82.

80 E. Martin Browne, quoted in 'Honesty in Mystery Plays Vital – Producer,' *Yorkshire Evening Press*, 10 November 1965: 8.

81 Stewart, 'Pageant for the People,' 210.

82 Hughes-Hallett, 'When the Little Devils Raised Hell,' 82.

83 Happé, 'Mystery Plays and the Modern Audience,' 99.

84 Ibid., 100.

85 Happé, 'The York Cycle: June 6–30, 1980,' 82.

86 Quoted in Elliott, 'Editor's Note,' 83.

87 'Mystery Plays Start with Some Surprises,' *Yorkshire Evening Press*, 7 June 1980: 6.

88 Ian Stewart, 'A Sense of Community,' *Country Life*, 10 July 1980: 122.

89 Robert Cushman, 'Travelling Nowhere,' *Observer*, 1 June 1980: 11.

90 'Mystery Plays Start with Some Surprises,' 6.

91 Ibid.

92 Irving Wardle, 'A Continuously Living Narrative: The Passion, Assembly Hall,' *The Times*, 20 August 1980: 9.

6. Storm Clouds over the Museum Gardens

1 Browne, 'Acting out of Doors,' 26.
2 Eric Keown, 'At the Play: The York Cycle of Mystery Plays,' *Punch*, 27 June 1951: 778.
3 Reynolds, *The Letters of Dorothy L. Sayers*, 11.
4 The royal couple met members of the cast and others involved in the 1957 production in the Tempest Anderson Hall and the duke hinted that there might be another visit in 1960. This visit did not eventuate and the queen has yet to see the York mysteries. HM Queen Elizabeth, the Queen Mother, saw the plays in 1961 when she was in York at festival time to open the restored Guildhall, and HRH Prince Andrew, the Duke of York, saw the Minster production of 2000.
5 York City Archives, BC 88, *Festival Minute Books*, 4 October 1950: 118–19, 8 November 1950: 126.
6 York City Archives, Purvis Papers, Acc 87:592, 'Second Report: York Season of Mystery Plays, Music, and the Arts 1954,' 30 September 1952, Appendix 2, 'Alternative for abandoned performance of Mystery Plays,' n.p.
7 York City Archives, BC 89/1, *Festival Minute Books*, 11 March 1953: 12.
8 Bruce R. Smith, *The Acoustic World of Early Modern England*, 49–51.
9 York City Archives, YDV, Festival 1960. Letters dated 20, 26, and 31 May, and 2 June 1960. Aircraft noise was always a problem. In 1954 the commanding officer of the Royal Air Force, No. 64 (Northern) Group issued instructions to local flying units not to fly within two miles of the centre of York for the duration of the festival; York City Archives, YDV, Festival 1954. Letter dated 22 March 1954.
10 York City Archives, YDV, Festival 1963. Letter dated 27 June 1963. The quip is in relation to the Beeching Report, 'The Reshaping of British Railways' (1963), which, according to Nuttgens and Nuttgens, 'A Future for the Past – York in the Twentieth Century,' 327, had 'resulted in the closing and demolition of many little branch lines that had linked the surrounding area to the city.'
11 E. Martin Browne Archive, University of Lancaster. Letter dated 8 July 1957.
12 Browne, 'Acting out of Doors,' 26.
13 York Minster, *Half a Millennium*, 35.
14 Elliott, 'The York Mystery Plays, 8 June – 2 July 1984,' 187–8.
15 'Five Floored by Lightning in City,' *Yorkshire Evening Press*, 1 July 1988: 1.
16 'Weather Boosts Mystery Plays,' *Yorkshire Evening Press*, 24 June 1976: 1.
17 'Move Mystery Plays from Gardens,' *Yorkshire Gazette*, 12 August 1976: 1.

18 'Lack of Concert Hall "is Biggest Festival Problem,"' *Yorkshire Evening Press*, 11 November 1976: 13.

19 'Festival Costs Rates £70,000: Move Plays If You Want to Prune,' *Yorkshire Evening Press*, 11 November 1976: 1.

20 'Cold Shoulder for Festival Referendum Suggestion,' *Yorkshire Evening Press*, 8 February 1977: 4.

21 ''76 Mystery Plays Pay for Themselves,' *Yorkshire Evening Press*, 12 November 1976: 6.

22 'Arts Council May Back 1984 Festival,' *Yorkshire Evening Press*, 21 February 1981: 1.

23 'City to Get 1984 Festival Despite Row,' *Yorkshire Post*, 4 August 1981: 6.

24 York City Archives, YDV, Festival 1984. Letter dated 4 July 1984.

25 Arts Council of Great Britain, *The Glory of the Garden*, 24–5.

26 York City Archives, YDV, Festival 1984. Richard Gregson-Williams, undated 'Memorandum': 2.

27 Ibid. Letter dated 28 June 1984.

28 York City Archives, YDV, Festival 1988. Board Meeting Paper regarding the contract to be drawn up with Scapegoat Production Company, dated 28 December 1987.

29 For discussion of the variations of the promenade method in these productions, see Happé, 'Mystery Plays and the Modern Audience,' 99–100.

30 Toby Robertson, quoted in Matthew Masters, 'Teaching the Beauty of Words,' *The Times*, 6 June 1984: 9.

31 Ibid.

32 York City Archives, YDV, Festival 1984. Letter dated 12 July 1984.

33 Toby Robertson, 'Director's Note,' 1984 program. This dialogue incorporated the headings from the original manuscript.

34 Elliott, 'The York Mystery Plays, 8 June–2 July 1984,' 187.

35 Masters, 'Teaching the Beauty of Words,' 9.

36 Elliott, 'The York Mystery Plays, 8 June–2 July 1984,' 187.

37 Irving Wardle, 'Mystery Plays: St Mary's Abbey,' *The Times*, 11 June 1984: 8.

38 John Peter, 'Arts,' *The Sunday Times*, 10 June 1984: 40.

39 Michael Coventry, 'Rare Delights of the York Festival,' *The Financial Times*, 11 June 1984: 15.

40 Jude Kelly, quoted in 'Mystery Plays Director Appointed,' *Yorkshire Evening Press*, 12 November 1987: 15.

41 Steven Pimlott and Jude Kelly, quoted in 'York Christ May Be Amateur,' *Yorkshire Evening Press*, 17 November 1987: 3.

42 York City Archives, YDV, Festival 1988. Letter dated 31 August 1987.

43 Ibid. Letter dated 15 September 1987.

44 Stacey Brewer, 'Victor's Jitters at Playing Christ,' *Yorkshire Evening Press*, 6 April 1988: 3.

45 Ibid.

46 Robert Beaumont, 'Sue Is to Be York's Virgin Mary,' *Yorkshire Evening Press*, 5 March 1988: 1.

47 The roles of the angels and a 'Young Lucifer' were also taken by schoolboys.

48 York City Archives, YDV, Festival 1988. Letter dated 1 March 1988.

49 Ibid. Undated letter. An internal reference to a meeting of the Friends of the York Festival on 9 March 1988 suggests that it was written shortly after that date.

50 York City Archives, YDV, Festival 1988. Letter dated 3 March 1988.

51 Jude Kelly, '"Friends" Make Enemies of Director,' *Yorkshire Post*, 9 July 1988: 20.

52 Jim Kelly, 'York Plays Orgy Scene Couple Decide to Improvise,' *Yorkshire Evening Post*, 11 July 1988: 11.

53 Laura Grayson, 'More Like a Pantomime?' *Yorkshire Evening Press*, 20 June 1988: 8.

54 Claire Field, 'Mysteries in All Their Splendour,' *Yorkshire Evening Press*, 22 June 1988: 13.

55 Jeremy Kingston, 'The York Cycle Survivors,' *The Times*, 18 June 1988: 20. John Peter in *The Sunday Times* notes the burning of the world, which was a borrowing from the Coventry cycle; 'How to Cash in on a Royalty,' *The Sunday Times*, 19 June, 1988: C9. Academic reviewer David Mills picked up other borrowings such as the gloating Judas of the 'Betrayal' as well as the 'Last Supper' episode from N-Town; Mills, 'The York Mystery Plays at York,' 70.

56 Heather Neill, 'Christian Unity,' *The Times Educational Supplement*, 24 June 1988: 30.

57 Robin Thornber, 'Mystery and Imagination,' *Guardian*, 13 June 1988: 19.

58 York City Archives, YDV, Festival 1988. 'York Cycle of Mystery Plays 1988: Scapegoat Productions Report and Observations for Future Productions', n.p.

59 Oakshott, 'York Guilds' Mystery Plays 1998,' 270–1, 286–7.

60 Mills, 'The York Mystery Plays at York,' 69.

61 For discussion of this novel, see Rogerson, 'REED: *York*, Volume 3, The "Revivals,"' 144–8.

62 'The Muddled Vision that Killed Festival,' *Yorkshire Evening Press*, 4 February 1993: 8.

63 Henri, *The Wakefield Mysteries*, v. For further discussion of Henri's Wakefield plays, see Normington, *Modern Mysteries*, 128–30.

64 York City Archives, YDV, Festival 1992. Letter dated 25 February 1991.

65 Ibid., Margaret Sheehy, 'Bringing Forth the Pageant,' 1992 York Festival Artistic Proposal, March 1991, 4.

66 'A Farce for the Elite?' *Yorkshire Evening Press*, 11 June 1991: 8.

67 Margaret Sheehy, quoted in 'Director Defends Mystery Plays,' *Yorkshire Evening Press*, 12 June 1991: 9.
68 Christopher Timothy and Jude Kelly, quoted in 'Star Backs Plays,' *Yorkshire Evening Press*, 11 June 1991: 1.
69 Edna Ward, 'Positive View,' *Yorkshire Evening Press*, 2 November 1991: 8.
70 Meg Twycross, 'Moving Story,' *Yorkshire Evening Press*, 2 November 1991: 8.
71 Ian Forrest, quoted in Charles Hutchinson, 'New Challenge in Old Plays,' *Yorkshire Evening Press*, 17 January 1992: 12.
72 York City Archives, YDV, Festival 1992. Liz Lochhead, 'Open Letter to Margaret Sheehy & Ian Forrest, Martin Johns, John Jansson, Mary Turner (and to myself),' dated July 1991, included as Appendix 2c, Mystery Plays Proposal, n.p. Lochhead had also read the 1988 York script and Tony Harrison's *Mysteries*.
73 Ibid. Letter dated 4 November 1991.
74 Mills, 'Recycling the Cycle, 75.

7. Indoor Mysteries

1 Bill Anderson, 'Banerjee's All Clued Up for York Mysteries,' *Stage and Television Today*, 23 June 1988: 13.
2 York City Archives, Acc. 159, Festival 1976. Phillip Gill, memorandum dated 17 February 1975.
3 The Theatre Royal had reopened in May 1992 with a York Amateur Operatic and Dramatic Society production of Cole Porter's *Kiss Me Kate*.
4 Derek Nicholls, quoted in Charles Hutchinson, 'New Ray of Hope in Theatre's Darkness,' *Yorkshire Evening Press*, 7 February 1992: 12.
5 York City Archives, YDV, Festival 1992. Letter dated 27 November 1991.
6 Luke Walton, 'Mystery Exercise: Drama in the Making at Fun-filled Workshop,' *Yorkshire Evening Press*, 28 November 1991: 10.
7 York City Archives, YDV, Festival 1992. Transcript of 'York Mystery Plays go Indoors,' broadcast during *Arts News*, 3 April 1992 (Interviewer Tony Jakes).
8 Ibid. Letter dated 29 June 1992.
9 Ibid. Letter dated 1 July 1992.
10 York Civic Trust, *Annual Report 1991–2*: 1.
11 York Civic Trust, *Annual Report 1990–1*: 19.
12 York Civic Trust, *Annual Report 1991–2*: 3.
13 York Civic Trust, *Annual Report 1990–1*: 19.
14 Ian Forrest, quoted in Charles Hutchinson, 'New Challenge in Old Plays,' *Yorkshire Evening Press*, 17 January 1992: 12. The seating capacity of the theatre was 863. The Museum Gardens seating-stands were typically constructed to hold around 1,500 people.

15 Charles Hutchinson, 'York Man to Take Plays Helm,' *Yorkshire Evening Press*, 15 January 1992: 3.

16 'Changes Afoot for Walkabout Plays,' *Yorkshire Evening Press*, 23 July 1991: 11.

17 'GBH Star May Be New Jesus,' *Yorkshire Post*, 13 January 1992: 8.

18 Charles Hutchinson, 'The Mystery Man: Jesus Actor is Set to Follow the Stars,' *Yorkshire Evening Press*, 7 March 1992: 3.

19 Green, *Robson Green: Just the Beginning*, 68.

20 Ibid. Robin Thornber, 'Mystery Plays,' *Guardian*, 16 June 1992: 46, comments that 'Green gives us a very human God Incarnate who's afraid of being hurt.' Kevin Berry, 'Full House,' *The Times Educational Supplement*, 19 June 1992: 38, was impressed with Green as 'an intense and vulnerable Jesus.' 'Mystery Man Robson Gets a Modern Look,' *Northern Echo*, 15 June 1992: 19, describes him as having 'an authority and presence that naturally – and rightly – sets him apart from the rest.'

21 Green, *Robson Green: Just the Beginning*, 68.

22 Elizabeth Jones, quoted in 'Cuts Continue on Mystery Plays,' *Yorkshire Evening Press*, 17 June 1992: 8.

23 Koren-Deutsch, 'A Mystery Cycle for the Modern World,' 23.

24 Ibid.

25 'Modern Slant on Tradition,' *Yorkshire Evening Press*, 23 June 1992: 11.

26 Tim Richardson, 'Tim Richardson Unravels the Mysteries at York,' *Country Life*, 13 June 1996: 151.

27 'Festival Must Shine Again,' *Yorkshire Evening Press*, 7 August 1995: 8.

28 George Austin, quoted in Ruth Gledhill, 'Woman Chosen to Play God in Mystery Plays,' *The Times*, 28 February 1996: 3.

29 John Doyle, 'A God for the Modern Audience: Another View,' *Independent*, 29 February 1996: 19. The debate over the ordination of women divided Anglicans during the 1980s and 1990s. The first women priests were ordained in 1994. Recently, Dr Rowan Williams, the archbishop of Canterbury expressed the view that the divisions had not been healed by the decision to allow women's ordination; see Ruth Gledhill, 'Archbishop Admits Doubts over Ordination of Women,' *The Times*, 16 November 2006: 8.

30 'Female God Faces Satan of Two Halves,' *The Times*, 19 March 1996: 5.

31 John Doyle, quoted in Charles Hutchinson, 'Mr and Mrs Lucifer: Satan to be Played by Both Man and Woman,' *York Evening Press*, 18 March 1996: 12.

32 Lynda Murdin, 'York Cycle of Mystery Plays,' *Yorkshire Post*, 8 June 1996: 9.

33 Charles Hutchinson, 'Rory Follows in Heavenly Footsteps,' *York Evening Press*, Mystery Plays Supplement, 1 June 1996: ii.

34 Lyn Gardner, 'Woman Works in Mysterious Ways,' *Guardian*, 13 June 1996: 2.

35 Charles Spenser, 'Divine Creation by Amateur Players,' *Daily Telegraph*, 8 June 1996: 6.

36 'The 1996 York Cycle of Mystery Plays, York Theatre Royal,' *Northern Echo*, 12 June 1996: 3.

37 Morris, *Poet in Residence.* For further discussion of Morris's work, see Rogerson, 'REED: *York*, Volume 3, The "Revivals,"' 136–41.

38 Morris, 'The Mystery of a Poet in Residence,' 16.

39 'Festival Must Shine Again,' 8.

40 'York Festival Must Not Be Allowed to Die,' *Yorkshire Evening Press*, 7 August 1995: 8.

41 For further discussion of the millennium production see Normington, *Modern Mysteries*, 61–3; Rogerson, '"Everybody Got their Brown Dress"'; and Gusick, 'A Review of the York Millennium Mystery Plays.'

42 Jane Oakshott, personal archive, Leeds. Letter dated 21 August 1996.

43 *St Erkenwald* was performed in The Other Place, Stratford, directed by David Hunt, who was the assistant director for the York mysteries in 2000.

44 Mike Poulton, quoted in 'The Mystery Men,' *York Evening Press*, 16 June 2000: 3.

45 Ibid.

46 Rosen, *The Transformation of British Life*, 174.

47 Ibid.

48 Rory Carroll, 'Vatican Endorses Superstar Musical,' *Guardian*, 15 December 1999: http://www.guardian.co.uk/world/1999/dec/15/rorycarroll.

49 Chester had mounted a full production in 1997 and was to do so again in 2003. Their next production is scheduled for 2008. For discussion of the Chester productions to 2003, see Normington, *Modern Mysteries*, 64–71.

50 The Coventry mysteries are performed every three years. For discussion of the Coventry production in 2000, see Normington, *Modern Mysteries*, 106–18; and Rogerson, '"Everybody Got their Brown Dress."'

51 The most recent production in Lincoln was in 2004 (dir. Karen Crow) and the next is scheduled for 2008. For an account of his work in Lincoln see Ramsay, 'The Lincoln Mystery Plays, 1978–1985' and *The Lincoln Mystery Plays 1978–2000.'* For discussion of Ramsay's productions to 2000, see Normington, *Modern Mysteries*, 71–3.

52 Blockley presented mysteries again in 2004, this time a set of episodes from the Old Testament (dir. Chris Jury). Other communities, large and small, that lack original mysteries have created their own 'medieval' cycles from time to time. The South Yorkshire village of Worsbrough put together a cycle of borrowed mysteries in 1977 that were played every three years up to 2001. They were not performed as scheduled in 2004 because of insufficient funding and lack of voluntary labour. For discussion of Worsbrough, see Normington, *Modern Mysteries*, 135–43. Every three years since 1994, the historic city of Lichfield in

Staffordshire has presented 'The Lichfield Mysteries,' an amalgam including the Durham Prologue, selections from the York, Chester, Towneley, and N-Town cycles, and parts of the Lichfield liturgical fragments. The next Lichfield Mysteries will be seen in 2009. For discussion of Lichfield, see Normington, *Modern Mysteries*, 73–5.

53 The *Greenwich Passion Play* (dir. John Doyle) involved the Greenwich, Blackheath, and Charlton Christian Alliance. It was performed as an audience-promenade in Greenwich Park on Good Friday, a community play with a cast of about 1,000 people. There were seven separate miracle episodes from the Gospel of St John followed by a Passion narrative with Ben Thomas, the only professional actor, as Christ. For a commentary on this event, see Lyn Gardner, 'Casting of the 1,000,' *Guardian*, 18 April 2000: G2, 14–15. *The Southwark Mysteries* were specially commissioned for the Year 2000 celebrations (text by John Constable). They were performed in Shakespeare's Globe Theatre and Southwark Cathedral (dir. Sarah Davey).

54 Johnston and Rogerson, *York*, 390.

55 'Drama in Minster to Aid Fund,' *Yorkshire Evening Press*, 27 March 1968: 7. The proceeds were donated to the York Minster Appeal Fund.

56 For discussion of these festivals, see Griffiths, *A Musical Place of the First Quality*, 83–102.

57 Ibid., 86–7.

58 Thomas Greatorex, quoted in ibid., 88.

59 Jeremy Kingston, 'Millennium Mystery Plays: York Minster,' *The Times*, 26 June 2000: 25.

60 The oboe was an apt choice to represent the raven. Speaking of the symbolic use of music in Shakespeare's theatre, Tiffany Stern points out the 'hautboys, the ancestors of the oboe, with their reedy, nasal sound, were taken to symbolize the fact that something bad was about to happen'; Stern, *Making Shakespeare*, 108.

61 Shepherd, 'York Millennium Mystery Plays,' n.p. I am grateful to Dr Shepherd for allowing me to quote from this lecture.

62 Several commentators mention *The Lion King* connection, including Paul Taylor who noticed 'shades of *The Lion King* and the Royal Enclosure at Ascot' in this scene; Taylor, 'York Millennium Mystery Plays: York Minster,' *Independent*, 27 June 2000: 14. *The Lion King* with music by Tim Rice, Elton John, Hans Zimmer, and Lebo M., opened in the United States in 1997 and at the time of writing is still playing in London and New York.

63 Shepherd, 'York Millennium Mystery Plays,' n.p.

64 Rastall, *The Heaven Singing*, 225.

65 Shepherd, 'York Millennium Mystery Plays,' n.p.

66 Rastall, *The Heaven Singing*, 225–32.

8. Theatre of the Streets

1 The Ark was shaped like a 'child's rocking horse'; the animals were 'painted …
on the pages of a folding picture book' and the audience was 'reminded of their
presence' once they were in the Ark by the 'zoological noises of the actors and
a few supernumeraries behind the cart'; the raven and dove 'circled round on
the invisible line of a fishing rod'; and the wooden rainbow 'unfolded in
hinged segments'; see Jaques, 'Ancient Magic Distilled, 84, 88.

2 In 1951 Olave Dench made a backcloth for Banker, the police horse ridden by
the herald, who issued the proclamation at the Mansion House, the Minster,
and the Museum Gardens on each performance day. In 1954 her task was to
outfit the second horse, Bonny, for the wagon play with a backcloth and a
hood; see A.L. Laishley, 'When a Bishop Made Devils' Tails! Behind the
Scenes at the Mystery Plays,' *Yorkshire Life Illustrated* 11.6 (1957): 13.

3 Browne, 'Medieval Plays in Modern Production,' 309.

4 Browne, 'Producing the Mystery Plays for Modern Audiences,' 11.

5 Browne, *Two in One*, 197–8.

6 Purvis scripts were used for the wagon plays until 1969 when it became traditional for the directors of the wagon plays to prepare their own texts. In 1969
Edward Taylor used the Purvis version for the 'river play' of the 'Flood,' but
in 1973, he used a version prepared by Howard Davies, who also provided the
script for the Museum Gardens production.

7 York City Archives, BC 89/1, *Festival Minute Books*, 14 April 1954: 99.

8 Jaques, 'Ancient Magic Distilled,' 86–7.

9 Browne, *Two in One*, 197.

10 John Buckingham, 'Returning One Day from the Middle Ages,' *British
Weekly: A Christian Journal of News and Comment*, 22 July 1954: 5.

11 Celia Henderson, 'York and the Festival,' *Time and Tide*, 26 June 1954: 847.

12 *Yorkshire Herald* review, 11 June 1954, quoted in Jaques, 'Ancient Magic Distilled,' 88.

13 York City Archives, YDV, Festival 1957. Letter dated 1 October 1956.

14 Ibid. Letter dated 20 September 1956.

15 J.S. Purvis, 'The "Play on the Wagon": Reason for Choice of Exodus,' *Yorkshire Evening Press*, York Festival Supplement, 1957: v.

16 Jaques, 'Ancient Magic Distilled,' 90.

17 Robert Speaight, 'The York Festival,' *New Statesman and Nation*, 29 June
1957: 837.

18 Jaques, 'Ancient Magic Distilled,' 96.

19 Twycross, 'The Theatricality of Medieval English Plays,' 47. John McKinnell
credits Lack's 1960 production among three 'end-on' staging experiments

before the 1988 productions in the York streets organized by Twycross; see McKinnell, 'The Medieval Pageant Wagons at York,' 101, n. 4.

20 Jaques, 'Ancient Magic Distilled,' 97.

21 For discussion of the off-wagon playing in Toronto (1998), see Rogerson, 'Raging in the Streets of Medieval York,' 118.

22 The symposium papers by Ralph Blasting, Margaret Rogerson, and Martin Walsh debating on- and off-wagon playing appear in *Early Theatre* 3 (2000).

23 Jaques, 'Ancient Magic Distilled,' 102.

24 For an account of the 1992 'Crucifixion,' see Butterworth, 'The York Crucifixion.'

25 Jaques, 'Ancient Magic Distilled,' 104.

26 For an account of Coghill's dramatic initiatives at Oxford, see Carpenter, *OUDS*, 134–63. Coghill was also approached regarding the Chester mysteries in 1951 as director of the mysteries there, an offer he turned down as he was directing the OUDS production for the Festival of Britain, and in the late 1950s as scriptwriter for a proposed new text, which he also declined; see Mills, 'The 1951 and 1952 Revivals of the Chester Plays,' 116, and *Recycling the Cycle*, 217.

27 Carpenter, *OUDS*, 136. See also 'Oxford Unemployed Camp: A Miracle Play,' *The Times*, 19 July 1934: 9, and King, 'Twentieth-Century Medieval-Drama Revivals,' 116–17.

28 York City Archives, BC 89/3, *Festival Minute Books*, 'York Festival 1966,' October 1964: between 112 and 114.

29 Sauer's wagon play was filmed by Clyde B. Smith, head of Film Production at the University of California (Berkeley) for educational and promotional purposes. A copy of this film is held in the Illumination Archive at the National Centre for Early Music, York.

30 York City Archives, YDV, Festival 1969. Mystery Plays Sub-Committee Minutes, 29 June 1968, n.p.

31 Wickham, *Early English Stages 1300 to 1660*, 173.

32 Jaques, 'Ancient Magic Distilled,' 109.

33 Ibid., 111.

34 Johnston and Rogerson (Dorrell), 'The Doomsday Pageant of the York Mercers, 1433.'

35 Lack provided an illustration for the cover of one of Browne's published lectures depicting Peter's Denial of Christ as he himself had played it under Browne's direction against the St Mary's Abbey ruins; see *Fifty Years of Religious Drama*.

36 A copy of Young's, 'The York Pageant Wagon,' annotated by Lack, is held in the E. Martin Browne Archive, University of Lancaster.

37 Marshall, 'Modern Productions of Medieval English plays,' 304.

38 Lack's interest in the 1433 document is also reflected in the two very similar cover illustrations of the 'Last Judgment' provided for R.M. Butler's *Medieval York* and Eileen White's, *The York Mystery Play*.

39 For discussion of this experiment, see Twycross, '"Transvestism" in the Mystery Plays.'

40 Hunter, *Archbishop Holgate's School York*, 78.

41 For further discussion of a number of the multiple-wagon productions considered here, see Normington, *Modern Mysteries*, 37–52.

42 Oakshott and Rastall, 'Town with Gown,' 224.

43 For an account of the Globe experiment with original pronunciation performances of *Romeo and Juliet*, see Crystal, *Pronouncing Shakespeare*.

44 Johnston and Rogerson, *York*, 109.

45 John Brown, 'The Devils in the York *Doomsday*,' 26.

46 Ibid., 38–9.

47 McKinnell, 'Producing the York Mary Plays,' 119.

48 Ibid., 120.

49 Twycross, 'Playing "The Resurrection,"' 273.

50 Ibid., 276.

51 Twycross had published various articles on these topics, for example, '"Places to hear the play,"' 'The Flemish *Ommegang* and Its Pageant Cars,' and (with Sarah Carpenter) and (with Sarah Carpenter) 'Masks in Medieval English Theatre.'

52 Happé, 'Acting the York Mystery Plays,' 112.

53 Johnston, 'Four *York* Pageants Performed in the Streets of York,' 101–2.

54 Ibid., 102.

55 Ibid., 104.

56 As Eileen White has pointed out, this square is on the original site of Christ Church at the intersection of Petergate, Goodramgate and Girdlergate, where the medieval audience had 'a chance to spread down the side streets' while the wagons performed in front of the church; this luxury is no longer available to modern audiences and the site remains problematic. See White, 'Places to Hear the Play,' 66.

57 Twycross, 'The Left-Hand-Side Theory: A Retraction,' 82.

58 Local wagon players have largely held to the 'side-on' orientation, with Mike Tyler commenting in 2002 that it had the 'advantage of practicality for the locations and audience deployment adopted' for the production; 'York Guild Mystery Plays,' 160.

59 Butterworth, 'The York Crucifixion,' 67.

60 Mills, '"Look at Me when I'm Speaking to You."'

61 Beadle and King, *The York Mystery Plays*, 212 (ll. 15–24).

62 Twycross, 'The Left-Hand-Side Theory,' 92.

63 Oakshott and Rastall, 'Town with Gown,' 220.

64 Ibid., 213.

65 Ibid., 224.

66 The production was for the Poculi Ludique Societas (PLS), a group formed at the University of Toronto in 1965. Parry was appointed as artistic director of the PLS in 1975. Later large-scale PLS productions of mysteries include Chester (1983); Towneley (1985); N-Town (1988); and a second full production of the York mysteries (1998).

67 Johnston, 'The York Cycle: 1977,' 2.

68 For reports of the minicycle, see Meredith, 'Stray Thoughts on Chester 1983'; Mills, 'The Chester Cycle of Mystery Plays'; and Twycross, 'The Chester Plays at Chester.'

69 Oakshott, 'York Guilds' Mystery Plays 1998,' 270.

70 Tyler completed an MA thesis at the Centre for Medieval Studies, University of York, 'Aquinas, Augustine and the Realist: The Shaping of the Passion Sequence from the York Corpus Christi Cycle' (2000). He then extended his studies at the Centre and completed his PhD project, 'Ideology and the Family in Late Medieval York,' in 2006. This research includes an analysis of the presentation of the family in selected episodes from the mysteries.

71 For reports on the 2002 production see Tyler, 'York Guild Mystery Plays,' 158–61; and Rogerson Review of the York wagon production 2002.

72 For reviews of the 2006 production, see Stevenson, 'The York Mystery Cycle, July 2006'; and Scherb, 'The York Mystery Plays 2006.'

73 I am grateful to Mike Tyler for providing me with a copy of this scheme.

74 Oakshott, 'York Guilds' Mystery Plays 1998,' 277.

75 St John's College also adopted the plainchant method for a number of lines in the play of the 'Fall,' giving particular emphasis to the words 'bite on boldly' with reference to the eating of the apple that is the central motif of the play.

76 Oakshott explains in 'York Guilds' Mystery Plays 1998,' 274–6, that the Merchant Adventurers, Merchant Taylors, and Butchers have enjoyed a continuous existence since the early Middle Ages, while the Scriveners were reconstituted in 1991 to include 'accountants, licensed insolvency practitioners, barristers, patent agents, actuaries (and) solicitors.' The choice of the 'Christ and the Doctors' play in which learned men pit their wits against the youthful Christ fits well with the profile of the current membership.

77 Tyler, 'York Guild Mystery Plays,' 158.

78 Meredith, 'The Two Yorks,' 163.

79 Papers from this symposium and reports from wagon directors are included in Early Theatre 3 (2000): The York Cycle Then and Now.

80 For example, Meredith, 'The Two Yorks,' 163; and Palmer, 'The York Cycle in Performance,' 141.

81 Patrons for the 1994 Oakshott production were the then mayor, David Wilde (a wagon play director in 1998, 2002, and 2006), and Dame Judi Dench. In 1998, Dame Judi was patron, to be joined in 2002 by the archbishop of York and the earl of Harewood, thus providing patronage from well-known figures with impeccable connections in the arts, the church, and the nobility. In 2006 the patrons were Dame Judi, the dean of York, and myself as a representative of the Academy. The Teacher's Pack compiled in association with the Minster production in 2000 took a cross-curricular approach; for the 2002 pack, Graham Sanderson, on this occasion assisted by Colin Jackson from the City of York Education and Leisure Services, focused on The National Literacy Strategy, Design Technology, and Art, with a special emphasis on production and performance.

Epilogue: Ongoing Mysterie

1 Minghella, *Plays: One*, introduction, n.p.
2 For the document and a commentary on it, see Hoskin, 'The Accounts of the Medieval Paternoster Gild of York.' Tom Stirling of the *York Evening Press* took up the 'origin' of the mystery plays issue from the press release issued by the University of York, 'Campus Team's Historic Find,' in *The Press*, 16 February 2007: 26. See also 'Mystery Play Scroll is Found,' *The Times*, 16 February 2007 http://entertainment.timesonline.co.uk/tol/arts_and_entertainment/stage/theatre/article1392690.ece.
3 *Yiimimangaliso: The Mysteries* was filmed at the Queen's Theatre by the BBC (first broadcast 6 March 2003 and repeated 10 March 2003). For a review of this production at the Wilton Music Hall, see Tucker, 'Yiimimangaliso: The Mysteries, A South African Interpretation of the Chester Mystery Plays.'
4 Mike Laycock, 'Plays Time for Young People,' *The Press*, 6 October 2007 http://archive.thisisyork.co.uk/2007/10/6/361477.html.
5 Nelson's pronouncements were published subsequently; see Nelson, 'Principles of Processional Staging.'
6 Rogerson (Dorrell), 'Two Studies of the York Corpus Christi Play.'
7 Stevens, 'Postscript,' 113.
8 Rogerson, 'A Table of Contents for the York Corpus Christi Play.' Richard Beadle suggests a thirty-four-episode play in 'The York Cycle,' 118–19.
9 Kahrl, *Traditions of Medieval English Drama*, 46. William Tydeman was unhappy with only 'two stops' and suggested a three-stop performance; *English Medieval Theatre*, 106–8. Another system of playing the episodes only twice has been advanced by Salvador-Rabaza, 'A Proposal of Performance for the York Mystery Cycle.' She suggests one performance of each episode at an authorized playing station with a second continuous performance of all the episodes on the

Pavement. Her hypothetical performance lasts a total of eighteen hours and thus the problems of the excessive duration of the event remain unsolved.

10 Johnston, 'York Cycle 1998: What We Learned,' 202.

11 Clopper, *Chester*, 355.

12 The total number of lines in the Chester mysteries is 11,202. The total number at York is 13,313. The number of lines by which York exceeds Chester is insignificant (only 2,111), but the 100 per cent increase in the number of separate episodes is a very significant factor, necessitating an increase in the time needed for the episodes to change over, that is, for one wagon to take down and another to set up, and also a possible increase in delays caused when plays of unequal length back up in the procession.

13 For discussion of the performance conditions in Chester, see Mills, 'The Chester Cycle,' 115–17. On day 1 the nine episodes from 'The Fall of Lucifer' to 'The Offerings of the Three Kings' were seen; on day 2, the eight from 'The Massacre of the Innocents' to 'The Harrowing of Hell'; and on day 3, the remaining seven from 'The Resurrection' to 'The Last Judgment.' Mills argues that when they were presented on one day at the Corpus Christi festival in the fifteenth century, Chester's mysteries were fixed-place productions, probably at the Church of St John, the final destination of the Corpus Christi procession; see *The Chester Mystery Cycle: A New Edition*, xiii.

14 Johnston, 'York Cycle 1998,' 199.

15 Johnston and Rogerson, *York*, 298, 356–7.

16 Syrett, *The Old Miracle Plays of England*, 92. Syrett's work and its relation to the medieval theatre scholarship of her time is discussed by David Mills, in 'Netta Syrett and "The Old Miracle Plays of England."'

17 There were fifteen plays for session 1 (Saturday May 17, 10 am to 3 pm, 'The Creation and Fall of Lucifer' to 'The Flight into Egypt'), ten for session 2 (Saturday May 17, 3 pm to 8 pm, 'The Massacre of the Innocents' to 'Christ before Herod'), and eleven for session 3 (Sunday May 18, 2 pm to 8 pm, 'The Way to Calvary' to 'The Last Judgement'). The total run-time was sixteen hours.

18 Johnston and Rogerson, *York*, 109.

19 Johnston, 'York Cycle 1998,' 200. Johnston refers to the delay caused in 1998 by having to reuse wagons for later episodes and suggests that the experience of lost time when there was a hold-up with one of the earlier performances 'makes great sense out of the 1476 city order.'

20 Nelson, 'Principles of Processional Staging,' 319.

21 Twycross, 'Forget the 4.30 a.m. Start.'

22 Mills, 'The 1951 and 1952 Revivals of the Chester Plays,' 113.

23 Elliott, *Playing God*, 142–3.

Appendix 1: Music in the Outdoor Mysteries

1 Rastall, 'Music in the Cycle Plays,' 213. See also the arguments that the Elizabethan theatre buildings were 'sound-devices' in Bruce R. Smith, *The Acoustic World of Early Modern England*, 206–45.
2 The visitors were attending the 2nd International Festival of Town Pipers and the International Pipe and Tabor Festival: the Taborers Society, Doncaster Waites, Gloucester Waites, King's Lynn Waites, Leeds Waites, and Stadspijpers van 's-Hertogenbosch.
3 Rastall, 'Music in the Cycle Plays,' 212.
4 Jaques, 'Ancient Magic Distilled,' 148.
5 York City Archives, YDV, Festival 1954. York Festival Society, 'Summary of Informal Meeting Held at the Art Gallery on Friday, 12th September, 1952': 4–5.
6 Browne, 'Medieval Plays in Modern Production,' 313.
7 'Denis Stevens: Obituary,' *The Times*, 15 April 2004: 34.
8 For an account of the music for 1954, see Jaques, 'Ancient Magic Distilled,' 168–72.
9 Ibid., 274.
10 Ibid., 273.
11 Ibid., 274.
12 Ibid., 322–3.
13 Ibid., 323.
14 Ibid., 381. Butchers also played Satan in the 1973 production.
15 Ibid.
16 Only one singer, a soprano, Chris Batty, is listed in the program for 1973.

Works Cited

References to newspaper and magazine articles are included in the notes.

Alakas, Brandon. 'Seniority and Mastery: The Politics of Ageism in the Coventry Cycle.' *Early Theatre* 9.1 (2006): 15–36.

Artaud, Antonin. *The Theatre and Its Double*. Trans. Mary Caroline Richards. New York: Grovepress, 1958.

Arts Council of Great Britain. *The Glory of the Garden: The Development of the Arts in England, A Strategy of a Decade*. London: Arts Council of Great Britain, 1984.

Banham, Mary, and Bevis Hillier, eds. *A Tonic to the Nation: The Festival of Britain 1951*. London: Thames and Hudson, 1976.

Beadle, Richard, ed. *The Cambridge Companion to Medieval English Theatre*. Cambridge: Cambridge University Press, 1994.

– ed. *The York Plays*. London: Arnold, 1982.

Beadle, Richard, and Pamela M. King, eds. *The York Mystery Plays: A Selection in Modern Spelling*. Oxford: Oxford University Press, 1984.

Beadle, Richard, and Peter Meredith, eds. *The York Play: A Facsimile of British Library MS Additional 35290*. Leeds: University of Leeds, Department of English, 1983.

– 'The York Cycle: Texts, Performances and the Bases for Critical Enquiry.' In *Medieval Literature: Texts and Interpretation*, ed. Tim William Machan, 105–19. Binghamton, NY: Centre for Medieval and Early Renaissance Studies, State University of New York at Binghamton, 1991.

Beal, Timothy K., and Tod Linafelt, eds. *Mel Gibson's Bible: Religion, Popular Culture, and* The Passion of the Christ. Chicago: University of Chicago Press, 2006.

Beckwith, Sarah. *Signifying God: Social Relation and Symbolic Act in the York Corpus Christi Plays*. Chicago: University of Chicago Press, 2001.

Bell, C.C. *Who's Who in the York Pageant: A Popular Historical Guide with Illustrations.* Leeds: Richard Jackson, 1909.

Billington, Michael. *State of the Nation: British Theatre Since 1945.* London: Faber, 2007.

Brecht, Bertholt. *Brecht on Theatre: The Development of an Aesthetic.* Trans. John Willet. London: Methuen, 1964.

Briscoe, Marianne G., and John C. Coldewey, eds. *Contexts for Early English Drama.* Bloomington, IN: Indiana University Press, 1989.

The British Drama League 1919–1959. London: British Drama League, 1959.

Brown, Ivor. '*Ane Satyre of the Thrie Estaits* at the Edinburgh Festival.' In *Sir David Lindsay: Ane Satyre of the Thrie Estaits*, ed. James Kinsley, 27–33. London: Cassell, 1954.

Brown, John. 'The Devils in the York *Doomsday.*' *Medieval English Theatre* 11 (1989): 26–41.

Browne, E. Martin. 'Acting out of Doors.' *Drama* ns 49 (1958): 26–8.

– 'The Amateur Theatre and the Universities.' In *The Universities and the Theatre*, ed. James, 75–83.

– 'Drama's Return to Religion.' *Theatre Arts* 41.8 (1957): 18–19; 92–3.

– 'The English Mystery Plays.' *Drama* ns 43 (1956): 34–6.

– *Fifty Years of Religious Drama.* Leicester: Department of Adult Education, University of Leicester, 1979.

– 'How Pilgrims Worked.' In *Pilgrim Story: The Pilgrim Players, 1939–1943*, by Henzie Browne, 57–64. London: Muller, 1945.

– 'A Look around Britain.' *Drama* ns 21 (1951): 36–40.

– *The Making of T.S. Eliot's Plays.* Cambridge: Cambridge University Press, 1969.

– 'The Medieval Play Revival.' *Contemporary Review* 219 (1971): 132–7.

– 'Medieval Plays in Modern Production.' In *Religious Drama 2: Mystery and Morality Plays*, ed. E. Martin Browne, 305–14. New York: Meridian, 1958.

– 'A Note on the Production at York, 1951.' In *The York Cycle of Mystery Plays: A Shorter Version of the Ancient Cycle*, ed. J.S. Purvis, 13–14. London: SPCK, 1951.

– 'Producing the Mystery Plays for Modern Audiences.' *Drama Survey* 3.1 (1963): 5–15.

– *The Production of Religious Plays.* London: Allan, 1932.

– 'The Words of My Mouth: A Producer Looks at Some Problems of Public Worship.' In *English Church Music, 1967*, 10–15. London: Royal School of Church Music, 1967.

Browne, E. Martin, and Henzie Browne. *Two in One.* Cambridge: Cambridge University Press, 1981.

Bruce, George. *Festival in the North: The Story of the Edinburgh Festival*. London: Robert Hale, 1975.

Bull, John. 'The Establishment of Mainstream Theatre, 1946–1979.' In *The Cambridge History of British Theatre*, vol. 3, *Since 1895*, ed. Baz Kershaw, 326–48. Cambridge: Cambridge University Press, 2004.

Butler, R.M. *Medieval York*. York: Yorkshire Architectural and York Archaeological Society, 1982.

Butterworth, Philip. 'Discipline, Dignity and Beauty: The Wakefield Mystery Plays, Bretton Hall, 1958.' *Leeds Studies in English* ns 32 (2001): 49–80.

– 'Substitution: Theatrical Sleight of Hand in Medieval Plays.' *European Medieval Drama* 9 (2005): 209–29.

– 'The York Crucifixion: Actor/Audience Relationship.' *Medieval English Theatre* 14 (1992): 67–76.

Carpenter, Humphrey. *OUDS: A Centenary History of the Oxford University Dramatic Society 1885–1985*. Oxford: Oxford University Press, 1985.

Cawley, A.C., ed. *Everyman and Medieval Miracle Plays*. London: Dent, 1956.

Cawley, A.C. 'Middle English Metrical Versions of the Decalogue with Reference to the English Corpus Christi Cycles.' *Leeds Studies in English* ns 8 (1975): 129–45.

– 'The Sykes MS of the York Scriveners' Play.' *Leeds Studies in English* 7 and 8 (1952): 44–80.

Cheetham, Francis. *English Medieval Alabasters*. Oxford: Phaidon, 1984.

Child, Harold. 'Revivals of English Dramatic Works, 1919–1925.' *Review of English Studies* 2 (1926): 177–88.

Clopper, Lawrence M. *Drama, Play, and Game: English Festive Culture in the Medieval and Early Modern Period*. Chicago: University of Chicago Press, 2001.

– 'Lay and Clerical Impact on Civic Religious Drama and Ceremony.' In *Contexts for Early English Drama*, ed. Briscoe and Coldewey, 102–36.

– ed. *Chester*. Records of Early English Drama. Toronto: University of Toronto Press, 1979.

Coffman, George R. 'A Plea for the Study of the Corpus Christi Plays as Drama.' *Studies in Philology* 26.4 (1929): 411–24.

Coldewey, John C. 'From Roman to Renaissance in Drama and Theatre.' In *The Cambridge History of British Theatre*, vol. 1, *Origins to 1660*, ed. Jane Milling and Peter Thomson, 3–69. Cambridge: Cambridge University Press, 2004.

Constable, John. *The Southwark Mysteries*. London: Oberon, 1999.

Coward, Noel. *The Lyrics*. London: Methuen, 1983.

Cowling, Douglas. 'The Liturgical Celebration of Corpus Christi in Medieval York.' *Records of Early English Drama Newsletter* 1.2 (1976): 5–9.

Craig, Hardin. *English Religious Drama of the Middle Ages*. Oxford: Oxford University Press, 1955.

– Review of Arnold Williams, *The Drama of Medieval England*. *Speculum* 36.4 (1961): 695–8.

Cross, Claire. 'Excising the Virgin Mary from the Civic Life of Tudor York.' *Northern History* 39.2 (2002): 279–84.

Crouch, David J.F. 'Paying to See the Play: The Stationholders on the Route of the York Corpus Christi Play in the Fifteenth Century.' *Medieval English Theatre* 13 (1991): 64–111.

– *Piety, Fraternity and Power: Religious Guilds in Late Medieval Yorkshire, 1389–1547*. York: York Medieval Press, 2000.

Cusick, Edmund. 'Religion and Heritage.' In *British Cultural Identities*, ed. Mike Storry and Peter Childs, 277–314. London: Routledge, 1997.

Crystal, David. *Pronouncing Shakespeare: The Globe Experiment*. Cambridge: Cambridge University Press, 2005.

Davidson, Clifford. 'York Guilds and the Corpus Christi Plays: Unwilling Participants?' *Early Theatre* 9.2 (2006): 11–33.

Davies, Leila. 'The York Mystery Cycle.' *Frontier* 2.8 (1951): 312–22.

Dobson, R.B. 'Craft Guilds and City: The Historical Origins of the York Mystery Plays Reassessed.' In *The Stage As Mirror: Civic Theatre in Late Medieval Europe*, ed. Alan E. Knight, 91–105. Cambridge: D.S. Brewer, 1997.

Dodsley, Robert. Ed. *A Select Collection of Old Plays*. Vol. 1. London: privately printed, 1744.

Douglas, Audrey, and Peter Greenfield, eds. *Cumberland, Westmorland, Gloucestershire*. Records of Early English Drama. Toronto: University of Toronto Press, 1986.

Eddershaw, Margaret. *Performing Brecht: Forty Years of British Performances*. London: Routledge, 1996.

Ede, Christopher. *Drama Festivals and Adjudications*. London: Jenkins, 1955.

Eliot, T.S. *On Poetry and Poets*. London: Faber, 1957.

– 'The Responsibility of the Man of Letters in the Cultural Restoration of Europe.' *The Norseman* 2.4 (1944), 243–8.

Elliott, John R. Jr. 'Editor's Note.' *Research Opportunities in Renaissance Drama* 33 (1980): 83.

– 'Medieval Acting.' In *Contexts for Early English Drama*, ed. Briscoe and Coldewey, 238–49.

– *Playing God: Medieval Mysteries on the Modern Stage*. Toronto: University of Toronto Press, 1989.

– 'Playing the Godspell: Revivals of the Mystery Cycles in England, 1973.' *Research Opportunities in Renaissance Drama* 15–16 (1972–3): 125–30.

– 'The York Mystery Plays, 8 June–2 July 1984.' *Research Opportunities in Renaissance Drama* 27 (1984): 187–8.

Fitzgerald, Christina M. *The Drama of Masculinity and Medieval English Guild Culture*. New York: Palgrave, 2007.

Forty, Adrian. 'Festival Politics.' In *A Tonic to the Nation*, ed. Banham and Hillier, 26–38.

Foulkes, Richard. 'Charles Kean and the Great Exhibition.' *Theatre Notebook* 58.3 (2004): 125–40.

Frayn, Michael. 'Festival.' In *Age of Austerity: 1945–51*, ed. Michael Sissons and Philip French, 330–52. Harmondsworth: Penguin, 1964.

Fuegi, John. *Bertolt Brecht: Chaos, According to Plan*. Cambridge: Cambridge University Press, 1987.

Gaskill, William. *A Sense of Direction*. London: Faber, 1988.

Germanou, Maro. 'Brecht and the English Theatre.' In *Brecht in Perspective*, ed. Graham Bartram and Anthony Waine, 208–24. London: Longman, 1982.

Gill, Peter. *The York Realist*. London: Faber, 2001.

Goldberg, P.J.B. 'Craft Guilds, the Corpus Christi Play and Civic Government.' In *The Government of Medieval York: Essays in Commemoration of the 1396 Royal Charter*, ed. Sarah Rees Jones, 141–63. York: University of York, Borthwick Institute of Historical Research, 1997.

– *Medieval England: A Social History 1250–1550*. London: Arnold, 2004.

Green, Robson, and Deborah Holder. *Robson Green: Just the Beginning*. London: Boxtree, 1998.

Griffiths, David. *'A Musical Place of the First Quality': A History of Institutional Music-Making in York, c. 1550–1990*. York: York Settlement Trust, 1994.

Gusick, Barbara I. 'A Review of the York Millennium Mystery Plays.' *Research Opportunities in Renaissance Drama* 40 (2001): 111–32.

Guthrie, Tyrone. Introduction. *The Satire of the Three Estates*, ed. Robert Kemp, vii–xi. Melbourne: Heinemann, 1951.

Happé, Peter. 'Acting the York Mystery Plays: A Consideration of Modes.' *Medieval English Theatre* 10.2 (1988): 112–16.

– 'Mystery Plays and the Modern Audience.' *Medieval English Theatre* 2.2 (1980): 98–100.

– *The Towneley Cycle: Unity and Diversity*. Cardiff: University of Wales Press, 2007.

– 'The York Cycle: June 6–30, 1980.' *Research Opportunities in Renaissance Drama* 33 (1980), 81–2.

Harding, Vanessa. 'Reformation and Culture 1540–1700.' In *The Cambridge Urban History of Britain*, vol. 2, *1540–1840*, ed. Peter Clark, 263–88. Cambridge: Cambridge University Press, 2000.

Harrison, P.A. 'The York Festival of 1951.' *York Historian* 8 (1988): 68–80.

Harrison, Tony. *Plays One: The Mysteries*. London: Faber, 1999.

Harwood, Elain, and Alan Powers, eds. *Festival of Britain.* London: Twentieth Century Society, 2001.

Hennessy, Peter. *Never Again Britain 1945–51.* London: Jonathan Cape, 1992.

Henri, Adrian. *The Wakefield Mysteries.* London: Methuen, 1991.

Hess, Hans. Editorial. *Preview* 15.4 (July 1951): 170.

Higgins, Anne. 'Streets and Markets.' In *A New History of Early English Drama,* ed. John D. Cox and David Scott Kastan, 77–92. New York: Columbia University Press, 1997.

Hill, Reginald. *Bones and Silence.* London HarperCollins, 1990.

Hill-Vásquez, Heather. *Sacred Players: The Politics of Response in the Middle English Religious Drama.* Washington, D.C. Catholic University of America Press, 2007.

Holford, M.L. 'Language and Regional Identity in the York Corpus Christi Cycle.' *Leeds Studies in English* 33 (2002): 171–96.

Homan, Richard L. 'Ritual Aspects of the York Cycle.' *Theatre Journal* 33.3 (1981): 303–15.

Horner, Olga. '"The Law that Never Was" – A Codicil: The Case of *The Just Vengeance.*' *Medieval English Theatre* 24 (2002): 104–15.

– 'The Law that Never Was: A Review of Theatrical Censorship in Britain.' *Medieval English Theatre* 23 (2001): 34–96.

Horsler, Val. *Elizabeth and Philip: 20 November 1947.* Kew: National Archives, 2007.

Hoskin, Philippa M. 'The Accounts of the Medieval Paternoster Gild of York.' *Northern History* 44.1 (2007): 7–33.

Hunter, Geoffrey, ed. *Archbishop Holgate's School York: 1546–1996, the First Four Hundred and Fifty Years.* York: Archbishop Holgate's School, 1996.

Jaques, Sister Bernarda. 'Ancient Magic Distilled: The Twentieth Century Productions of the York Mystery Plays.' PhD diss., Tufts University, 1971.

James, D.G., ed. *The Universities and the Theatre.* London: Allen & Unwin, 1952.

Jellicoe, Ann. *Community Plays: How to Put Them On.* London: Methuen, 1987.

Johnston, Alexandra F. 'Four *York* Pageants Performed in the Streets of York: July 9, 1988.' *Research Opportunities in Renaissance Drama* 21 (1992): 101–4.

– 'Medieval Drama in England – 1966.' *Queen's Quarterly* 74 (1967): 78–91.

– 'The Plays of the Religious Guilds of York: The Creed Play and the Pater Noster Play.' *Speculum* 50.1 (1975): 55–90.

– 'William Revetour, Chaplain and Clerk of York, Testator.' *Leeds Studies in English* ns 29 (1998): 153–71.

– 'The York Corpus Christi Play: A Dramatic Structure Based on Performance Practice.' In *The Theatre in the Middle Ages,* ed. Herman Braet, Johan Nowé, and Gilbert Tournoy, 362–73. Leuven: Leuven University Press, 1985.

– 'The York Cycle: 1977.' *University of Toronto Quarterly* 48.1 (1978): 1–9.
– 'York Cycle 1998: What We Learned.' *Early Theatre* 3 (2000): 199–203.
– 'The York Cycle and the Libraries of York.' In *The Church and Learning in Late Medieval Society: Studies in Honour of Professor R.B. Dobson*, ed. Caroline Barron and Jenny Stratford, 355–70. Donnington: Shaun Tyas, 2002.
Johnston, Alexandra F., and Margaret Rogerson (Dorrell). 'The Doomsday Pageant of the York Mercers, 1433.' *Leeds Studies in English* 5 (1971): 27–34.
– eds. *York*. 2 vols. Records of Early English Drama. Toronto: University of Toronto Press, 1979.
Jones, Ian. *Brass Bands in York 1833–1914*. York: Borthwick Institute for Historical Research, University of York, 1995.
Kahrl, Stanley J. 'Medieval Drama in England, 1973: Chester and Ely.' *Research Opportunities in Renaissance Drama* 15–16 (1972–3): 117–23.
– *Traditions of Medieval English Drama*. London: Hutchinson, 1974.
Kelly, Mary. *How to Make a Pageant*. London: Pitman, 1936.
Keown, Eric. 'Festival Time.' In *Theatre Programme*, ed. J.S. Trewin, 179–96. London: Muller, 1954.
King, Pamela M. 'Twentieth-Century Medieval-Drama Revivals and the Universities,' *Medieval English Theatre* 27 (2007), 105–30.
– *The York Mystery Cycle and the Worship of the City*. Cambridge: D.S. Brewer, 2006.
– 'The York Plays in Performance: *Civitas* versus *Templum*.' *Medieval English Theatre* 25 (2003): 84–97.
King, Pamela M., and Clifford Davidson, eds. *The Coventry Corpus Christi Plays*. Kalamazoo, MI: Medieval Institute, 2000.
Kirk, Russell. 'York and Social Boredom.' *Sewanee Review* 61 (1953): 664–81.
Knight, G. Wilson. 'The Kitchen Sink: On Recent Developments in Drama.' *Encounter* 21.6 (1963): 48–54.
Koren-Deutsch, Ilone. 'A Mystery Cycle for the Modern World.' *Western European Stages* 5 (1993): 21–3.
Lambourne, Norah. 'Designing for the York Cycle of Mystery Plays in 1951, 1954 and 1957.' *Costume* 30 (1996): 16–36.
– 'Recollections of Designing for the Religious Plays of Dorothy L. Sayers.' *Costume* 25 (1991): 1–17.
Langhans, Edward A. 'The Theatre.' In *The Cambridge Companion to English Restoration Theatre*, ed. Deborah Payne Fisk, 1–18. Cambridge: Cambridge University Press, 2000.
Legg, F.S.H. 'Religious Life in York since 1800.' In *York: A Survey 1959*, ed. G.F. Willmott, J.M. Biggins, and P.M. Tillott, 143–9. York: British Association, 1959.
Lerud, Theodore K. 'Quick Images: Memory and the English Corpus Christi Drama.' In *Moving Subjects: Processional Performance in the Middle Ages and*

the Renaissance, ed. Kathleen Ashley and Wim Hüsken, 213–37. Amsterdam: Rodopi, 2001.

Loney, Glenn. 'Summer Production at York, England.' *Educational Theatre Journal* 18.3 (1966): 284–5.

Lowenthal, David. *Possessed by the Past: The Heritage Crusade and the Spoils of History.* New York: Free Press, 1996.

Mandler, Peter. 'Nationalising the Country House.' In *Preserving the Past: The Rise of Heritage in Modern Britain*, ed. Michael Hunter, 99–114. Stroud: Alan Sutton, 1996.

Marshall, John. 'Modern Productions of Medieval English Plays.' In *Cambridge Companion to Medieval English Theatre*, ed. Beadle, 290–311.

McCaw, Dick. 'Lifelong Listening: An Appreciation of the Fifty-Year Career of Teacher and Choreographer Geraldine Stephenson.' *Dance Theatre Journal* 17.1 (2001): 20–4.

– 'Old Theatre for New: The Cambridge Medieval Players (1974–1977), The Medieval Players (1980–1992).' *Leeds Studies in English* ns 32 (2001): 275–88.

McKinnell, John. 'The Medieval Pageant Wagons at York: Their Orientation and Height.' *Early Theatre* 3 (2000): 79–104.

– 'Producing the York Mary Plays.' *Medieval English Theatre* 12.2 (1990): 101–23.

McNeir, Waldo F. 'The Corpus Christi Passion Plays as Dramatic Art.' *Studies in Philology* 48 (1951): 601–28.

Meredith, Peter. 'The City of York and Its "Play of Pageants."' *Early Theatre* 3 (2000): 23–47.

– 'The Fifteenth-Century Audience of the York Corpus Christi Play: Records and Speculation.' In *'Divers toyes mengled': Essays on Medieval and Renaissance Culture in Honour of Andre Lascombes*, ed. Michel Bitot, Roberta Mullini and Peter Happé, 101–11. Tours: Université François Rabelais, 1996.

– 'John Clerke's Hand in the York Register.' *Leeds Studies in English* ns 12 (1981): 245–71.

– 'Stray Thoughts on Chester 1983.' *Medieval English Theatre* 5.1 (1983): 42–4.

– 'The Two Yorks: Playing in Toronto and York.' *Early Theatre* 1 (1998): 160–3.

Miller, Eileen. *The Edinburgh International Festival 1947–1996.* Aldershot: Scolar, 1996.

Miller, John. *Judi Dench with a Crack in Her Voice: The Biography.* London: Weidenfeld & Nicholson, 1997.

Mills, David. 'The 1951 and 1952 Revivals of the Chester Plays.' *Medieval English Theatre* 15 (1993): 111–23.

Mills, David, ed. *The Chester Mystery Cycle: A New Edition with Modernised Spelling.* East Lansing: Colleagues, 1992.

- 'The Chester Cycle.' In *Cambridge Companion to Medieval English Theatre*, ed. Beadle, 109–33.
- 'The Chester Cycle of Mystery Plays.' *Medieval English Theatre* 5.1 (1983): 44–51.
- '"Look at Me When I'm Speaking to You": The "Behold and See" Convention in Medieval Drama.' *Medieval English Theatre* 7.1 (1985): 4–12.
- 'Netta Syrett and "The Old Miracle Plays of England."' *Medieval English Theatre* 10.2 (1988): 117–28.
- 'The "Now" of "Then."' *Medieval English Theatre* 22 (2000): 3–12.
- 'Recycling the Cycle: The Chester Mystery Plays.' *Manchester Memoirs* 131 (1991–3): 75–95.
- *Recycling the Cycle: The City of Chester and Its Whitsun Plays.* Toronto: University of Toronto Press, 1998.
- 'Replaying the Medieval Past: Revivals of Chester's Mystery Plays.' In *Medievalism in England II*, ed. Leslie J. Workman and Kathleen Verduin, 181–93. Cambridge: D.S. Brewer, 1995.
- 'Who Are Our Customers? The Audience for Chester's Plays.' *Medieval English Theatre* 20 (1998): 104–17.
- 'The York Mystery Plays at York.' *Medieval English Theatre* 10.1 (1988): 69–72.
- Minghella, Anthony. *Plays: One.* London: Methuen, 1992.
- Mitchell, Katie, and Edward Kemp. 'How Do We Live?' In *Moral Mysteries: Essays to Accompany a Season of Medieval Drama at The Other Place*, ed. David Jays, 40–54. Stratford, Royal Shakespeare Theatre, 1997.
- Morris, Tony. 'The Mystery of a Poet in Residence: The Art of The Oral.' *Spoken English* 30.1 (1997): 16–18.
- *Poet in Residence, Poems by Tony Morris: The Process and the People of the York Mystery Plays at the Theatre Royal.* Selby, North Yorkshire: Woodman's, 1996.
- Murdoch, Brian. *Cornish Literature.* Cambridge: D.S. Brewer, 1993.
- Nelson, Alan H. *The Medieval English Stage: Corpus Christi Pageants and Plays.* Chicago: University of Chicago Press, 1974.
- 'Principles of Processional Staging: York Cycle.' *Modern Philology* 67.4 (1970): 303–20.
- Normington, Katie. *Gender and Medieval Drama.* Cambridge: D.S. Brewer, 2004.
- 'Little Acts of Faith: Katie Mitchell's "The Mysteries."' *New Theatre Quarterly* 54 (1998): 99–110.
- *Modern Mysteries: Contemporary Productions of Medieval English Cycle Dramas.* Cambridge: D.S. Brewer, 2007.

Nuttgens, Patrick, and Bridget Nuttgens. 'A Future for the Past – York in the Twentieth Century.' In *The History of York: From the Earliest Times to the Year 2000*, ed. Patrick Nuttgens, 302–58. Pickering: Blackthorn, 2001.

Oakshott, Jane. 'York Guilds' Mystery Plays 1998: The Rebuilding of Dramatic Community.' In *Drama and Community: People and Plays in Medieval Europe*, ed. Alan Hindley, 270–89. Turnhout: Brepols, 1999.

Oakshott, Jane, and Richard Rastall. 'Town with Gown: The York Cycle of Mystery Plays at Leeds.' In *Towards the Community University: Case Studies of Innovation and Community Service*, ed. David C.B. Teather, 213–29. London: Kogan Page, 1982.

O'Donoghue, Bernard. Introduction. *Plays One: The Mysteries*, by Tony Harrison, 1–8. London: Faber, 1999.

Palliser, D.M. *Tudor York*. Oxford: Oxford University Press, 1979.

Palmer, Barbara D. '"Townelye Plays" or "Wakefield Cycle" Revisited.' *Comparative Drama* 21 (1987–8): 318–48.

– 'The York Cycle in Performance: Toronto and York.' *Early Theatre* 1 (1998): 139–43.

Parker, Louis N. Foreword in *The Book of the York Pageant 1909: A Dramatic Representation of the City's History in Seven Episodes, from B.C. 800 to A.D. 1644*. York: Ben Johnson, 1909.

– *Several of My Lives*. London: Chapman and Hall, 1928.

Pascoe, Charles Eyre. *York Historic Pageant Souvenir*. York: Ben Johnson, 1909.

Pickering, Kenneth W. *Drama in the Cathedral: The Canterbury Festival Plays 1928–1948*. Worthing, West Sussex: Churchman, 1985.

Powers, Alan. 'The Expression of Levity.' In *Festival of Britain*, ed. Harwood and Powers, 47–56.

Priestley, J.B. *Festival at Farbridge*. London: Heinemann, 1951.

Proceedings of the Colloquium Held at the University of Leeds 10–13 September 1974 on The Drama of Medieval Europe. Leeds: Graduate Centre for Medieval Studies, University of Leeds, 1975.

Pugh, Ben. 'York Mystery Plays Feasibility Report.' 4 February 2004.

Purey-Cust, Arthur P. *Last Words on the York Pageant of 1909: A Sermon Preached at York Minster, 9th Sunday after Trinity, August 8th, 1909*. York: John Sampson, 1909.

Purvis, J.S., ed. *The York Cycle of Mystery Plays: A Shorter Version of the Ancient Cycle*. London: SPCK, 1951.

– *The York Cycle of Mystery Plays: A Complete Version*. London: SPCK, 1957.

Ramsay, Keith. 'The Lincoln Mystery Plays, 1978–1985.' In *Acting Medieval Plays,* ed. Peter Meredith, William Tydeman, and Keith Ramsay, 47–54. Lincoln: Honywood, 1985.

– The Lincoln *Mystery Plays 1978–2000: A Personal Odyssey*. Lincoln: Nerone, 2008.

Rastall, Richard. *The Heaven Singing: Music in Early English Religious Drama*. Vol. 1. Cambridge: D.S. Brewer, 1996.

– 'Music in the Cycle Plays.' In *Contexts for Early English Drama*, ed. Briscoe and Coldewey, 192–218.

Reed, George. *1900th Anniversary Celebrations: The York Pageant 1971*. Bound typescript, n.d.

Rees-Mogg, William. Preface. *The Glory of the Garden: The Development of the Arts in England, A Strategy of a Decade*. London: Arts Council of Great Britain, 1984.

Reynolds, Barbara, ed. *The Letters of Dorothy L. Sayers*, vol. 4, *1951–1957: In the Midst of Life*. Cambridge: Dorothy L. Sayers Society, 2000.

Richardson, Gary. 'Craft Guilds and Christianity in Late-Medieval England: A Rational-Choice Analysis.' *Rationality and Society* 17.2 (2005): 139–89.

Rio [pseud.]. 'The Mystery Plays.' *Chatter* 2 (1951): 7.

Roddy, Kevin. 'Revival of the Cornish Mystery Plays in St. Piran's "Round" and of the York Cycle, 1969.' *New Theatre Magazine* 9 (1968–9): 16–21.

Rogerson (Dorrell), Margaret. 'Two Studies of the York Corpus Christi Play.' *Leeds Studies in English* ns 6 (1972): 63–111.

Rogerson, Margaret. '"Everybody Got Their Brown Dress": Mystery Plays for the Millennium.' *New Theatre Quarterly* 66 (2001): 123–40.

– 'Living History: The Modern Mystery Plays in York.' *Research Opportunities in Renaissance Drama* 43 (2004): 12–28.

– 'Raging in the Streets of Medieval York.' *Early Theatre* 3 (2000): 105–25.

– 'REED: *York*, Volume 3, The "Revivals."' In '*Bring furth the Pagants': Essays in Early English Drama Presented to Alexandra F. Johnston*, eds. David N. Klausner and Karen S. Marsalek, 132–61. Toronto: University of Toronto Press, 2007.

– 'Rediscovering Richard Eurich's "York Festival Triptych."' *Medieval English Theatre* 23 (2001): 3–16.

– Review of the York wagon production 2002. *Research Opportunities in Renaissance Drama* 42 (2003): 161–9.

– 'A Table of Contents for the York Corpus Christi Play.' In *Words and Wordsmiths: A Volume for H.L. Rogers*, ed. Geraldine Barnes, John Gunn, Sonya Jensen, and Lee Jobling, 85–90. Sydney: Department of English, University of Sydney, 1989.

Rosen, Andrew. *The Transformation of British Life, 1950–2000: A Social History*. Manchester: Manchester University Press, 2003.

Rosenfeld, Sybil. *The York Theatre*. London: Society for Theatre Research, 2001.

Rosser, Gervase. 'Crafts, Guilds and the Negotiation of Work in the Medieval Town.' *Past and Present* 154 (1997): 3–31.

Rowntree, B. Seebohm. *Poverty and Progress: A Second Social Survey of York.* London: Longmans, 1941.

Rubin, Miri. *Corpus Christi: The Eucharist in Late Medieval Culture.* Cambridge: Cambridge University Press, 1991.

Sahlins, Bernard, and Nicholas Rudall, eds. *The Mysteries: Creation.* Chicago: Dee, 1992.

St Olave's Marygate, York. *A Christmas Play: A Series of Scenes from the Mystery Plays Performed in York in the 14th, 15th and 16th Centuries.* York: H. Morley, 1909.

Salvador-Rabaza, Asunción. 'A Proposal of Performance for the York Mystery Cycle: External and Internal Evidence.' *Selim* 9 (1999): 181–90.

Samuel, Raphael. *Theatres of Memory,* vol. 1, *Past and Present in Contemporary Culture.* London: Verso, 1994.

Savidge, Dale E. 'E. Martin Browne and the Revival of Verse Drama in England.' PhD diss., University of South Carolina, 1991.

Sayers, Dorothy L. *The Just Vengeance: The Lichfield Festival Play for 1946.* London: Gollancz, 1946.

– Preface. *Dressing the Play,* by Norah Lambourne, 6–8. London: Studio, 1953.

– 'Types of Christian Drama: With Some Notes on Production.' In 'Dorothy L. Sayers and the Other Type of Mystery,' by John R. Elliott Jr. *Seven* 2 (1981): 84–99.

Schofield, John, and Alan Vince. *Medieval Towns.* London: Leicester University Press, 1994.

Scherb, Victor I. 'The York Mystery Plays 2006.' *Research Opportunities in Renaissance Drama* 46 (2007): 21–4.

Shapiro, James. *Oberammergau: The Troubling Story of the World's Most Famous Passion Play.* New York: Pantheon, 2000.

Shellard, Dominic, and Steve Nicholson. *The Lord Chamberlain Regrets ... : A History of British Theatre Censorship.* London: British Library, 2004.

Shepherd, Richard. 'York Millennium Mystery Plays.' University of the South, Sewanee, Tennessee, 2000.

Shepherd, Simon, and Peter Womack. *English Drama: A Cultural History.* Oxford: Blackwell, 1996.

Smith, Bruce R. *The Acoustic World of Early Modern England: Attending to the O-Factor.* Chicago: University of Chicago Press, 1999.

Smith, Laurajane. *Uses of Heritage.* Abingdon, Oxon: Routledge, 2006.

Southern, Richard. *The Medieval Theatre in the Round: A Study of the Staging of* The Castle of Perseverance *and Related Matters.* London: Faber, 1957.

Sponsler, Claire. *Ritual Imports: Performing Medieval Drama in America.* Ithaca, NY: Cornell University Press, 2004.

Stern, Tiffany. *Making Shakespeare: From Stage to Page.* London: Routledge, 2004.

Stevens, Martin. *Four English Mystery Cycles: Textual, Contextual, and Critical Interpretations*. Princeton, NJ: Princeton University Press, 1987.
– 'Illusion and Reality in the Medieval Drama.' *College English* 32.4 (1970): 448–64.
– 'Postscript.' *Leeds Studies in English* ns 6 (1972): 113–15.
– 'The York Cycle: From Procession to Play.' *Leeds Studies in English* ns 6 (1972): 37–61.
Stevenson, Jill. 'The Material Bodies of Medieval Religious Performance in England.' *Material Religion* 2.2 (2006): 206–32.
– 'The York Mystery Cycle, July 2006; Negotiating Past and Present.' *Research Opportunities in Renaissance Drama* 46 (2007): 10–20.
Stratman, Carl J. *Bibliography of Medieval Drama*. Berkeley: University of California Press, 1954.
Styan, J.L. *The English Stage: A History of Drama and Performance*. Cambridge: Cambridge University Press, 1996.
Swanson, Heather. 'The Illusion of Economic Structure: Craft Guilds in Late Medieval English Towns.' *Past and Present* 121 (1988): 29–48.
Swanson, R.N. *Church and Society in Late Medieval England*. Oxford: Blackwell, 1989.
– 'The Origins of the *Lay Folks' Catechism*.' *Medium Aevum* 60.1 (1991): 92–7.
Syrett, Netta. *The Old Miracle Plays of England*. London: Mowbray, 1911.
Taylor, Jefferey H. *Four Levels of Meaning in the York Cycle of Mystery Plays: A Study in Medieval Allegory*. Lewiston, NY: Mellen, 2006.
Toulmin Smith, Lucy, ed. *York Plays*. Oxford: Oxford University Press, 1885.
Trewin, J.C. 'The Drama of Daybreak.' *Drama* ns 22 (1951): 26–8.
Trussler, Simon. *The Cambridge Illustrated History of British Theatre*. Cambridge: Cambridge University Press, 1994.
Tucker, Betsy Rudelich. 'Yiimimangaliso: The Mysteries, A South African Interpretation of the Chester Mystery Plays.' *Theatre Journal* 54.2 (2002): 303–5.
Twycross, Meg. 'The Chester Plays at Chester.' *Medieval English Theatre* 5.1 (1983): 36–42.
– 'Civic Consciousness in the York Mystery Plays.' In *Social and Political Identities in Western History*, ed. Claus Bjorn, Alexander Grant, and Keith J. Stringer, 67–89. Copenhagen: Academic Press, 1994.
– 'The Flemish *Ommegang* and Its Pageant Cars.' *Medieval English Theatre* 2:1 (1980): 15–41, and 2.2 (1980): 80–98.
– 'Forget the 4.30 a.m. Start: Recovering a Palimpsest in the York *Ordo Paginarum*.' *Medieval English Theatre* 25 (2003): 98–152.
– 'The Left-Hand-Side Theory: A Retraction.' *Medieval English Theatre* 14 (1992): 77–94.

- 'Medieval English Theatre: Codes and Genres.' In *A Companion to Medieval English Literature and Culture c. 1350–c.1500*, ed. Peter Brown, 454–72. Oxford: Blackwell, 2007.
- '"Places to Hear the Play": Pageant Stations at York 1398–1572.' *Records of Early English Drama Newsletter* (1978:2): 10–33.
- 'Playing "The Resurrection."' In *Medieval Studies for J.A.W. Bennett*, ed. P.L. Heyworth, 273–96. Oxford: Oxford University Press, 1981.
- 'The Theatricality of Medieval English Plays.' In *Cambridge Companion to Medieval English Theatre*, ed. Beadle, 37–84.
- '"Transvestism" in the Mystery Plays.' *Medieval English Theatre* 5.2 (1983): 123–80.
Twycross, Meg, and Sarah Carpenter. *Masks and Masking in Medieval and Early Tudor England*. Aldershot, Hants: Ashgate, 2002.
- 'Masks in Medieval English Theatre: The Mystery Plays.' *Medieval English Theatre* 3:1 (1981): 7–44, and 3:2 (1981): 69–113.
Tydeman, William. *English Medieval Theatre 1400–1500*. London: Routledge, 1986.
Tyler, Mike. 'York Guild Mystery Plays.' Report by Director Mike Tyler. *Research Opportunities in Renaissance Drama* 42 (2003): 158–61.
Walker, Greg. ed. *Medieval Drama: An Anthology*. Oxford: Balckwell, 2000.
- *The Politics of Performance in Early Renaissance Drama*. Cambridge: Cambridge University Press, 1998.
Waugh, Evelyn. *Love Among the Ruins: A Romance of the Near Future*. London: Chapman & Hall, 1953.
Weissengruber, Erik Paul. 'The Corpus Christi Procession in Medieval York: A Symbolic Struggle in Public Space.' *Theatre Survey* 38.1 (1997): 117–38.
White, Eileen. 'Places for Hearing the Corpus Christi Play in York.' *Medieval English Theatre* 9.1 (1987): 23–63.
- 'Places to Hear the Play: The Performance of the Corpus Christi Play at York.' *Early Theatre* 3 (2000): 49–78.
- 'The Tenements at the Common Hall Gates 1550–1725.' *York Historian* 6 (1985): 32–42.
- 'The Tenements at the Common Hall Gates: The Mayor's Station for the Corpus Christi Play in York.' *Records of Early English Drama Newsletter* 7.2 (1982): 14–24.
- *The York Mystery Play*. York: Yorkshire Architectural and York Archaeological Society, 1984.
Wickham, Glynne 'Conclusion: Retrospect and Prospect.' In *The Universities and the Theatre*, ed. James, 102–15.
- *Early English Stages 1300 to 1660*, vol. 1, *1300 to 1576*. London: Routledge, 1966.

- 'Introduction: Trends in International Drama Research.' In *The Theatre of Medieval Europe: New Research in Early English Drama*, ed. Eckehard Simon, 1–18. Cambridge: Cambridge University Press, 1991.
- 'A Revolution in Attitudes to the Dramatic Arts in British Universities, 1880–1980.' *Oxford Review of Education* 3.2 (1977): 115–21.
- *Shakespeare's Dramatic Heritage: Collected Studies in Mediaeval, Tudor and Shakespearean Drama*. London: Routledge, 1969.
Wiles, David. *A Short History of Western Performance Space*. Cambridge: Cambridge University Press, 2003.
Williams, Arnold. *The Drama of Medieval England*. East Lansing: Michigan State University Press, 1961.
Williams, J. Hadley. 'Lyndsay and Europe: Politics, Patronage, Printing.' In *The European Sun: Proceedings of the Seventh International Conference on Medieval and Renaissance Language and Literature*, ed. Graham Caie, Roderick J. Lyall, Sally Mapstone, and Kenneth Simpson, 333–46. East Linton: Tuckwell, 2001.
Withington, Robert. 'The Corpus Christi Plays as Drama.' *Studies in Philology* 27.4 (1930): 573–82.
Wright, Paul H. *The Word of God: A Miracle Play Adapted from the Mediaeval York Cycle*. York: Church Shop, 1926.
Wyatt, Diana. 'The English Pater Noster Play: Evidence and Extrapolations.' *Comparative Drama* 30.4 (1996–7): 452–70.
Wyatt, Euphemia van Rensselaer. 'What Religious Drama Owes to E. Martin Browne.' *Drama Critique* 4.1 (1961): 31–7.
Yates, Kimberley M. 'The Critical Heritage of the York Cycle.' PhD diss., University of Toronto, 1997.
York Minster. *Half a Millennium: York Minster After 1472*. York: York Minster Centre for School Visits, 1997.
Young, M. James. 'The York Pageant Wagon.' *Speech Monographs* 34.1 (1967): 1–20.

Index

acoustics, 123–4, 159, 177–8
affective piety, 84–5, 100, 244–5n95
Alexander, Ray, 211, 220, 222
amateur theatre movement, 13–14,
   102–3, 105
anachronism, 19–20, 85, 135, 189
Anderson, John Stuart, 110, 216
Andrew, Prince, 249n4
Anne, Queen, 195
anti-Semitism, 56–7, 235n69
The Archers, 196
Artaud, Antonin, 82, 84–5
Arts Council of Great Britain, 3, 9–10,
   29, 126–7, 208
audiences: medieval, 25–6, 40, 85;
   modern 16, 30, 32–4, 40, 45–6
Austin, George, 150

Banerjee, Victor, 132–4, 216
Barber, John, 68, 116
Beadle, Richard, x, 21, 43, 52–3, 174
Beckwith, Sarah, 16, 113
Belgrade Theatre, 155
Bell, Charles, 35–6, 158
Bell, George, 14, 61, 81
Benfield, T.C., 15, 34, 106, 164
Berliner Ensemble, 83, 86

Blanshard, Peter, 107, 108, 216
Blockley, 155
Bowman, Philip, 221–3
Bradley, David, 111, 114, 216
brass bands, 114, 118. *See also* York,
   bands
Brecht, Bertolt, 13, 82–6, 88–9, 91–2,
   95, 99
Bretton Hall, 13, 75–6, 178, 219,
   239n76
Bridge, Harry, 131, 209
British Drama League, 4, 29, 61–2,
   103, 104–6
Brook, Peter, 87, 99–100
Brown, James, 206
Brown, John, 175, 218
Browne, E. Martin, 4, 8, 14, 16, 87;
   advice on change, 58–9, 112; and
   amateur actors, 71–3, 97, 103, 106;
   and Brecht, 86; and British Drama
   League, 13, 29, 103; as model director, 88–9, 99; and music, 206–7;
   and Oberammergau, 7, 47–8; and
   rehearsals, 63, 68, 97; and theatre of
   cruelty, 95, 99–100; as York mystery
   play director (Museum Gardens),
   29–30, 33–4, 41, 45–81, 124, 216–17;

York mystery plays (*continued*)
220, 222; Temptation, 221, 223;
Woman Taken in Adultery/Raising
of Lazarus, 222
York Nativity Play, 50, 62, 236n5

York Repertory Company, 84
York waits, 205, 247n57
Yorkshire Musical Festivals, 159
Young, James, 172